# THE BARCELONA INHERITANCE

## PREVIOUS BOOKS BY JONATHAN WILSON

*Behind the Curtain: Travels in Eastern European Football*

*Sunderland: A Club Transformed*

*The Anatomy of England: A History in Ten Matches*

*Brian Clough: Nobody Ever Says Thank You*

*The Outsider: A History of the Goalkeeper*

*The Anatomy of Liverpool: A History in Ten Matches*

*Angels with Dirty Faces: The Footballing History of Argentina*

*The Anatomy of Manchester United: A History in Ten Matches*

*Inverting the Pyramid: The History of Football Tactics*

## ABOUT THE AUTHOR

Jonathan Wilson's *Inverting the Pyramid* was football book of the year in the UK and Italy and was shortlisted for the William Hill Sports Book of the Year Award. He writes for the *Guardian, Sports Illustrated,* and *World Soccer,* and is the editor of *The Blizzard.*

# THE
# BARCELONA
## INHERITANCE

### THE EVOLUTION OF WINNING SOCCER
### TACTICS FROM CRUYFF TO GUARDIOLA

## JONATHAN WILSON

NATION
BOOKS
New York

Nation Books
116 East 16th Street, 8th Floor New York, NY 10003
www.nationbooks.org
@NationBooks
Printed in the United States of America

Published in the United Kingdom as *The Barcelona Legacy* by Blink Publishing in 2018

First US Trade Paperback Edition: November 2018

Published by Nation Books, an imprint of Perseus Books, LLC, a subsidiary of Hachette
Book Group, Inc.

Nation Books is a co-publishing venture of the Nation Institute and the Perseus Books.

The Hachette Speakers Bureau provides a wide range of authors for speaking events. To
find out more, go to www.hachettespeakersbureau.com or call (866) 376-6591.

The publisher is not responsible for websites (or their content) that are not owned by
the publisher.

Library of Congress Control Number: 2018956694

ISBN: 978-1-56858-785-1 (paperback)

ISBN: 978-1-56858-853-7 (e-book)

LSC-C

10  9  8  7  6  5  4  3  2  1

# CONTENTS

*PHOTO SECTION APPEARS AFTER PAGE 150*

# CHAPTER ONE
# THE GREAT TRADITION

Few great men get the end they deserve. For football managers as for so many others, professional lives tend to conclude in failure. Johan Cruyff's dismissal by Barcelona was grimly acrimonious as he was escorted from the training ground following a season of turmoil in which Barcelona had finished third amid an ongoing civil war between coach and president. Cruyff was 49 but he never managed again: his coaching career comprised just 11 years and two clubs. But managers are not judged on their final seasons; they are defined by their legacy. By the time Cruyff died 20 years later, his ideas had shaped the game more profoundly than those of perhaps any other thinker in history. At least two major clubs played to an overtly Cruyffian philosophy, while his influence was felt far more widely. Yet when he was sacked after eight years in the Barcelona job, nobody was surprised and many, perhaps even most, fans seemed to consider it the correct decision.

On 18 May 1996, the day before the final home league game of the season against Celta Vigo, Cruyff was visited at the training ground by Joan Gaspart, the vice president of Barcelona. Everybody knew what the conversation would be about: the end had been inevitable for at least a week, and probably a long time before that.

The problems, in truth, had begun in Athens two years earlier, when Barcelona had lost 4-0 to Fabio Capello's AC Milan in the final of the Champions League. After four seasons that had brought four

Spanish titles as well as Barça's first European Cup, that was the end of the Dream Team. Perhaps it was a natural conclusion – all teams, even the very best, have a lifespan – but Cruyff ensured his first great team was finished.

On the bus from the stadium back to the hotel, Cruyff told a number of players they would be sold. He undertook a radical rebuilding and the churn that had characterised his first seasons in charge began again. The goalkeeper Andoni Zubizarreta, the playmaker Michael Laudrup, the attacking midfielder Ion Andoni Goikoetxea and the centre-forward Julio Salinas didn't play another minute for the club. Romário was sold in the January. Eusebio Sacristán, Hristo Stoichkov, Ronald Koeman and Txiki Begiristain all went the following summer. By then, Barça were no longer champions, having finished fourth, nine points behind Real Madrid.

The new signings – Gică Popescu, Robert Prosinečki and Gheorghe Hagi – struggled to settle. The 1995-96 season brought a series of disappointments. On 10 April, Barça lost to Atlético in the Copa del Rey final. Six days later, Bayern Munich won 2-1 at the Camp Nou to complete a 4-3 aggregate win in the semi-final of the UEFA Cup. There were persistent rumours that Cruyff was to be ousted for the former England manager Bobby Robson, but he kept working; a couple of weeks before the end of the season, he persuaded the midfielder Luis Enrique to leave Madrid for Barça.

By mid-May, though, Cruyff's exit was all but certain. On the 15th, *Diario Sport*, under the headline 'The board opens another front against Cruyff', reported that Josep Lluís Núñez, the club president, thought the club's injury problems were the result of Cruyff's training methods. The board, the piece went on, planned to restructure the weekly schedule, having players work with a fitness coach before training with Cruyff, something that would have represented a drastic diminution of his influence. Cruyff's unease was evident. 'Johan Cruyff is starting to get tired,' said a report in *Mundo Deportivo*. 'The Dutchman had intended to respond to the attitude of the board when the season ended but he is losing his patience. He faced the media yesterday, focused, serious, but biting his tongue. Four or five answers were enough to work out that Johan is in an unsettled state, tense, angry even.'

Cruyff, meanwhile, accused the board of sleeping when it came to transfers, furious that Zinedine Zidane was leaving Bordeaux, not for Barça but for Juventus. 'He's going to Italy, no?' Cruyff asked. 'I had him signed in January.'

That night, Barcelona had to complete the final 82 minutes of their third-last league game of the season, against Espanyol, after an abandonment because of torrential rain the previous Saturday. 'Tonight they are playing the derby in Sarrià,' wrote the columnist Josep Casanovas, 'but until the start of the game the attention will be focused on the match which Cruyff and Núñez are playing as if they were cat and dog. It's an absurd and damaging war for the club, a very unedifying spectacle that leaves the players aghast and the fans furious.'

A 1-1 draw in a spiky game that ended with red cards for Luís Figo and Guillermo Amor ended whatever hope Barça had of closing the gap on Atlético at the top of the table. The following day came the confirmation of what everybody had expected. 'He will be sacked,' read the headline in *Diario Sport*. 'The marriage between Núñez and Cruyff seemed like it was going to be for life,' the article beneath read. 'However, bad results in Europe signified the end of an idyllic love story.' Fans agreed that it was time for radical action with 83.6 per cent of those polled by the newspaper saying they believed the relationship between Cruyff and Núñez was broken and 79 per cent saying it had affected the performance of the team. Many clearly felt

Cruyff was to blame, with only 21.4 per cent saying he was in the right and 60 per cent believing neither party was.

'*FIN*,' read the headline on the front page of *Mundo Deportivo*. 'The film is reaching its end,' said an editorial. 'The last episode is being written and the scriptwriters took away the uncertainty yesterday, although they provided a dramatic turn of events. Núñez has axed Cruyff. The coach will not continue at Barcelona … and now they are working out who should replace him…

'Cruyff doesn't understand why they offered him continuity two weeks ago and now they want to get rid of him, although nobody has told him anything officially. Barcelona fans are stunned at the end of a cycle with glorious times and huge potholes, looking towards a somewhat unknown future.'

By then, the only question was the manner of Cruyff's departure. 'The greatness of a club and a town are measured by the details a lot of the time,' said Ernesto Valverde, who had played as a forward under Cruyff. 'Because of all the good he gave to Barcelona, and because being well-mannered is the sign of a good upbringing, Johan should be waved goodbye like a myth, like a hero.'

But there was none of that, little gratitude and no dignity. When Gaspart greeted him in the dressing room, the manager asked, 'Why are you giving me your hand, Judas?' He then accused Núñez of lacking the guts to sack him personally. Players heard the shouting from next door. A chair was thrown. As the pair almost came to blows, Gaspart told him to leave the Camp Nou before he called the police, saying, 'You no longer belong here.'

Yet no figure has ever belonged at a club more than Cruyff belonged at Barça. No club has ever so owed its identity to one man. 'It hurts not to be able to wave goodbye to the fans,' Cruyff said. 'If they need me I will come back but never with Núñez.'

As it turned out, Cruyff never really left but, in the immediate aftermath, the sense of shock and distaste was clear. 'To sack him like this is a lack of respect,' said Ronald Koeman, who was by then back in the Netherlands with Feyenoord. 'It's hard to see him sacked like this, I don't know how they can doubt Johan.'

The following day, with Cruyff's long-time assistant Charly Rexach in charge of the side, his son Jordi Cruyff, a tidy forward, inspired a comeback as Barça won 3-2. Jordi was taken off to a huge ovation with a few minutes remaining as the crowd chanted, '*Cruyff sí, Núñez no!*'

Cruyff had taken a faltering side and not merely made them the dominant team in Spain, had not merely ended the quest for that first European Cup, but had defined the style of the club and had established a tactical ideal that would inspire coaches across the world. Even to speak of philosophies before Cruyff might have seemed a little strange but he redefined what it was to be a manager, turned him from a general seeking to inspire his troops into a visionary preaching a creed. He added to tactics a spiritual dimension that went far beyond the old platitudes of trying to entertain. It wasn't a template he created so much as an aspiration, a way of thinking about the game that would shape football for two decades and probably more.

\* \* \*

At Ajax and then at Barça, as a player and as a manager, Cruyff was seen as a revolutionary, or at least to be enacting the philosophy of revolutionaries, but the ideas that he imposed with such stunning effect in Barcelona stood in a direct line that reaches back to the very first international, played between Scotland and England in Partick in 1872. He was a radical, for sure, but a radical who was part of a great tradition.

England had been expected to win that inaugural international. They were more experienced, had more players to draw upon and were between a stone and two stone per man heavier, depending whose account you believe.* Disadvantage, though, was the mother of innovation. Senior members of Queen's Park, from which, as the only serious club in Scotland, the entire national side was drawn, considered how best to combat the problem. The answer, they concluded, was to try as far as possible to avoid the charging game prevalent at the time and instead to keep the ball away from England by focusing on passing which, back then, was a minority pursuit if it was practised at all. A player was withdrawn from the forward line to operate as a back, so Scotland met England's 1-2-7 with a 2-2-6.

The ploy worked and Scotland secured a 0-0 draw. Queen's Park began to focus on passing while the English game remained focused on dribbling and charging. Scotland lost only two of their first 16 internationals, a record of success that, allied to the coming of professionalism in England (which took the game away from amateurs intent on playing the game the right way and made it far more focused on winning), led to passing being widely accepted by the mid-1880s. Queen's Park, though, remained the masters and became famed for their 'pattern-weaving' approach, as the ball was worked in a zigzag shape along the forward line.

In the 1890s, Robert Smyth McColl emerged as perhaps the finest centre-forward Queen's Park had ever had. In 1900, he scored a hat-trick as Scotland beat England 4-1 at Celtic Park, taking his international record to 13 goals in 13 games. It turned out to be his final match for his country as the following year he left Glasgow to

---

* There have been some recent suggestions that this is a post hoc myth but it was reported in the *Glasgow Herald* at the time and there seems little reason to dispute their account.

join Newcastle United. He received £300 as a signing-on fee and used a third of that to go into business with his brother Tom, setting up the newsagent RS McColl and acquiring the nickname 'Toffee Bob'. McColl stayed in Newcastle for three years before returning to Glasgow with Rangers. It was long enough for his ideas on the value of passing to take root.

The left-half Peter McWilliam, another Scot, was particularly enthused and, when he became manager of Tottenham Hotspur in December 1912, he took McColl's ideas with him. He left Tottenham for Middlesbrough in 1927, but returned in 1938 for a further four years. In his second spell, he brought through three players who would themselves go on to have successful coaching careers: Arthur Rowe, Bill Nicholson and Vic Buckingham.

Rowe was broad-minded enough to travel to Hungary in 1939, giving a series of lectures and exchanging ideas with local coaches who had emerged from the vibrant and innovative coffee-house culture of Budapest, before being forced to return home by the outbreak of the Second World War. He became Tottenham manager in 1949 and led them to the Second Division title in 1949-50 and the First Division championship in 1950-51, as well as First Division runners-up in 1951-52, playing a style of football known as 'push and run'.

Nicholson took charge at Spurs in 1958 and guided them to the double in 1961, adding further FA Cups in 1962 and 1967, when his side included Terry Venables, Barcelona manager between 1984 and 1987. Nicholson's football was very much in the McWilliam–Rowe mould.

But it was Buckingham who would have the greatest impact on the world game. He was appointed manager of West Bromwich Albion in 1953 and, in his first season, almost won the double, leading them to victory over Preston North End in the 1954 FA Cup final and second place in the league. That side included Bobby Robson, who succeeded Cruyff at Barcelona. Buckingham left for Ajax in 1959, won the league, came back to England with Sheffield Wednesday in 1962 and returned to Amsterdam two years later. His second spell at Ajax lasted just a season and ended with the club battling relegation, but during that time he gave Johan Cruyff his debut.

Ajax were already a club with pass-and-move principles, instilled by Jack Reynolds, a Manchester-born former winger who managed the club for 27 years in three stints between 1915 and 1947. Buckingham built on that legacy, laying the foundations for his successor Rinus Michels and the coming of Total Football.

Buckingham spent three acrimonious seasons with Fulham and had a brief time in Athens with Ethnikos before being appointed manager of Barcelona in 1969-70. There too he instilled the principles he had been taught by McWilliam, a modern variation on the passing game invented by Queen's Park a century previously. He won the Copa del Generalísimo in 1971 but by then he was plagued by back problems and decided to return to England. To replace him, Barcelona turned to the man who had succeeded him at Ajax. Michels had been stunningly successful with a team based around Cruyff and playing hard-pressing, possession-based football, winning four league titles, three Cups and a European Cup in six seasons.

Two years later, Cruyff followed Michels to Barcelona, cementing the Spanish club's link with Ajax. But the tradition wasn't just Cruyff and Michels. It stretched back beyond that, through Buckingham to McWilliam and before him to 'Toffee Bob' McColl and Queen's Park. Cruyff's radicalism had a proud lineage.

\* \* \*

More immediately, Cruyff had been born into the Ajax tradition. His father was a fan and he grew up on Akkerstraat, five minutes' walk from De Meer, Ajax's home until they moved into the Amsterdam ArenA in 1996. He would play on a sandy patch of ground that happened to be overlooked by a house where Jany van der Veen, a coach at Ajax, lived. Van der Veen, who had worked with Jack Reynolds, saw the skinny kid from his window and offered him a trial at Ajax. 'He always played football with older boys, and he had bossed them,' Van der Veen said. 'It seemed like he was fused to the ball.' Cruyff joined Ajax on his tenth birthday.

Van der Veen, Cruyff said, was his first major football influence, becoming 'a second father' after the death of his own father when he was 12. It was Van der Veen who made him two-footed and helped him to develop strength in his ankles by strapping weights to them and having him raise them up and down.

The next big influence was Buckingham, who picked him for the Ajax first team when he was 17. Buckingham, though, was more than just a coach. He had two sons who were roughly Cruyff's age so the teenager spent a lot of his time at Buckingham's house, where his mother worked as a cleaner. It was the Buckinghams, Cruyff said, who really taught him English.

Within a year Buckingham was gone, but Cruyff would form an even stronger bond with the man who replaced him – Rinus Michels. The first game under him ended in a 9-3 victory over MVV Maastricht. Cruyff had stood out and was suddenly a minor celebrity. Michels quickly realised he was far more than a rapid and highly skilled player; even when Cruyff was as young as 18, Michels would discuss tactical matters with him. So precocious was he that his first contribution to *Voetbal International* was not as an interviewee but in a letter he sent to the editor in which, aged 20, he took issue with various points raised in the magazine's coverage of Ajax's 1-1 draw with Real Madrid.

Right from the start, Cruyff was aware of the 'importance of organisation on the field' and loved the 'mental arithmetic' of tactics. 'Once you understand completely how to organise a team,' he wrote in his autobiography, published shortly after his death in 2016, 'then you know what the possibilities are.'

Cruyff found possibilities in other sports. He was a gifted baseball player and was catcher for the Netherlands under-15s national team. Baseball taught him the importance of knowing where you were going to throw the ball before you caught it, a principle he took into football. Cruyff seems always to have been blessed with an awareness of space and the possibilities around him. He made his debut for Ajax's baseball team in 1961 in a vital game against WV-HEDW, despite his coach, Rien van 't Hof having reservations about the lack of power in his arms. 'At his first ball,' Van 't Hof recalled, 'he hesitated for so long that I was afraid the game would be gone. But at the right moment, Johan turned and threw the ball to third base, where WV-HEDW's player had strayed too far. He was out and Ajax were champions.'

The Cruyff turn, similarly, although he always insisted it was an instinctive response to a situation, has a very clear parallel in hockey. For Cruyff the key skills of Total Football – awareness, visualisation, an ability to innovate while appreciating the disposition of others on the field – were learned so early that they seemed almost innate. 'The good player,' he said, 'is the player who touches the ball just once and knows where to run… I say, don't run so much. Football is a game you play with your brain. You have to be in the right place at the right moment, not too early, not too late.'

That was true not merely of attacking situations but also of setting up to win the ball back. In his autobiography, Cruyff gives some idea of the sort of pressing that had developed at Ajax under Michels. 'When putting pressure on a right-footed defender,' he said, 'I would close him down on his right, forcing him to pass with his weaker left foot. Meanwhile Johan Neeskens would be coming up from midfield on his left, forcing the opponents to make the pass quickly. That made the problem even worse. To do that, Neeskens had to let his man go. That meant that *his* opponent was unmarked but that guy didn't track Neeskens because, from our defence, Wim Suurbier had pushed up to fill Neeskens's position. Quickly and effectively we'd created a three-on-two situation.'

After Michels's departure, the success continued under the Romanian Ştefan Kovács with two more Dutch titles and the 1972 and 1973 European Cups. Kovács was a less authoritarian, less dictatorial figure than Michels, which allowed Ajax greater freedom of self-expression and so, perhaps, hastened the process of decay.

Concerned by his team's defence, Michels had approached the combative Partizan libero Velibor Vasović in October 1966. Defeat to Sparta Prague in the quarter-final of the 1966-67 European Cup made the situation critical and he signed the Yugoslav the following summer. Vasović, by his own account, added 'toughness and discipline and a winning mentality' to the side. Aged only 31 but suffering from asthma, he retired after captaining Ajax in the 1971 European Cup final and was replaced as libero by the more attack-minded Horst Blankenburg.

With the German shaping play from the back and the avuncular Kovács in the dugout, Ajax produced arguably their best – or at least most attacking – football between 1971 and 1973. 'Kovács was a good coach,' the midfielder Gerrie Mühren said, 'but he was too nice. Michels was more professional. He was very strict, with everyone on the same level. In the first year with Kovács we played even better because we were good players who had been given freedom. But after that the discipline went and it was all over. We didn't have the same spirit. We could have been champions of Europe for ever if we'd stayed together.'

Ajax became too free, too expressive and that led to decline. It's as though at the precise moment the fruit becomes fully ripe, it begins to rot; a coach's job in a sense then becomes to delay maturation for as long as possible. It was a lesson that was not lost on Cruyff. 'If you have less discipline coming from the coach,' he said, 'you end up with lots of different opinions coming from the squad.'

That, perhaps, is the central paradox of Total Football. On the one hand it is the most egalitarian football there is; as David Winner makes clear in *Brilliant Orange*, there were links, direct and indirect, between Ajax and the radicalism that transformed Amsterdam. In the space of a decade it went from being the drab city Albert Camus described in which 'for centuries, pipe smokers have been watching the same rain falling on the same canal' to become the thriving centre of the youth movement. The loose ethos of both was rooted in a vague idea of self-expression directed towards a common good. 'The Dutch,' as the journalist Hubert Smeets wrote in *Hard Gras* magazine in 1997, 'are at their best when they can combine the system with individual creativity. Johan Cruyff is the main representative of that. He made this country after the War. I think he was the only one who understood the sixties.' Cruyff, as he liked to say, was to the Netherlands in the sixties what the Beatles were to Britain.*

That idea is encapsulated by the term Total Football ('*totaalvoetbal*' in Dutch) which appeared only in response to performances of the national side in the 1974 World Cup, but the prefix '*totaal*' came originally from architecture. The theorist J.B. Bakema, for

---

* See, for instance, Simon Kuper and David Winner's article 'Comparing Apple with *Oranje*' in Issue Three of *The Blizzard*.

instance, spoke of 'Total Urbanisation', 'Total Environment' and 'Total Energy'. 'To understand things,' he said in a lecture given in 1974, 'you have to understand the relationship between things… Once, the highest image of interrelationship in society was indicated by the word "God" and man was allowed to use earth and universal space under the condition that man should care for what he used. But we have to actualise this kind of care and respect since man came by his awareness nearer the phenomenon of interrelationship called the relation of atoms. Man became aware of his being part of a total energy system.'

At the same time, though, while players at Ajax may similarly have derived their meaning from their interrelationship with other players, there were dangers in breaking top-down hierarchies. In 1973, in the ballot to elect a captain, Ajax voted not for Cruyff but for Piet Keizer. Cruyff decided he had to leave. 'I had suffered the kind of injury you can't see with the naked eye,' he said. As he saw it, he had been betrayed by 'not just fellow players but also close friends'.

Cruyff always seemed at his best when he had a point to prove. He made his debut for Barcelona against Granada at the end of October 1973. Barça had begun the season poorly, winning two and losing three of their opening seven games, but they won that match 4-0. They went unbeaten until February when they faced Real Madrid at the Bernabéu. Cruyff's wife Danny had a Caesarean section in Amsterdam to ensure their son – Jordi – was born in time for Cruyff to play, but his availability wasn't Michels's only concern. He had heard from Theo de Groot, a Dutch friend who lived opposite the Madrid centre-back Gregorio Benito, that Madrid intended to combat Cruyff by marking him zonally. Michels told Cruyff to drop back from his usual centre-forward position and play more as a creator, and so devised the role that would later be known as the false nine.* 'If they don't follow me, I'm free,' Cruyff said, explaining the position in 1977. 'If they follow me, they're one man short in the defence.'

That first implementation of the ploy worked spectacularly and Barça beat Madrid 5-0, a *manita*, a goal for every finger on the hand. That, said the forward Charly Rexach, later a long-serving coach at the club, was the birth of the current Barcelona. It was a watershed, the moment at which all the old sense of victimhood, the belief that Barça would always be undone by greater forces from Madrid, fell away.

Only when the title, their first for 14 years, was secured did Barça lose their first league game with Cruyff in the team. It wasn't just that he was a supremely gifted player, blessed with quick feet and preternatural balance, he seemed to invigorate the whole side. 'There are some players who might have better technique than me,' he said soon after joining Barça, 'and some may be fitter than me, but the main thing is tactics. With most players, tactics are missing.'

That March 1974, Michels was appointed coach of the Netherlands national side to lead them through the World Cup. It was that tournament that introduced the wider world to Total Football as the Dutch, playing brilliant, swaggering football, reached the final. At the time, it was their inter-movement and the pace of the attacking

---

* It would be inaccurate, though, to describe Cruyff as the first false nine (just as it would be misleading to suggest that Cruyff did not anyway instinctively drop deep seeking space; this merely formalised or made more conscious the process). From as early as the 1890s, strikers experimented with dropping deep away from their markers. G.O. Smith of the Corinthians was the first to gain a reputation for doing so, standing at the head of a proud line that included various *conductors* in Argentinian football in the 1920s, Matthias Sindelar of Austria's 1930s Wunderteam, Nándor Hidegkuti in the great Hungary side of the early fifties and even, arguably, Real Madrid's Alfredo Di Stéfano who described his role as *delantero retrasado* – a delayed centre-forward.

play that drew most of the attention, but the pressing that gave them control of the ball was unprecedentedly ferocious, often seven or eight orange-shirted players charging at the man in possession. By contrast with modern pressing it looks perhaps a little unsophisticated, but the aggressive intent was often enough.

Brazil's captain in that World Cup, Marinho Peres, reacted to the tactic with bemusement. 'The Dutch players wanted to reduce the space and put everybody in a thin band,' he explained. 'The whole logic of the offside trap comes from squeezing the game. This was a brand new thing for me. Theoretically what people thought in Brazil was that you could chip the ball over and somebody starts running. But it's not like that because you don't have time.'

Marinho joined Barça before the start of the 1974-75 season and had to learn the new style of defending. 'In one training session I pushed up and we caught four or five players offside,' he said. 'I was pleased, but Michels came and shouted at me – what he wanted was that we then went to the guy with the ball with extra players, because they had men out of the game. That's how offside becomes an offensive game.'

Johan Neeskens also moved to the Camp Nou that summer* and together he and Cruyff developed Barça's pressing game, giving it greater focus. But further success largely eluded them as Barça finished third and then runners-up three years running before winning the Copa del Rey in 1978. Yet somehow Cruyff was always about more than trophies, more even than football.

There have been various claims that he identified from the start with the Catalan cause, but the truth is rather that he was a contrarian

---

* He had been knocked unconscious by Marinho in the Netherlands' 2-0 win over Brazil at the World Cup, but seems to have borne him no ill will.

who instinctively resisted authority. He only joined Barça because Ajax had tried to sell him to Real Madrid. He called his son Jordi not because he wanted to salute the patron saint of Catalonia but because he liked the name; when he was told Jordi was not on the list of names permitted by the Spanish state, he objected because objecting was what he did (and he argued, not unreasonably, that his son was Dutch). His decision to send a signed photograph to the jailed Communist Josep Solé i Barberà, who had been arrested on the day of his debut against Granada with two tickets for the game in his pocket, was an act of anti-authoritarian mischief-making rather than part of some wider ideological campaign. Just as his attitude had made him a figure of cultural revolution in the Netherlands, so in Barcelona he became symbolic of a far wider movement. That was implicit right from the start. The morning after that Granada game, *La Vanguardia* had run a headline, '*El Barça es más que un club*', echoing a statement made by Narcís de Carreras in January 1968 just before he became Barcelona president. It was from then that '*més que un club*', the same sentiment expressed in Catalan, became the club slogan. Initially it expressed Barça's political and cultural significance but increasingly it came to refer to an aesthetic philosophy that became an identity in itself. In terms of silverware, Cruyff was only moderately successful as a player at Barcelona; in terms of giving the club self-belief, he was essential.

Fearing kidnap, Cruyff refused to travel to the World Cup in Argentina, where the Netherlands again lost in the final. At 31, he probably would have retired that summer but lost most of his money in an ill-advised pig-farming venture and so moved to the US, playing first for LA Aztecs and then Washington Diplomats.

While playing for the Diplomats in 1980, Cruyff became a technical advisor at Ajax. Inevitably his tendency to assume he knew best and everybody would be grateful to him for pointing out their mistakes brought conflict. With Ajax trailing 3-2 at home to Twente, he left his place in the stand and made his way down to the bench where he took a seat next to the coach Leo Beenhakker and, seemingly without consultation, made a number of changes to the shape of the team. Ajax won 5-3, but Beenhakker was undermined and left the club the following year.

After a ten-game stint at Levante in which he scored twice, Cruyff rejoined Ajax as a player in 1981, winning another two league titles with them. By then Cruyff was 36 and Ajax decided not to offer him a new contract. He responded with typical bravura and bloody-mindedness, signing for Ajax's great rivals Feyenoord, playing all but one game that season and being named Dutch Footballer of the Year as they won the league for the first time in a decade. His point made, Cruyff retired.

He worked as a part-time advisor to Roda JC Kerkrade and then helped out with youth training with MVV before, in June 1985, returning to Ajax as manager. His aim, he said, 'was to give the Ajax school an identity of its own again'. He wanted, in other words, to re-establish Total Football. What that actually meant is not quite as clear as it might be.

Total Football, after all, is a term that has become debased, used retrospectively for almost any side that likes to keep the ball and favours the inter-movement of players, from the Uruguayans of the twenties to the Austrians of the thirties to the Hungarians of the fifties. What differentiated the Dutch of the seventies was their combination of that swirl of players with pressing and an aggressive offside trap.

Cruyff's philosophy was, at heart, very straightforward: win possession and retain possession. 'There's a ball and either they've got it or you've got it,' he said in his autobiography. 'If you've got it, they can't score. If you use the ball well, the chances of a good outcome are greater than the chances of a bad outcome.' This, he explained, was the legacy of the 1974 World Cup and the world's recognition of Total Football: the Dutch example had shifted the focus 'to quality and technique' rather than 'effort and hard work'. That may be so, but it did not come without effort and hard work: by Guardiola's time, Barça would soon be seen as a fusion of the two.

Michels's sides had tended to play a 4-3-3, with the back four not flat, as in the English version of the offside game, but with one of the centre-backs liberated to step out into midfield. Believing wingers vital to stretch an opposing defence and create lateral space, Cruyff wanted to maintain a front three and he also wanted a creator operating behind them. But he was aware that with so many sides operating a 4-4-2 by the mid-eighties, it was a huge risk to play with only three midfielders, particularly if one was essentially a playmaker. To combat that, he needed an extra man in midfield and he found him in the defence, coming to prefer a 3-3-1-3, a 3-4-3 that could morph into 4-3-3 when out of possession, something made possible by the high offside line, a compact shape with no more than '10 to 15 metres' between the lines, and by the use of the goalkeeper as an auxiliary outfield player. What he most 'loved' about coaching, Cruyff said, was 'to puzzle about positioning and match strategy'. This was the method he passed on, the influence of his strategical thinking seen in Guardiola's preferred term for his philosophy: '*juego de posición*'.

Cruyff had very clear and controversial ideas about the role of the goalkeeper. He himself had continued playing in goal for Ajax's third team even as he made his debut for the senior side and it seems reasonable to assume his practical experience had shaped his understanding that a goalkeeper was not just somebody to stop the ball going in the net, but was another player. 'Goalkeeping at a high level,' he insisted, 'is largely a matter of vision.' That meant the goalkeeper had to be willing to play outside his box. To accept that, Cruyff acknowledged, required a leap of faith from the keeper and a mental readjustment from everybody else. 'You have to learn that the great fear of goalkeepers that they will be beaten by a ball lobbed over their head from the halfway line,' Cruyff said, 'is not based in reality. If he plays like that, in the interests of his team, then it doesn't matter ... if once in a while he doesn't save a high ball.'

That theory of the keeper as libero had had at least some bearing on the selection of Jan Jongbloed of FC Amsterdam over PSV's Jan van Beveren for the 1974 World Cup (although Van Beveren was struggling with a groin injury and fell out first with Michels, after insisting on playing only half of a pre-tournament friendly, then Cruyff, after revealing details of the unequal division of the players' sponsorship pot to other squad members). 'The great thing was,' Cruyff said, 'that in his youth Jongbloed had been an attacker. As a goalkeeper, he didn't just like joining in, he was also very good at it.' It was at Ajax, though, that he was really able to explore the possibilities of his thinking, in part because he had control, and in part because he had in his squad Stanley Menzo, whom he described as 'a keeper who was emphatically an outfield player'.

Cruyff's Ajax scored 120 goals in the 34 games of the 1985-86 season, but they finished second in the league behind PSV, who also beat them to the title the following season. Ajax did, though, win the Cup in both seasons and in 1986-87 won the Cup Winners' Cup, beating Lokomotive Leipzig in the final to bring their first European honour since Cruyff had left the club after winning the European Cup in 1973.

But this was Cruyff and this was Ajax and discord was never far away. His always troublesome relationship with the board had been fraying for some time and reached a critical point when they refused to sanction the signing of the Coventry City forward Cyrille Regis to replace Marco van Basten when he was sold to AC Milan in 1987. Cruyff left 18 games into the following season and, the following summer, replaced Luis Aragonés as manager of Barcelona. It was the beginning of an extraordinary eight years, a period far more successful than anything Barcelona had ever experienced before, a reign that transformed the nature of the club and ultimately crafted the whole course of football history.

\* \* \*

The Barcelona Cruyff took over were a big club but not an especially successful one. When Terry Venables led them to the championship in 1985, it was their first league title since Cruyff the player had inspired them in 1974, just their second in a quarter of a century. But defeat on penalties to Steaua Bucharest in the European Cup final the following year was devastating. Barça had staged a remarkable comeback to win the semi-final, beating IFK Gothenburg 3-0 in the second leg to force a penalty shoot-out and, with the final staged in Seville and only 40 Romanian fans allowed to travel, victory had seemed pre-ordained and inevitable. They drew 0-0 and missed all four penalties as they lost the shoot-out 2-0. It was, Joan Gaspart said, 'a terrible trauma, horrifying, desperately sad'. If they couldn't win the European Cup in those circumstances, when could they?

The defeat caused a general depression that undermined Venables, who came to be perceived as favouring the British players he'd signed. It didn't help that, against Steaua, he'd selected Steve Archibald, who'd just returned from injury and later admitted he wasn't fully fit, ahead of the Spanish forward Pichi Alonso.

Aragonés was appointed in 1987 but was forced out towards the end of a grim season after the so-called Mutiny of Hesperia. 'Aragonés stuck behind the players rigidly,' said Gary Lineker, one of those brought in by Venables. 'It probably cost him his job.' A number of Barcelona players had been paid for their image rights on top of their salary as a means of effectively raising their income by lowering tax liability. After the scam had been exposed, Núñez demanded that the players rather than the club should pay what was owed. They rebelled and, following a meeting at the Hotel Hesperia in Madrid, called on Núñez to resign. Crowds had fallen and those who did still go to games were split on whether to support the players or the president. With elections coming up that June, Núñez needed a dramatic move to regain popular approval. Cruyff was an obvious solution. Bringing him back turned out to be perhaps the best decision in Barcelona's history but it was one effectively forced on Núñez by the weakness of his position. In easier times, he may not have been so willing to work with such a headstrong figure.

Cruyff's self-belief was vital in dispelling the disillusionment around the Camp Nou, while the fact that everything seemed to be going so badly meant he was able to impose fundamental changes without much resistance. 'As a footballer and a trainer* I was always an idealist,' Cruyff said. There was a purge of the squad that summer, largely because of Hesperia. Fifteen players were offloaded, including

---

* The usual Dutch word for 'coach' is 'trainer'. It does not imply, as the term does in English, a physio, but it does suggest the extent to which the role in the Netherlands is seen as being about teaching and improving players rather than managing a club. The British preference for the term 'manager' seems unique in this regard.

Víctor Muñoz, Ramón Calderé and Bernd Schuster, although the captain Alexanko, who had been the mouthpiece of the revolt, remained thanks to the intervention of Cruyff.

Cruyff, recognising the problems Venables had faced with his British influx, self-consciously Hispanicised – or Catalanised/Basquified – the squad, in which he was benefited by a gifted generation emerging from La Masia, Barcelona's academy. 'Barça fans like seeing players from the *cantera**in the first team,' Cruyff said. 'It makes them feel that the coach somehow is more a part of Barcelona. I tried to produce a game that they could claim as Catalan. That way, the fans are less likely to whistle if things go wrong.'

In his first season, he promoted the midfielders Guillermo Amor and Luis Milla and the left-back Sergi from the academy side to the first-team squad. In addition, 12 players were signed, among them the winger Txiki Begiristain, the forward José Mari Bakero, the striker Julio Salinas and the midfielder Eusebio Sacristán.

'From the start,' Eusebio said, 'he wanted to impose a style that was revolutionary: playing a 3-4-3, with only three defenders, four midfielders in a diamond and three up front, two of them very wide. It was, wow, something we'd never seen. It surprised us, but for me it was very exciting because I was a player whose qualities were technique, vision, decision-making… All my career I found it hard to make my way in professional football. It was all physique, strength and technical quality but very much in an individual sense, one on one. I was a passer, I needed my teammates to be positioned in a way that allowed my attributes to be useful.'

Almost through force of will, Eusebio had forged a career at Valladolid and Atlético, but always playing wide in a 4-4-2. In Cruyff's

---

* Literally 'the quarry', but used to mean the youth system.

3-4-3, though, he could play in any of the three more advanced midfield positions or on the wing. 'A whole load of possibilities opened up for me,' he said.

That didn't suit everybody, though. Salinas's arrival meant Lineker being pushed into a wide role. 'I was ill at the beginning of the season with hepatitis,' he said.* 'I was out for a few months and Cruyff wanted his own foreign players to come in. He messed me about. He deliberately played me on the wing to try to wind me up so I'd have a hissy fit. But I saw through that, so I just carried on professionally and played on the wing the whole season... He just said I was fast and therefore suited. He played ... Salinas up front, who was a decent centre-forward. The most frustrating thing was that with his system of play, if he'd have played me in the central role, it would have been absolutely made for my game. But it wasn't for him. He was entitled to do that and I understood it.'

That, of course, is the other side of Cruyff. Genius he may have been, but he was also extremely difficult. 'He didn't like one-to-one stuff,' Lineker said. 'He was a brilliant coach and a great visionary and a wonderful footballer and I admired a lot about him, but he was also an incredibly arrogant man. Super-confident, know-it-all about everything.'

Yet Lineker, for all his problems with Cruyff, acknowledges he benefited from playing under him. 'I learnt a load: spatial awareness, how to make the pitch as large as you possibly can when you attack,' he said. 'His whole training thing was about that, that when you have the ball you make everything large, when you don't, you make everything small. I was fascinated by the way he got that across. It was all possession football: nine v seven, seven v five, all different numbers. It was very, very interesting and clever.'

---

* In an interview with Tom Williams in Issue 27 of *The Blizzard*.

'Players would run everywhere,' Eusebio said, 'and Johan would be, "No, stop. Stop, don't invade the space your teammate is occupying, don't let a defender mark both of you, separate." His idea was: "I have technical players, let's put them in positions where the opponent can't take the ball off them. Let's always have a line of pass open; let's open up the wingers so that the defenders who want to stop them have to spread right across the pitch... The other teams all have four defenders; that means they have players they don't use. We're going to use ten players and as we will always have a free man, we're going to pass the ball to each other. When one man comes to you, you pass it on to the next." It was about decision-taking, choosing the right moment: when to pass the ball, whom to pass it to.'

Training was not just about ball retention but about using the ball in the most efficient way. 'We played positional games in reduced spaces,' Eusebio explained, 'generating situations of [numerical] superiority, so that when we got onto a big pitch, this same thing we were doing in a small space is applied and easier. If he saw that your body position was wrong, if he saw that you were passing to the nearest man, he would say, "No, pass it to the furthest [available]... If you overcome lines of pressure, you allow this player, a line further on, to face forward and he has more passes, in different lines..."'

'These were details that he told us about from the very first day – details that only he knew, or had discovered, or saw ... it was different, vanguard, revolutionary, exciting ... what can I say? For me, I found my religion and I am faithful to it.'

In Cruyff's first season, 1988-89, Barça finished second in the league, five points behind Madrid. Crucially, though, playing in that idiosyncratic style, Barça beat Sampdoria 2-0 in Bern to lift the Cup Winners' Cup, their first European silverware in seven years. As Cruyff continued his rebuilding, Lineker and Francisco Lobo Carrasco left, effectively to be replaced by Michael Laudrup and, crucially, Ronald Koeman, who had just won the European Cup with PSV and the European Championship with the Netherlands.

Koeman, powerful, blond, intelligent and blessed with a fearsome shot, had a disappointing first season and Barça slipped to third, 11 points behind Madrid, but a 2-0 win over Madrid in the Copa del Rey final kept Cruyff in a job. Still, there was discontent that summer with many questioning the high turnover of players. Núñez had to head off a motion of no confidence in Cruyff that might have seen him dismissed.

The churn of players went on as Cruyff sought the right balance while insisting he would keep only those who were most committed. Milla, Alonso, Ernesto Valverde and Roberto were all offloaded, while the goalkeeper Carles Busquets (father of Sergio) and the forward Ion Andoni Goikoetxea were promoted from the youth side and the turbulent Bulgarian striker Hristo Stoichkov was signed from CSKA Sofia. Stoichkov was a player of huge importance, not just gifted but headstrong, self-assured and unpredictable.

Although La Masia provided Cruyff with a handful of players, he wasn't happy about how it was run. When he became manager, the academy was still employing its *prueba de la muñeca* – the test of the wrist – which sought to weed out by means of a bone scan players who weren't going to reach 1.80m in height. Cruyff didn't care about size. He wanted touch, energy and tactical intelligence and scrapped the test, while insisting every side, from under-eights upwards, should play the 3-4-3 and become comfortable with his system.

They were long-term plans that would have a profound impact, but there was also a need for short-term success. An attempt to sign Jan Mølby from Liverpool failed and led to Cruyff doubting the board, whom he suspected had never wished to sign the Dane. Koeman was injured and with Milla sold, Barça were left short of holding midfielders. Cruyff asked Rexach, his assistant, who in the youth set-up could step up. His reply was instant: Pep Guardiola.

Cruyff had already given him his debut in a friendly against Banyoles 18 months earlier but Guardiola, then 18, hadn't impressed, with the manager dismissing him as 'slower than my granny'. Cruyff went to watch the B-side to refresh his memory but found Guardiola was on the bench. When he asked why, he was told that for that game they'd preferred bigger, more dynamic players. Cruyff was furious. 'A good player,' he said, 'doesn't need a strong physique.'

Growing up at La Masia, Guardiola had idolised Guillermo Amor, who was four years his senior, turning up two hours early for practice to watch the midfielder train. It was a suspension for Amor that gave him his opportunity in the first team as, aged 19, he made his competitive debut in December 1990 in a 2-0 win over Cádiz. 'Before he was a coach, before he was a teacher, Pep was an excellent apprentice,' said the goalkeeper Andoni Zubizarreta. 'When he came through at Barça for the first time, his idea was not to teach us how to play football. His obsession was to learn how to play in that system. And he overwhelmed us with questions, watched, put things right and learned.'

That 1990-91 season was when everything crystallised. A memorable 2-1 win over Real Madrid in January gave Barcelona control of the title race and they weren't derailed even when Cruyff suffered a heart attack a month later. By the end of the season he was back on the bench, replacing his cigarettes with Chupa Chups lollies. Barça lost to Manchester United in the Cup Winners' Cup final, undone by two goals from Mark Hughes, a player who had never settled at Barça after being signed by Venables, but that was a minor disappointment: six years after their previous title, Barça won the league. Just as important as the success was the means of the success: there was a sense of Cruyff's philosophy coming to fruition. This was what would become known, a year later, as the 'Dream Team'.

Although it was their technical quality that caught the eye, Cruyff was adamant that at the heart of their success was pressing and passing. Give an opponent five metres of space and he'll look like a good player; reduce that distance to three and he may not. 'To be able to play like that,' Cruyff wrote in his autobiography, 'you need to be fast, and you have to keep switching gear. It took more than 10,000 hours of training to finally reach the level of the Dream Team.'

Positioning was vital and Cruyff would stop training every few seconds to suggest minor adjustments. It was infuriating but effective. 'It isn't the man on the ball who decides where the ball goes, but the players without the ball,' he explained. 'Constantly creating triangles means ball circulation isn't interrupted.' Practice was everything. 'The more instinctive our play becomes,' Cruyff said, 'the less mental energy it would require.' And the more the opponent is pinned back in their own half, the less running Barça had to do. This was the origin of the *juego de posición* Guardiola would later evangelise. 'If you do not have discipline, it is impossible to play soccer,' said Stoichkov. 'When the strikers lose the ball, even the strikers come behind the ball, everyone presses very quickly to pick up the ball. No space. That was Cruyff's concept.'

Guardiola had played only four games in 1990-91, but the following season he was a regular. 'Guardiola had to be clever,' Cruyff explained. 'He didn't have any other choice back then. He was a bit like me. You must have a lot of technique, move the ball quickly, avoid a collision – and to avoid it you must have good vision. It's a domino effect. You soon get a sharp eye for detail, for players' positions. You can apply this when you are a player and a coach too. Guardiola learnt that way – thanks to his build – and he was lucky enough to have a coach who had experienced the same thing.'

Guardiola tended to operate as the holding midfielder just in front of Koeman. There could have been no more overt symbol of Cruyff's determination to play the ball out from the back, his rejection of defenders whose only function was to defend. 'They weren't fast and they weren't defenders,' Cruyff acknowledged. That, he reasoned, didn't matter because Barça spent most of the game in the opposition half. So long as his goalkeeper was alert and prepared to play out of his box, the chances of Barça being undone by a long ball from deep hit over Koeman and Guardiola were minimal. To make sure Zubizarreta could do that, Cruyff would play him in midfield in training so he could get used to having the ball at his feet under pressure. Cruyff had 'fast full-backs who were trained as wingers' and so had the pace and awareness to get back to intercept cross-field balls. 'The third option was the pass down the middle. Guardiola and Koeman had such positional strength that they always intercepted it, even though they were clearly not the ideal midfielder-defenders.'

The league was won again as Real Madrid, having been 2-0 up on the final day, lost 3-2 away to a Tenerife side managed by their former striker Jorge Valdano and Barça beat Athletic Bilbao. Of even greater consequence, though, was what happened in the European Cup as Barça beat Sampdoria 1-0 in the final at Wembley thanks to a 112th-minute Koeman free kick. Appropriately, they did so wearing orange. That success, Eusebio said, 'was necessary as a confirmation that the idea was good. We needed that to be confirmed by results because results lay down the judgement.'

And it was necessary because Barça had never previously won the European Cup; if they hadn't won it with that side, hadn't won it with Cruyff, then when could they have won it? That night, the vice president Joan Gaspart, fulfilling a vow he had made earlier in the season, paddled in the Thames in celebration. The following day as the squad gathered on the balcony of Barcelona's City Hall, Guardiola consciously echoed the Catalan president Josep Tarradellas on his return from exile after the death of Franco, adjusting his declaration, 'Citizens of Catalonia, I am here' to announce, 'Citizens of Catalonia, you have it here.'

The following year brought a repeat of the final-day drama. Again Real Madrid lost away to Valdano's Tenerife and again Barcelona won to overhaul them, this time beating Real Sociedad. The season after, with Romário up front, Barça claimed a fourth title in a row. The Brazilian forward scored a hat-trick in a 5-0 win over Madrid, but that season their closest rivals were Deportivo La Coruña. They too faltered on the final day of the season, having foolishly mocked Cruyff with giant Chupa Chups the week before. After a 6-2 defeat at Zaragoza in February, Cruyff had promised each member of his squad new contracts if they won the league. They went on to take 28 points from the final ten games of the season. Still, though, they won the league on the final day only because Depor's Miroslav Đukić missed a last-minute penalty against Valencia. Cruyff's Dream Team were good, but they were also lucky.

Four days later, the luck ran out and Barça were hammered 4-0 in Athens by Milan. Barça, perhaps, had got too used to winning, had prevailed so often in the previous four years that it seemed success was inevitable, that they, playing football in what their manager assured them as the right way, were somehow elect. 'Barcelona are favourites,'

Cruyff had said before the game. 'We're more complete, competitive and experienced than at Wembley [in 1992]. Milan are nothing out of this world. They base their game on defence, we base ours on attack.'

The result was a fatal complacency. 'We didn't prepare,' his assistant, Charly Rexach, admitted. 'We lacked concentration. Athens was the beginning of the end.'

Except it wasn't an end. 'Along the route,' Eusebio said, 'there are things that mean that the narrative thread gets lost, but it's always there.' Cruyff may have been seen as such a problem that he wasn't invited when, three years later, they began their centenary year with a game against Atlético, but his influence would live on. With no official role, he became effectively the conscience of the club, a floating eminence always there in the background, ready to offer advice or intervene in times of crisis; Cruyff had always railed against the *entorno* – literally 'environment' – that he said undermined Barça, yet in time he became that *entorno*. That sense of distance, perhaps, was essential: his theories unsullied by such mundane issues as results, Cruyff could get on, from above the fray, with shaping the football of the first two decades of the 21st century.

# CHAPTER TWO

# THE GREATEST SEMINAR IN HISTORY

Bobby Robson had turned down Barcelona twice before, once out of loyalty to Ipswich Town and once out of loyalty to England. The third time, he was not going to miss the opportunity. In his autobiography he wrote, perhaps a little optimistically, that his past record earned him respect but the truth is that whoever had followed Cruyff was facing an immensely difficult task. Cruyff, Robson admitted, 'haunted my early days'.

The tendency now is to write off that 1996-97 season, to see it as a disappointing campaign largely notable for the performances of the Brazilian striker Ronaldo, who was signed from PSV Eindhoven for US$20m. Robson even suggested that it was intended or at least expected that he should fail, that the terms of his contract which stipulated that he could be shifted into a role as director of football after a year were an indication that he was regarded primarily as a post-Cruyff buffer. Yet that year brought both the Cup Winners' Cup and the Copa del Rey, while Barça finished the league just two points behind Madrid, who played 14 fewer games than them that season.

The issue, supposedly, was style, although it's not clear how anybody could have followed Cruyff in that regard. 'Robson was more heart,' said Hristo Stoichkov. 'He liked contact. Johan wanted to play more soccer. Robson wanted to play football but to play hard. With heart.' Nor is it clear to what extent even the carping was motivated by background machinations. Certainly it's easy to see why Robson was bewildered after his side was criticised following a 6-0 win over Rayo Vallecano. But then he never understood that side of life at the Camp Nou. 'It was a highly political environment and I wasn't a political animal...' he said. 'Hysteria would sweep around the ground at the smallest invitation.'

Robson's claim that he had 'embarrassed' Barça with his success is perhaps an overstatement, but it certainly made it harder to bring in Louis van Gaal after one season. In the end, as the two men realised Núñez had signed contracts with both of them, Robson effectively stepped aside and clearly enjoyed his year acting as a sort of scout-cum-ambassador, travelling the world, watching football. His year in charge thus became an interregnum between the two great avatars of the Total Football philosophy and that perhaps is why it tends to be overlooked. Yet, having learned the game under Vic Buckingham at West Brom, Robson was at least connected to the same tradition.

Robson also helped nurture the tradition's antithesis, the man who would eventually become Barcelona's nemesis. When he arrived at Barcelona, he brought with him a sharp-featured, fresh-faced, dark-haired translator. But José Mourinho was always more than a translator. The 33-year-old had been born into football. His great uncle had been president of Vitória de Setúbal. His father, José Manuel Mourinho Félix, had been a goalkeeper – he saved a penalty from Eusébio on the forward's debut and won one international cap, albeit playing for just eight minutes – and then went into coaching. Mourinho wanted to be a player but after spells at Rio Ave, where his father was coach, Belenenses and Sesimbra, he recognised that his future lay in coaching.

Mourinho had grown up on an estate near Setúbal owned by that great uncle, Mário Ascensão Ledo, who oversaw a number of sardine canneries and was a prominent supporter of the dictator António de Oliveira Salazar, who ruled Portugal between 1932 and 1968. The young Mourinho would play football in the garden, having a servant go in goal while he took shots at him. He was no rebel: he didn't drink or smoke growing up and seems never to have wanted to do anything other than follow his father into football.

Mourinho was five when Salazar suffered a cerebral haemorrhage, slipped in the bath and was replaced as prime minister. He was 11 when the Estado Novo, the right-wing Catholic dictatorship* Salazar had forged, was finally dissolved. His mother's family lost much of their estate as a result. 'It may be that from this traumatic event,' the Argentinian full-back Javier Zanetti, who played for Mourinho at Inter, speculated, 'that Mourinho has drawn the ethics of work, of precision, the horror of entrusting himself to fortune.'

Certainly the aspiring coach had few illusions about the world to which he was committing himself; his father's experiences had demonstrated how ungrateful football can be. Mourinho has often referred to one Christmas when he was 'nine or ten' when his father was sacked on Christmas Day. Actually, it happened in 1984 when Mourinho was 21, but the general point remains: no matter what you've done in the past – Mourinho Sr had taken Rio Ave to promotion and a Portuguese Cup final – a run of bad results can bring the end.

---

* It was perhaps not strictly fascistic, but as the US historian David L. Raby puts it, 'of para-fascistic tendency'.

From being a teenager, Mourinho had helped his father, preparing scouting reports on opponents – perhaps significantly, looking for ways their way of playing could be hampered. As Félix Mourinho oversaw Amora's promotion to the Portuguese top flight in 1979-80, José took charge of the ballboys, passing on messages to players from his father.

Struggles with maths meant that Mourinho Jr failed to get into university at the first attempt. At his mother's urging he tried business school, but lasted just a day before following his father north as he managed Rio Ave. He continued his studies, resat the exam and this time passed, being accepted at the Instituto Superior de Educação Física in Lisbon. There, he came under the influence of Professor Manuel Sérgio, who believed that football knowledge was not enough, that a coach also had to be a psychologist, a public speaker and have a grasp of the sciences. Specifically, he gave lectures on emotions and how they could be manipulated. Mourinho followed them with a rapacious curiosity. 'He looked,' Manuel Sérgio said, 'like a cat catching birds.'

In 1987, Mourinho left the college and worked for a while as a PE teacher at various primary schools, specialising in helping children with disabilities. The following year, he went to Largs in Scotland and got the first part of his UEFA licence. A year later, Vitória de Setúbal, a club where his father had played and worked, took him on as a youth team coach. The senior coach was the former Portugal forward Manuel Fernandes, who took Mourinho with him to act as fitness coach when he was appointed at Estrela da Amadora. When Estrela were then relegated, Fernandes was sacked and Mourinho returned to Setúbal, before following Fernandes to Ovarense where he acted as scout.

When, after winning the league in each of his two seasons at PSV, Bobby Robson was appointed manager of Sporting in 1992, Fernandes, a legend at the club, was named as his assistant. He suggested Mourinho be brought in as a translator; this was the 29-year-old's big break. Robson liked Mourinho, recognising his translator conveyed not only the sense but also the tone of what he was saying to players. The great Hungarian Béla Guttmann, a peripatetic coach whose irascibility meant he never stayed anywhere long, said a manager had to be like a lion tamer, able to dominate his players. This, perhaps, is the first real evidence of Mourinho, another wanderer, possessing that quality: he had the force of personality to deliver a rollicking to top-class players without any sense of hiding behind the excuse that he was just passing on what Robson had said (and Robson, for all the cuddliness of his image, was not one to avoid a ferocious dressing-down when he deemed it necessary).

Robson led Sporting to third in the league in his first season despite describing the club as being 'in a terrible state' but was sacked in December the following year following a UEFA Cup defeat to Casino Salzburg – even though Sporting were top of the league. The following month, in January 1994, Porto named Robson as the successor to Tomislav Ivić with Mourinho alongside him as his translator and a little bit more. A naturally open and garrulous man, Robson had taken to discussing tactics with Mourinho and he began to give him more and more responsibility, getting him to plan training sessions and prepare dossiers on opponents, recognising that the younger man's meticulousness and natural caution were a useful counterbalance to his own spontaneity and attacking instincts. Robson described Mourinho's scouting reports as being 'as good as anything I've ever received' but at the same time was always clear that, 'I never gave him a coaching job: he assisted.'

The level of that assistance, though, increased as time went by. 'Bobby Robson's work concentrates mainly on the final part – finishing, scoring,' Mourinho told his biographer Luís Lourenço, explaining that he fitted into the gaps and did the homework and the preparation. Robson's official number two was Augusto Inácio but, according to Joel Neto in his biography of Mourinho, after he had held a private meeting with the players, the translator began to machinate against him with the result that Inácio was forced to leave. That's a trait that has surfaced again and again, a sense that Mourinho is always politicking, for his own status within the club as well as for the advancement of the club.

Porto beat Sporting, by then managed by Carlos Queiroz, in the Portuguese Cup final in Robson's first season and they won the league in each of the next two. In late spring 1995, the Barcelona vice president Joan Gaspart had telephoned Porto, ostensibly to discuss whether he should sign Luís Figo from Sporting. That opened a channel of communication and a year later he ended up offering Robson the job from which Cruyff was about to be ousted. Mourinho followed Robson to Catalonia.

That summer, Barça signed Ronaldo, who was then 19 but already one of the best strikers in the world. It was, the Dutch journalist Frits Barend suggested, a populist move to get fans back onside after Cruyff's departure (although quite how well known Ronaldo was in Catalonia is debatable), just as Cruyff's appointment had been a populist move to following the Mutiny of Hesperia. Nonetheless, replacing Cruyff was always going to be an all but impossible job.

Robson's geniality might have made an effective contrast but whatever doubts the players had were magnified one morning soon after he'd arrived as he attempted to explain his tactics, drawing in chalk on the dressing-room floor with Mourinho translating. After Cruyff, Robson seemed very traditional and he lacked the clarity of expression of his predecessor. Mourinho took to adding supplementary, clearer instructions.

'I watched Mourinho every day for a year,' said Stoichkov. 'Mourinho looked every day, reading the conversations, the attitude of the players, the sessions. He's the typical guy who watches every-thing – changing room, bus, control. Everything. That's the reason he has a tough character. He liked everything to be 100 per cent, in the room, good discipline, good organisation...'

Stoichkov acknowledged that as a coach he is like Mourinho in demanding absolute discipline in his desire for control, but he also made a more surprising comparison. 'Maybe people don't like his attitude,' he said. 'OK, sometimes you like it, sometimes you don't. And if you don't, so what? ... Don't be saying sorry all the time. If people don't like it, tough luck. He is very hard but he is very close to the guys; maybe he says sorry to them, speaks to them. He has a big heart. He's like Johan. Johan spoke very hard, very hard. After games he would say, "You're the best, I love you all: ... that's work. That's no problem. Sometimes he's tough, sometimes he hits you, sometimes he hugs you.'

Back then, Guardiola and Mourinho had a cordial relationship. Guardiola, for instance, intervened to protect Mourinho when the Athletic bench swarmed towards him during a league game at San Mamés. Footage of the celebrations after Barça had won the Cup Winners' Cup final against Paris Saint-Germain in Rotterdam, meanwhile, shows them hugging on the pitch. Perhaps in the context of winning a European trophy that means little, but the way Guardiola reacts when he sees Mourinho approaching, with a point and a grin, suggests at least a measure of mutual respect and possibly even affection.

Still, there seem to have been few if any long and detailed debates about the game even if Mourinho did effectively serve as a liaison between Robson and the players, in particular, the so-called 'gang of four' – Guardiola, Luis Enrique, Sergi and Abelardo – who ran the dressing room. Guardiola, Robson said, 'was a big fish. A good player too… He'd say we couldn't play this way or we couldn't do that – he had an opinion on everything. José saw that he was an important figure within the club and said to himself, "I've got to get to know him. I've got to get in with this guy." And he did. José and Pep were quite friendly.'

In his 2001 memoir *La meva gent, el meu futbol* [*My People, My Football*], Guardiola said that the players did eventually come round to Robson's way of thinking but that the three to four months it took them to adjust after Cruyff was too much, that by then the title had gone and minds were made up. 'The synchrony [of the thinking of Robson and the players],' he wrote, 'was interpreted as self-management.'

Perhaps it was. At half-time in the 1997 Copa del Rey final against Real Betis, Barça were drawing 1-1. The players wanted to focus attacks on the left side of the Betis defence and discussed their plan with Mourinho as Robson watched on. Perhaps Robson was a lame duck, or perhaps he merely encouraged players to think for themselves and managed by consensus: either way, the tweak worked and Barça won 3-2 after extra time. Just because a manager isn't dictatorial doesn't mean he is somehow inferior; arguably being willing to listen to advice is a sign of strength.

Guardiola was already taking a lead in directing tactics, with Laurent Blanc euphemistically speaking of his 'perseverance'. 'I was up to my balls with Pep,' said the France captain. 'All day, this and that and this and that in the dressing room. He made my head spin.'

To the end, Robson remained baffled by the politics of the club. In England, he protested, he'd have been 'a bloody hero' for his successes in the Copa del Rey and the Cup Winners' Cup, while the 90 points they took in the league was more than they'd won in all but one season under Cruyff (making the necessary adjustment for the switch from two to three points for a win). His fate, though, had already been decided and a couple of days after the cup final, Robson was shunted aside for Louis van Gaal.

Núñez, having seemingly already informed Robson of his fate, only told Van Gaal he was taking over at a meeting with his predecessor and his translator. 'Mourinho,' Van Gaal recalled, 'went out of his mind and said all the things that he said. It was not nice for Núñez and not nice for me either.'

The reason for the change was almost entirely ideological. 'Robson was a typical English manager,' said Van Gaal. 'He inspired his players in a certain way – he was a father for his players, that kind of thing. He did not play like the school of Holland. He was only there one year and won three titles but in spite of that, the board of Barcelona was more indoctrinated with the vision of Michels and Cruyff.'

I met Van Gaal in a central London hotel on the morning of the League Cup final in 2018, in which Guardiola won his first trophy in English football as his Manchester City beat Arsenal. Van Gaal was an exhausting interviewee, forever asking questions – Who were my defenders? What was the situation? – but he also expressed scepticism about a City side that until that point had seemed imperious. He was worried about the way Guardiola at times had his full-backs 'inside at the moment they lose the ball'. This was why he preferred a slightly more conservative approach, protecting possession: to play like City, he said, was 'a big risk because when the opponent overcomes the pressure of City, Guardiola starts at once that pressure with the full-backs a line higher. Until this moment Premier League clubs did not find a solution, but in the Champions League I have to see.'

In that, Van Gaal was prescient but he was generally positive about how City were playing, seeing them as the most recent incarnation of that philosophy derived ultimately from Rinus Michels. 'The most important thing,' he said, 'is the positions on the pitch.' Although he proved increasingly flexible and increasingly willing to adapt to circumstance as his career progressed, he still has a fundamental belief that the best way of achieving that is 'the 1-4-3-3 or 1-3-4-3 system that I played with Ajax when I started: then you have always triangles. That's the point you want to reach when a player has the ball that he has always two or three options – in front. You can go back but I prefer to go forward. That's one of the key principles. With 4-4-2 it's not good if you play flat. Yes, you can do it by moving five metres and then you are free but then you have to do it, and at the right moment. In the other system this is more natural already. And you can improve also by finding the open lines. But this depends on the quality of the players.'

It's significant that Van Gaal insists upon including the goalkeeper in his designation of formations. The convention is to speak of 4-3-3 or 3-4-3 and take the position of the goalkeeper for granted, but for Van Gaal he is effectively an auxiliary outfielder: 'The goalkeeper has to play football.'

There are then three other key principles: 'I always insist that the team is more important than the individual. That is also very important.' That was a tenet that caused problems not only for Van Gaal but also at times for Guardiola.

The next principle: 'We want to attack, so everything is built up to attack. Even when you don't have the ball, you have to attack, and that is the pressing that we also did, so direct pressing. That direct pressing means that your defenders are on the halfway line because you have to make the space short and that also determines the profile of the players.' There are many, particularly at Manchester United, who would claim that Van Gaal's football was far from attacking, but the term 'attack' is a slippery one in football. Much of the most thrilling football is actually the result of counter-attacking producing sudden, sweeping moves from one end of the pitch to the other. For Van Gaal, to attack is to be proactive, either to have the ball or to be seeking to win it back by pressing.

'So another principle,' he went on, 'is that because you have to attack, you know in advance that your opponent is defending and in a short space and are only playing counter-football.' That is to say that by pressing, by pushing high up the pitch to squeeze the opponent in possession, the Van Gaal philosophy risks leaving space behind the defensive line and is vulnerable to the counter-attack. That's why it's so important to have a goalkeeper who can sweep up in that space and why countering the counter – *Gegenpressing*, to give it the term under which the theory was popularised in Germany – has become such a feature of the modern game. It's perhaps no coincidence that no manager has troubled Guardiola as much as the arch-exponent of *Gegenpressing*, Jürgen Klopp.

In some ways, if Robson had to go, Van Gaal was the obvious appointment. Having led a startlingly young Ajax side to the Champions League title in 1995, he was regarded as one of the foremost emerging managers in Europe. From Barcelona's point of view, what was significant wasn't just that he'd been successful, but that he'd been successful at Ajax. Who better to pick up from Cruyff than the man who had effectively carried on his legacy in Amsterdam, who idolised Michels? 'When I was 15, I was looking only at Michels, not at the players,' Van Gaal said. 'All my friends were looking at the players, but I wanted a signature from him.'

It wasn't, though, as simple as that. Their football education may have been similar but Cruyff and Van Gaal were contrasting types. Van Gaal was only four years younger than Cruyff, although acclaim came to him much later. Like Cruyff, he had grown up within walking distance of De Meer and, like Cruyff, he had the typical arrogance of the Amsterdammer. But where Cruyff was slight and graceful, Van Gaal was heavy-set and had a face that a satirical Spanish television show later depicted as a brick wall.

Van Gaal was the youngest of nine children in a family dominated by a strict father who gave each of his offspring a specific chore: one set the table, one did the dishes. Louis's job was peeling potatoes. Footballing philosophy tends always to be a compromise between ideology and circumstance; whatever grand theoretical thoughts Van Gaal may have been attempting to enact, it's also impossible not to see the similarity between how he ran his teams and how his father ran his family.

After high school, Van Gaal had enrolled at the Academie voor Lichamelijke Opvoeding (the Academy of Physical Education). A big influence there was John Rijsman, his psychology tutor. 'I learned,' Van Gaal said, 'that it is better to deal with people in a positive than a negative way. I am the harmony type. Rinus Michels and Johan Cruyff were the war type.' There are plenty of former players who would raise their eyebrows at that self-description.

While training to be a PE teacher, Van Gaal played football for the local amateur side RKSV De Meer, dreaming always of playing for Ajax. He joined them in 1972 and played for a season in their reserve side, but never managed a game for a first team that was, at the time, dominating Europe under the captaincy of Cruyff.

As a player, Cruyff said Van Gaal lacked 'rhythm … [but] his vision was good. The technical quality was very good. But … when there was pressure, it was all over. It had to be faster.' Van Gaal's own assessment was relatively similar and, just before Cruyff moved to Barcelona, he joined Royal Antwerp. There he tended to be the fourth foreigner when the Belgian league allowed only three, with the manager Guy Thys also regarding him as too slow to play at the highest level.

Van Gaal returned to the Netherlands in 1977 and worked as a PE teacher at the Don Bosco school in Amsterdam, a tough environment. While teaching, he played for Telstar and, when they were relegated, moved to Sparta Rotterdam where he played alongside Danny Blind, who would later be his captain at Ajax. Nobody could have called him elegant, but in 248 league games there he proved himself an effective playmaker. It says much for his style of play – and perhaps his personality – that he was only ever booked five times, on each occasion for dissent. His mouth also earned him the only red card of his career: 'If you want to make the newspapers, moustache man,' he supposedly said to the referee, 'you should give me a yellow card. If you want to make the front pages, you should give me another one.' Teammates at Sparta remember how Van Gaal would organise them on the pitch, frequently making small adjustments to rebalance the side.

In 1986, deciding the commute from Amsterdam to Rotterdam had become too much – he had twice crashed his car through exhaustion – Van Gaal joined the Alkmaar club AZ as a player-assistant coach. He stopped playing a year later and, as the coach Hans Eijkenbroek fell ill, took on greater responsibility, giving full rein to the disciplinarian streak he had shown as a teacher: lateness was punished, players were forced to polish their shoes and the polite form of the second-person pronoun was insisted upon (he also makes his daughter use it when talking to him, as he used it to his mother). 'I am a consistent, honest and direct person,' Van Gaal said. 'And sometimes that strikes people as being hard.'

Like Cruyff he would repeatedly stop training to correct positioning, always trying to ensure the passing lanes were kept open. And like Cruyff his intensity caused problems. Morale dropped, with both players and directors finding him too intense, too demanding, and in 1988 he was sacked.

The turmoil at Ajax, though, offered an opportunity. After the success of 1986-87, the following season had been hard, with Marco van Basten leaving for AC Milan and Frank Rijkaard going to Real Zaragoza before the departure of an infuriated Cruyff. He was replaced initially by a trio of coaches and then by the German former Marseille and Young Boys boss Kurt Linder before, in October 1988, the Luxembourg-born former Twente striker and manager Spitz Kohn was placed in interim charge for the remainder of the season. He brought in Van Gaal as his assistant. The start to the season had been shambolic, but under Kohn and Van Gaal they recovered to finish second. Van Gaal had hoped he might be appointed full time, but Ajax instead turned to the tough-talking, cigar-smoking Leo Beenhakker who, after effectively being ousted by Cruyff in 1981, had managed Real Zaragoza, the Netherlands national side and Real Madrid. Van Gaal went back to working with the youth set-up, where he helped develop Clarence Seedorf, Patrick Kluivert, Edgar Davids and Michael Reiziger. In 1989, he began a Dutch football federation (KNVB) coaching course which included a stint observing Cruyff at Barcelona. The following year, he replaced Kohn as Beenhakker's assistant and in September 1991, when Beenhakker returned to Madrid, he took over as head coach.

Van Gaal was not an instant success. He moved Jan Wouters from the centre to the right, then clashed with the popular winger

Bryan Roy. 'The supporters have always adored Bryan because in the Netherlands the emphasis is on kicking the ball around nicely and not in all the other disciplines I find equally important,' Van Gaal explained. He eventually decided Roy lacked 'football intelligence' and sold him.

The Roy issue was symptomatic of a wider debate, with many traditionalists unhappy at how Ajax were playing – and Ajax, perhaps, stand alongside Barcelona as the two clubs most obsessed by style as a facet of identity. On the wall of his office hung a framed slogan: 'Quality is the exclusion of coincidence.' There was a desire to control that Van Gaal argued underpinned spontaneity on the pitch; his detractors felt it inhibited it.

Van Gaal's Ajax may have played the Cruyffian 3-4-3, but even at their most successful they were never as fluid, never as obviously aesthetically pleasing as their counterparts of two decades earlier. 'The Ajax number ten,' Henny Kormelink and Tjeu Seeverens wrote in *The Coaching Philosophies of Louis van Gaal and the Ajax Coaches*, 'has to set an example by pursuing his opponent.' Van Gaal used Dennis Bergkamp in the role and then Rob Alflen but his ideal was always the industrious Jari Litmanen. 'When Ajax lose possession,' Kormelink and Seeverens continued, 'he immediately carried out his defensive tasks, and when Ajax are in possession, he chooses the right moment to appear alongside the centre-forward as the second striker.'

That sounds as though Van Gaal was obsessed with work rate, yet he argued he was one of the few coaches who wanted his players to run less, not more. 'We talked always about speed of the ball, space and time,' his assistant coach Gerard van der Lem told David Winner in *Brilliant Orange*. 'Where is the most space? Where is the player who has the most time? That is where we have to play the ball. Every player had to understand the geometry of the whole pitch.'

Whatever the doubters said, though, that season did end with a remarkable success. Ajax beat Gent and Genoa to reach the UEFA Cup final, where they faced a Torino side that had overcome Beenhakker's Madrid in the semi. Twice Ajax took the lead in the first leg at the Delle Alpi and twice Torino equalised. Bergkamp missed the second leg through illness and Stefan Pettersson played on with a broken collarbone.* Torino hit the woodwork three times, but Ajax survived for a 0-0 draw and an away goals victory. Nobody would realistically deny they had been fortunate, but the spirit Van Gaal had generated was equally obvious.

Ajax lost five players to Serie A that summer, including Bergkamp and Wim Jonk, but success in the Cup in 1992-93 suggested the promise of the emerging young talents. Rijkaard returned to the club before the start of the 1993-94 season and was joined by two Nigerian forwards, Nwankwo Kanu and Finidi George.

Van Gaal had married his wife Fernanda, whom he had met at a handball game, when he was 19 and had two daughters with her. In summer 1993, while on a cruise to celebrate 20 years of marriage, she complained of severe stomach pains. She had cancer of the pancreas and liver. That autumn, Van Gaal nursed her, looked after their two daughters and also oversaw the flowering of the second great Ajax generation. She died in January 1994, four months before he won the league for the first time. Van Gaal had grown up in a Catholic family and had been a regular churchgoer; he lost his faith during Fernanda's illness and would have given up football had his daughters not persuaded him to carry on.

---

* Ajax's preparations were also hampered by the fact that Van Gaal had recorded the first leg off the television for his players to watch before the second leg, only for his daughter to tape over it with an episode of the long-running Dutch soap opera *Goede Tijden, Slechte Tijden*.

The following season, Ajax won the league without losing a single game and, more importantly, won the Champions League, following up a 5-2 win over Bayern Munich in the second leg of the semi with a 1-0 win over Milan in the final. Of the 13 players used that night in Vienna, eight – Edwin van der Sar, Michael Reiziger, Frank Rijkaard, Frank de Boer, Clarence Seedorf, Edgar Davids, Ronald de Boer and Patrick Kluivert – were home-grown. Only two of the squad were over 25 and yet, by the time of that final, each of the starting XI had been at the club for an average of eight years. For Van Gaal, this was profound vindication: his version of Total Football may have been criticised by traditionalists, but where Cruyff had lost 4-0 to Fabio Capello's side, he had triumphed.

And yet even then there was a curious note of conflict. Van Gaal took Seedorf off for Nwankwo Kanu eight minutes into the second half and spent most of the second half arguing with the midfielder before another substitute, Kluivert, poked in the 85th-minute winner.

Ajax lost on penalties to Juventus in the following season's Champions League final and Van Gaal's side began to disintegrate in 1996-97. In part it was a simple issue of money: Reiziger had been on £500 a week, Seedorf and Kluivert £600, Davids £800. The move to the Amsterdam ArenA proved troublesome with the poor pitch at the new stadium hampering their passing game. The tensions that had undermined the Dutch squad at Euro 96 also gnawed away at Ajax and were in part responsible for the departures of Seedorf, Davids and Reiziger (who noted the De Boer brothers were on £4,000 a week). Marc Overmars suffered a long-term injury. Rijkaard had retired to set up an underwear company. There were suggestions, as there often are when results deteriorate, that Van Gaal's intensity had led to fatigue. Cruyff, meanwhile, had accused Van Gaal of 'choking' the academy, saying first-team results had disguised the problems in other parts of the club. Ajax finished fourth in the league and lost in the semi-final of the Champions League; the club and Van Gaal were both ready for a change.

But if Barcelona thought they were getting a second Cruyff, they were misguided. 'Their styles have nothing to do with each other,' Eusebio insisted, although that is an extreme view. 'There's no similarity, they're nothing like each other.' Where Cruyff was deft and ludic in his public pronouncements, Van Gaal's discourse was didactic and bombastic and, if his words could at times take on a strange poetry, particularly when drink had been taken – 'I have seen a lady saxophone player...' – he tended to the bluntly literal, never more so than on the notorious occasion when he demonstrated the concept of 'balls' to his Bayern team by dropping his trousers and waving his genitals in the face of a startled Luca Toni.

Cruyff had never been convinced by Van Gaal. Even in February 1995, with Ajax three months from a league and Champions League double, Cruyff wrote a critical column in *Nieuwe Revu*. 'A lot of things are going wrong at Ajax...' he said. 'Ajax have a traditional way of playing, their own style that no one can ever change. It's been like that for 20 years and luckily Van Gaal is not trying to change it.' He predicted a collapse within three years – although given the economics of football and the inevitability of Ajax selling their best talent, that wasn't the most startling prophecy. Their disagreements could, at times, seem like Marxist theorists squabbling over obscure minutiae of doctrine, but Cruyff, without question, saw Van Gaal's interpretation of the Ajax philosophy as inferior to his own.

For Van Gaal, the differences were minor. 'With Michels it was fixed,' he explained. 'Right winger is right and left winger is left. With Cruyff there was more freedom for the players, and it could be a left-sided man on the right wing and Cruyff would play with the striker dropping off. He would put the striker back so sometimes there was a rhomboid in midfield and the two wingers came in.' Van Gaal always preferred a more traditional striker: at Barcelona, Sonny Anderson and Patrick Kluivert, at Bayern Miroslav Klose and Mario Gomez, with the national team Robin van Persie.

The other difference was at the back. 'Michels,' Van Gaal said, 'played always with big defenders, like Mourinho – Hulshoff, Vasović ... strong, big players and then Cruyff had a building-up defender in the two. But the building up was always done in midfield.' That's why the shape became 3-4-3 rather than the 4-3-3 of Michels. Van Gaal, though, disliked having the 'building-up' player in front of the central defender. 'The opponent can put a man there,' he said, 'and then the other central defender had to build up and he doesn't have that quality because he is the more defending central defender. My preference was two building-up central defenders like I played with Ajax in 1995 with Danny Blind and Frank Rijkaard, so the opponent has to choose. And then you can create a man more in midfield where at that moment the time and space is. That is much more difficult for the opponent to defend against. But when I started as a coach in 1991, we played at Ajax with Wim Jonk and Danny Blind, two tactical small central defenders. Nevertheless we won the UEFA Cup in the first season because most of the time in the match we played with our defenders on the halfway line. But of course with Frank Rijkaard as a central defender we were more stable in defence, especially in the air. That is the process of building a team.'

Cruyff wasn't the only one to wonder whether something essential had been lost in Van Gaal's version of Total Football, with its risk-averse emphasis on maintaining possession. Sjaak Swart, who had been a winger in the great Ajax side of the early seventies, was appalled by the way his nineties counterparts, Finidi George and Marc Overmars, would always check back if faced with two defenders. 'I never gave the ball back to my defence, never!' Swart told David Winner in *Brilliant Orange*. 'It's unbelievable! But that was the system with Van Gaal. Many games you are sleeping! On television, they say: "Ajax 70 per cent ball possession." So what? It's not football. The creativity is gone.'

The differences between Cruyff and Van Gaal weren't merely doctrinal. 'We have a bad chemistry,' Cruyff admitted. When Van Gaal had observed him in 1989, they had got on perfectly well, but they were said to have fallen out that Christmas at a dinner hosted by Cruyff. Van Gaal received a telephone call telling him his sister had died and left hurriedly. In his autobiography, he claimed that Cruyff had been angered that he hadn't taken the time to thank him before leaving. 'Nonsense,' said Cruyff. 'If anyone thinks that of me he has lost the plot. He has probably lost the whole trilogy.'

Throughout the nineties, they had a habit of winding each other up. When Van Gaal announced he was the most successful coach Ajax had ever had, Cruyff regarded it as a slight. When Cruyff, during his time at Barça, was asked which other sides in Europe played good football, he listed only Parma and Auxerre, both of whom had beaten Ajax in the previous couple of years; Van Gaal, probably rightly, saw that as a deliberate snub. And then there was the basic fact that when Van Gaal took over at Barça, he was doing the job Cruyff had left acrimoniously a year earlier and that he still desired.

If Robson felt any similar envy, he didn't show it. He recommended Mourinho to Van Gaal who, despite Mourinho's outburst when he learned of the change of manager, appointed him as his 'third assistant'. In his first season in charge, when Barcelona won the league, Van Gaal used Mourinho principally to analyse the opposition. By the second year, when Barça retained their title, he had him working with the first team. 'I am a believer in ball possession and positional play,' Van Gaal said. 'So we do a lot of positional play in a session. Then you can see if someone can really coach. And he could.' So much confidence did Van Gaal have in Mourinho that he let him take charge of the team for some friendlies and the Catalan Cup. For the 34-year-old, that was a huge step, the first sign that he was respected by figures at the very top of the global game.

And yet he remained an outsider. He hadn't played at Ajax or Barcelona – or even West Brom – so although much of his experience at the top end of football had been under Cruyffian thinkers, those ideals perhaps weren't as deeply ingrained in him as they were in others. As Mourinho became increasingly confident, Van Gaal found 'an arrogant young man, who didn't respect authority that much, but I did like that of him. He was not submissive, used to contradict me when he thought I was in the wrong. Finally I wanted to hear what he had to say and ended up listening to him more than the rest of my assistants.'*

There was friction and debate but the discussions during Van Gaal's three seasons at the Camp Nou were effectively the greatest seminar in the history of the game. At no other time have so many coaches who would go on to play such significant roles been gathered at one club at the same time. Guardiola and Luis Enrique were already together in midfield when Van Gaal took over. Julen Lopetegui, a back-up goalkeeper who would later manage Porto and Spain, and Laurent Blanc, who became manager of France, departed as Van Gaal arrived. A year later, Phillip Cocu, twice a league winner as manager of PSV, joined the midfield and Ronald Koeman, later a league champion as manager of Ajax, arrived as an assistant coach.

---

* From Patrick Barclay's biography of Mourinho.

Frank de Boer, who would win four Dutch titles with Ajax, more than anybody else in history, and consecutive titles at that, was signed the year after.

And at the top of it all was Van Gaal, stubbornly insisting things were done his way, even as Cruyff sniped in the background. 'He is,' Guardiola said, 'alongside Juanma Lillo, the manager whom I talked to most.' Lillo at the time was managing Tenerife, having made his name by becoming, at 29, the youngest man ever to coach in the Spanish top flight by leading Salamanca to promotion in 1994-95. Although he was never given his chance at one of Spain's biggest clubs, Lillo remained one of the country's most forthright and intriguing thinkers on the game.

The assumption often seems to be that, because Van Gaal's approach was a little less aggressive than Guardiola's later would be, there must have been tension between them but that seems not to have been the case. Guardiola's admiration for Van Gaal's Ajax is clear. 'That Ajax team always gave me the impression that they tried to and could do all of the following: play, sacrifice themselves as a team, shine individually and win games,' he said. 'All the players of different quality, without exception, were aware of their mission on the field of play. They demonstrated a tactical discipline and enormous capacity to apply all of that at just the right time.'

The respect was mutual. 'I came to Spain,' said Van Gaal, 'and there the habit was that always the oldest player – at that time Amor – was the captain and Nadal was assistant captain under Robson. And I said, no, not the oldest player will be my captain but the player with the best characteristics to be a captain. I analysed it for six weeks and made Guardiola captain because Guardiola was tactically very good but also he had a lot of influence with his fellow players. And he thought in football tactics, and this is very important. He was the most tactically intelligent player I worked with. I never saw that Luis Enrique would be a great trainer-coach but he is. Koeman and Mourinho yes.'

Guardiola had missed most of Van Gaal's first season with a muscle problem that first surfaced as he dashed across a road to get to a deli. Van Gaal had been concerned that he lacked a number four, the position Rijkaard had occupied for him at Ajax, the deep-lying playmaker. He considered bringing in Davids, but when Guardiola recovered he proved the perfect fit. 'From there,' Van Gaal said, 'he can see the game and he had the personality to dominate it.' By his second spell in charge, as Guardiola increasingly struggled with injury, Van Gaal would leave him out for a younger model, another less than physically imposing product of La Masia: Xavi.

The Barça scout Antoni Carmona had wanted the club to sign Xavi when he was six, but concerns over his lack of height and bulk meant it was a further five years before he was picked up. Van Gaal may have promoted him, but the two had an uneasy relationship, not least because the manager insisted Xavi was a *pivote*, a deep-lying midfielder; something the player internalised to the extent that he was initially resistant when Frank Rijkaard moved him into a more advanced position. Ultimately, of course, it was Guardiola, perhaps understanding his role better than anybody, who got the best out of Xavi, using him to the right of a midfield three with Sergio Busquets as the *pivote*.

For the goalkeeper Vítor Baía, Guardiola's potential as a coach was 'plain to see'. 'He would give his opinion in the team talks and discuss them with the coach. His interest in tactics and the game itself was clear. You could see that he was really into being a part of the team's strategy preparation for each game, although that was clearer with Bobby Robson than Van Gaal.'

Luis Enrique's capacities were less obvious. 'He didn't get involved in the tactical talks,' Vítor Baía explained, 'but his leadership was impressive, and he was always willing to help everyone.'

And then there was Mourinho. Although, having got to Manchester United, he would cast aspersions on the work done by his predecessor, as he did in every job, Mourinho has always been clear how significant Van Gaal was in his development as a coach. 'He gave me confidence,' Mourinho said. 'He gave me complete control in training sessions and I became, with him, a coach on the pitch.'

What most impressed Mourinho seems to have been the attention to detail that, as manifested in his notorious notebooks, drew ridicule from others at Barcelona. 'With Van Gaal the practice sessions were set out already,' he said. 'I would know everything we were going to do in training beforehand, from the aims to the exact time each exercise was going to take place. Nothing was left to chance; everything was programmed to fine detail.' In *Fear and Loathing in La Liga*, Sid Lowe cites an anonymous player who had told him that Van Gaal was more meticulous than Cruyff, perhaps even a better coach, but lacking his charisma.

After Robson had gone, Vítor Baía said, Mourinho 'adapted really well, because Van Gaal knew he had something special and knew how to take advantage of that capacity he had for analysis. Van Gaal put him analysing our opponents and he was great at that.'

Although Cruyff carped from the sidelines, few had too many quibbles about Barcelona's style under Van Gaal – or at least, not initially. Perhaps he did prioritise maintaining possession a little more than Cruyff had, perhaps there was a little more aversion to risk and he certainly brought in a lot of Dutch players (three in his first season, five in his second) but when Barça won the league in Van Gaal's first season, 1997-98, they scored 78 goals, 15 more than anybody other than Atlético, and conceded 56, the fourth-worst defensive record in the league. They were more dominant the following year, scoring 87 as they finished 11 points clear of Madrid.

'It was the system of Ajax,' Van Gaal explained. 'It was 4-3-3 but it was not so easy because all the systems against which we played had five defenders. Our right and left attacker had to close the fifth defender. So we had to look for another system. So there was a lot of 3-4-3 but also with an extra full-back. Ronald de Boer played full-back because opponents were not playing with a right or left winger. On the flanks there was time to create so I chose a better player in that position. Inside, a man behind two, which is why I bought Litmanen.'

In his use of goalkeepers, Van Gaal was classically of the Ajax school. 'We would be integrated with the rest of the team during training,' said Vítor Baía, who moved to Barça from Porto in 1998. 'Van Gaal wanted the keepers to be constantly involved in the game. This involvement meant we were the first ones starting the offensive process by searching for our references, which could be the full-backs, the defensive midfielder, or even the wingers, if we were in need of more direct football.'

But gradually, Van Gaal's demands, his insistence that players assimilate his philosophy, began to grate. By his third season, as Barcelona finished second in the league, and lost in the semi-final of both the Copa del Rey and the Champions League, there was almost constant friction with the Brazilians Rivaldo, Giovanni and Sonny Anderson. Rivaldo wanted to play as a number ten but Van Gaal knew he lacked the discipline to fulfil the role as Litmanen had. 'Rivaldo wanted a free trip in the game,' Van Gaal explained. 'That was the problem of that team at that moment. When Rivaldo was playing as a ten, I had a midfielder less so that was not possible. That's why I kept him always on the left. In that position he won the Ballon d'Or then he comes in my office – he had never come to my office – and said, "I want to say something in the dressing room." I thought he would thank the players because I had adjusted my team for him, always the pressing was behind him because he was not doing that automatically. But OK, that's not a problem. He could do what he wants and then the rest had to adapt so we pressed always to the left side because of him. He came in the dressing room and said, "I don't ever play at 11 any more." He wanted to play as a ten. So I said, "Second team. Maybe you can convince me.'"

But Barça lost the first game without Rivaldo. 'He was very important,' Van Gaal went on. 'He scored the goals from the left side. Straight away after one loss the players were interfering and Guardiola came to me and said, "Let him play at ten, because without him we don't score enough." I said, OK. When the team is thinking it is bad I have to change, because I am the trainer-coach but they are doing it. Then he played at ten and we didn't win anything any more because it was chaos.' The issue of players who refused to subjugate themselves to the greater philosophy was a persistent one for Barça.

'Van Gaal was a really disciplined person, really focused on the objectives, really methodical, but he lacked communication skills and interpersonal relations with the squad,' said Vítor Baía. 'He was a real mess when it came to revealing his feelings. He was too cold, too harsh in speaking to the players, which created some opposition inside the dressing room. However, in terms of knowledge of the game, training philosophy and discipline, he's one of the best there is. For you to understand how bad he was with his communication skills, even when he wanted to tell a joke, or make us laugh, he couldn't, because he was too harsh in the way he told it.' As another player put it, Van Gaal would tell jokes as though he was going to murder a child with an axe.

During his final season at the club, for instance, Van Gaal visited a former vice president of the club at his home and was introduced to his grandson, a promising 12-year-old central defender in Barça's youth set-up. He looked him up and down and then, without warning, gave him a sharp shove to the chest. The 12-year-old fell over, at which Van Gaal peered down at him and said, 'Not strong enough for a centre-back.' The child was Gerard Piqué.

Mourinho effectively became the good cop alongside Van Gaal's bad cop. '[Van Gaal] got mad with us a lot,' said the winger Simão Sabrosa. 'Everywhere, in training, in matches. He was very demanding. Mourinho was very relaxed, always making jokes. He was very attentive.'

Or perhaps Simão simply found a compatriot easier to understand. Certainly Vítor Baía felt at least some of the difference was cultural. 'Mourinho took almost everything from Van Gaal to evolve,' the goalkeeper said, 'but being as Latin as he is, his relationship skills were perfect. He would want to know every player individually, to know how to act with each of them. He would do this to get the best out of each player, which was precisely what Van Gaal couldn't do. Mourinho added his own mental and communication skills to Van Gaal's original qualities.'

By then, for different reasons, Mourinho was also unsettled. He lived very close to Van Gaal in Sitges and clearly felt loyal to him, but in the Dutchman's final season he became 'an anguished assistant coach', keen to set out on his own. Thinking about decisions Van Gaal had made, he would become 'harsh and overly critical'. He had outgrown his role at Barça, where he was perhaps undervalued. Núñez, for instance, always referred to him as 'the translator'. The sense is that he wasn't especially disappointed when his contract wasn't renewed as Van Gaal left the club.

Whether Van Gaal's time at the Camp Nou was successful is a slightly more complex question. History has been kind to him and a recognition of his place in the continuum that runs from Cruyff to Guardiola – exemplified by the fact he gave debuts to such significant figures as Xavi, Carles Puyol, Víctor Valdés and Andrés Iniesta – has led to a rehabilitation of his reputation, but there were many at the time, in the dressing room, in the stands and in the boardroom, who grew weary of a style that seemed to favour possession over excitement.

By the end, he seemed frustrated at his inability to force change. He acknowledged that other nations weren't as used to his style of blunt criticism as the Dutch but also highlighted the politicking that had undermined Robson, Cruyff and countless others before them. There had been constant wrangling over the presidency as the *Elefant Blau* (Blue Elephant) group, which had been co-founded by the future president Joan Laporta, opposed Núñez and brought an unsuccessful vote of no confidence in 1998. Had it been successful, Van Gaal would have been deposed and Cruyff appointed in his place. 'I was loyal,' Van Gaal said. 'That was why I went away. A lot of politics, eh? *Més que un club.*'

The press never really seemed to warm to his brusque manner and as soon as results began to go awry he was subjected to ferocious criticism. There had been group-stage exits in the Champions League in both 1998 and 1999; then, in 1999-2000, Barça finished second in the league behind Deportivo La Coruña and lost to Valencia in the Champions League semi-final. 'Friends in the press,' he sneered at his farewell press conference that May. 'I'm going. Congratulations.'

Yet realistically, for all the ill feeling, two league titles and a second-place finish, achieved in a close approximation of the requisite style, cannot be considered a failure: that Van Gaal was effectively drummed out after that – with typical pride and stubbornness, he refused a pay-off – says more about the club than about his tenure.

# CHAPTER THREE

# SPECIAL

Barcelona had been Mourinho's education. The next step was to put that into practice. Let go by Barcelona with Van Gaal in 2000, he returned to Setúbal where he spent his summer reading, thinking and compiling his thoughts on football and coaching into what came to be known as his 'bible'. In that last season at Barça he had turned down an offer to coach Braga, hoping for something a little more high-profile. It had been a difficult decision: he was aware both of how damaging a poor spell at a smaller club could be, particularly in Portugal where the landscape is so dominated by the big three of Benfica, Sporting and Porto, but he was also aware, as he told his biographer and long-time confidant Luís Lourenço, that he was not part of the 'clan' – 'those who deal the cards and set up the game'.

The point was clear: Mourinho was an outsider – or at least felt like an outsider, or wanted to portray himself as such – even back in his home country. In the context of the Apito Dourado (Golden Whistle) scandal that broke in 2004, and led to Boavista's relegation for attempting to influence referees, the terminology Mourinho used is intriguing. Several other clubs were implicated and Porto were, much later, docked six points which were returned on appeal. The league president, Valentim Loureiro, who was also chairman of Boavista, ended up receiving a suspended jail sentence of three years and two months. Given the rumours of corruption in Portuguese football going back years, perhaps it's safest to say that when Mourinho returned home, it was to a country in which accusations of match-fixing and the influencing of referees were commonplace.

Outsider or not, an offer came and at the beginning of 2000-01 Mourinho took up the assistant manager's position at Benfica, reasoning that the path to the top would be shorter back in Portugal. Sure enough, Jupp Heynckes left the club four games into the season and Mourinho was invited to replace him.

There was, though, a complication: Benfica's upcoming presidential election in which the incumbent, the lawyer João Vale e Azevedo, was being challenged by a businessman, Manuel Vilarinho. Vale e Azevedo offered Mourinho a six-month contract, on the understanding it would be extended to two and a half years should he, as expected, win the election. There was widespread scepticism – overt opposition from some within the club who felt Mourinho lacked the requisite experience and doubts expressed from pundits on the outside. Immediately, the conditions of a siege were created, perhaps bringing to the surface in Mourinho an approach to management that was already in his nature.

His reign was brief and antagonistic. He dropped Sabry, Colado, Serhiy Kandaurov and Chano, all of whom were popular with fans. He told five youth-team players they had no future at the club. He protested at the signings of Rui Baião, Ricardo Esteves, Roger and Andre, saying he hadn't endorsed them, and then criticised the director of football António Simões. His manner and his radical training methods unsettled the squad.

But then, perhaps it needed unsettling.

Benfica's first game under their new manager was against Boavista. Mourinho had José Augusto Peres Bandeira scout the opposition and give a presentation at which, at least in Mourinho's version of events, only ten opponents were discussed. The 11th, the Bolivian forward Erwin Sánchez, was the key player as Boavista won 1-0. Mourinho raged at the lack of organisation at the club and paid from his own pocket for an old college friend to carry out scouting of the opposition.

Boavista's goal came from a near-post cross, something about which Mourinho had specifically warned his players. He was furious; that frustration at the disjunction between him offering advice and players being able to act upon it in the moment would be a persistent theme over the years that followed.

Slowly, though, Mourinho's particular form of man-management began to take effect. The midfielder Maniche was sent off in a training game and told to run around the pitch as punishment. After eight minutes he had completed just two laps at which Mourinho sent him to the showers. The following day he made him train with the B-team and it seemed he would join the list of players on their way out of the club. But four days later, Maniche apologised and paid a €1,000 fine. He knuckled down, was named as captain before the end of the season and ended up following Mourinho to Porto and Chelsea.

Perhaps the capacity to dominate players, to break them down psychologically and remould them as his loyal followers, wasn't so well developed then as it would become, but it was there. 'He wasn't an easy person to get on with,' the centre-back Paulo Madeira said. 'He was opinionated, said anything that came into his head and, at the beginning, his arrogance was a shock to the team. But after a while we got to like him.'

Performances improved and, after that initial game, Mourinho lost just one of his other 11 matches in charge. But Vale e Azevedo was defeated in the election and Vilarinho had made clear that his preference as coach was Toni. The problem for the anti-Mourinho elements at the club was that Benfica kept winning and that the coach was becoming more and more confident at applying his methods. In the week before the derby against Sporting, for instance, Mourinho happened to see a number of opposition players at a tennis tournament and spied an opportunity. What arrogance they were showing, he said to his own side, what an affront it was that they weren't cloistered away in preparation. It was nonsense, as he well knew, but he used the sighting to 'poison our brood' and was rewarded with a 3-0 win. It was his greatest triumph as Benfica manager – and his last.

The night before the win over Sporting, Benfica's directors had mysteriously changed the hotel the team were using without bothering to consult their manager. Mourinho saw that as evidence of a plot to destabilise the side – quite possibly correctly; at the very least it showed a level of contempt for a manager for whom control was essential – and decided the board was waiting to sack him.

That night, as Mourinho drove back to Setúbal, a storm raged. As he crossed a bridge, he felt the wind pulling at his car and, seized with a sense of his mortality, decided he had to act: his position was precarious, but he also knew his hand would rarely be stronger than it was at that moment. He called Vilarinho and asked for a one-year contract (rather than the two he would have got had Vale e Azevedo won the election). The president fudged, saying that he would love to offer the deal but that the board would never accept it. Mourinho resigned.

Seven months later, in July 2001, Mourinho was appointed coach of União de Leiria. They are a small club and their budget was extremely limited, but Manuel José had taken them to a highly creditable seventh place the previous season. Playing hard-nosed counter-attacking football, Mourinho did even better and had them third by January.

What's striking, given his later reputation, is how he inspired his players on a personal level. 'I could stand here and say that he was brilliant tactically but we all know that,' said Silas, an attacking midfielder signed from the Spanish second-division side Ceuta. 'In my opinion, the most important aspect of his personality is definitely the human relationship he creates with his players, his one-on-one conversations and the way he worries about each player. He is also really generous.'

By the time Ceuta's season had finished, Leiria were already in their third week of training for the following campaign. Silas travelled to Portugal assuming he would have to carry on through without a break, only to be sent on holiday by Mourinho. 'He told me: "You are very important to the team and I need you to have a fresh and relaxed head,"' Silas recalled. 'This attitude touched me. You could see he cared. Then when I got back, we were one week from the kick-off of the season, and our starting winger, [Emmanuel] Duah, got injured. I only had five or six days of training and he said, "Silas, do you think you can do well as a left winger?" My position was always as a central attacking midfielder, but I had played some matches as a winger before, and he knew that I could do well as a winger and so I did. I started the first match and was never out of the starting XI. He gave me the time I needed to rest and then he gave me the confidence and belief I could do well despite not having been with the team for long.'

Immediately, Mourinho put into practice the principles of periodisation he had learned from Vítor Frade. 'Training was completely different from everything I had experienced until then,' Silas said. 'He really made an impact in Portuguese football with his methods. When he started as a head coach there were very few people coaching like he was coaching, but now we see a lot of coaches doing the same. It's a kind of training that's completely focused on game situations, all game situations, all really specific. He created a school. He was looked at by the new coaches as an example and we can now see the good coaches we have in Portuguese football spread across the world. It all happened after Mourinho. He was way ahead of his time.'

The nature of the Portuguese league, with its three giants and the rest, is that pressure comes quickly – and that means there will always be opportunities for the ambitious. At the end of November 2001, Porto were top of the table, but they won only one of the six games that followed and slipped to fifth, leading to the dismissal of Octávio Machado. To replace him, Porto turned to the manager of the team two places above them: Mourinho was appointed on 23 January 2002, having impressed the Porto president Jorge Nuno Pinto da Costa with a PowerPoint presentation in which he laid out his vision for the club based around his 'bible'.

'I think this document is extremely important, because it guides and directs an entire process,' Mourinho explained. 'The very first diagram sets out the idea that is the basis for the whole programme: "The concept of club is more important than any player." This concept is presented by itself on the first slide and is the basis for the entire structure of the document. It is a belief that must be taken on by everyone in the club, especially in the junior ranks.'

Mourinho presented similar documents to Roman Abramovich before getting the Chelsea job and to Barcelona's directors when he was seeking to be named as Frank Rijkaard's successor there. He also sent a précis of a report to Manchester United's board when he was being lined up as Louis van Gaal's replacement at Old Trafford. That's significant for what it suggests about his meticulousness and level of preparation, but also for psychological reasons. As Roy Henderson outlined in an article in *The Blizzard*, the presentation serves as a sort of constitution, a written document that validates his authority. He reinforced that by writing to the players outlining what was expected of them.

The German sociologist Max Weber theorised that there are three categories of authority: traditional – a leader has authority because that's how it's always been; rational-legal – there is an acceptance the leader has a mandate; and charismatic – a leader has authority because people want him to have authority. Mourinho's PowerPoint is effectively a formulation of his ideas as a pre-existing code helping establish him as having both traditional and rational-legal authority. More powerful, though, is his charisma, defined by Weber as 'the authority of the extraordinary and personal gift of grace (charisma)... Men do not obey him by virtue of tradition or statute, but because they believe in him.' He inspires his players while simultaneously creating an environment in which his authority comes to seem habitual, perhaps even divinely sanctioned.

Machado had been fighting against the tide. Although the two titles Robson, with Mourinho alongside him, had claimed had been the start of a run of five in a row, Porto had then gone three seasons without success. Fans were disenchanted, calling the players 'rubbish' and describing them as 'clowns'. Other managers might have ignored the chants or asked supporters to stop; Mourinho embraced them. He had his players learn the chants and practise them in the dressing room so they became a form of motivation rather than intimidation.

Leiria, having lost just three times that season up to Mourinho's departure, lost their next four matches and ended up seventh. Porto, meanwhile, dropped only ten points in the 15 games they played under Mourinho that season. It was there that his ideas were first tested on a stage he saw as befitting his talents; there that, very gradually, the dark angel of the post-Cruyffians began his turn away from the principles that had guided Barcelona. It was there that he first achieved the sort of control over a side that he demanded, there that

THE BARCELONA INHERITANCE

he was competing for titles rather than scrapping to avoid relegation. That allowed him to be more expansive in his approach. 'At Porto he practised attacking football, but in Italy he played differently, because he didn't have a team that gave him the same guarantees offensively speaking,' said the centre-back Jorge Costa, the captain of that Porto side, who was recalled by Mourinho from a loan spell at Charlton Athletic. 'I think it's a huge mistake to say a coach is either offensive or defensive, because we should always coach according to the reality we are inserted in. Mourinho is a great example of that. He didn't separate offence from defence, instead he worked the tactic as one.'

But even in Portugal, where the top sides would expect to steam-roller most teams in the division, there were limits to how much freedom Mourinho was prepared to give players. 'He didn't let me or any of the other centre-backs go up the pitch with the ball,' said Costa. 'I did it sometimes and he hated it, clearly letting me know later that this would unbalance the team. He would allow the full-backs to go up but that would always be compensated by one of the midfielders.'

Mourinho took charge of everything: diet, timetable and training. He imposed a strict discipline. Benni McCarthy, for instance, was dropped for going out in Vigo to celebrate his girlfriend's birthday two days before a game. When Porto played away at Benfica, Mourinho made a point of walking out first to draw the hostility of the crowd onto himself rather than his players. There were complaints, of the sort that would become familiar, about Benfica and how the establishment supposedly favoured them. He was the leader as father figure, always protecting his players while at the same time demanding they give him more, but he was also something a little more sinister, a Svengali who played with the emotions of his team and outsiders, alleging conspiracy to generate a siege mentality.

As Porto's form improved, there was only one dissenting voice, that of Machado, who believed that he should have won the league in his first season. He accused Mourinho of bringing back Rubens Junior, Nelson and Miran Pavlin, players he had jettisoned, even putting Pavlin on penalty duty 'simply to try to prove that I had been wrong about everything'. At the time it just seemed like sour grapes, but the idea that Mourinho selected his team with a view not merely to winning games but also making points soon gained currency.

That summer, after Porto had finished third, Mourinho signed four players from Leiria: Paulo Ferreira, Derlei, Nuno Valente and Tiago. Paulo Ferreira was immediately struck by his 'incredible sense of organisation', 'the will he has to win, and the way he passes that on to the players' and by the modernity of what Mourinho was doing. 'His training methods were different, more advanced than the ones I had had until then,' the full-back said. 'He was really demanding, and his personality was strong, really focused on details.'

In a world that was dominated by former players and a spirit of intellectual conservatism, often complacency, Mourinho brought levels of professionalism that many players hadn't experienced before. 'Maybe other coaches have the same qualities as Mourinho,' said Deco, 'but nobody works as hard as him.'

And few were as prepared to push the boundaries of the rules quite as hard. In a pre-season tournament in the summer of 2002, Porto drew with Paris Saint-Germain, leading to a penalty shoot-out. Maniche, who had been substituted at half-time, took one of the kicks as Porto won. It was a pre-season game of little consequence and Lourenço plays the story for laughs. Ultimately, though, however unimportant the game, Porto cheated.

That tone endured throughout his stint at Porto. He was successful, but his methods were at times disreputable. In 2002-03, Mourinho's first full season, Porto lost just twice in the league and won the title by 11 points from Benfica. A Portuguese Cup and the UEFA Cup completed a treble. Aged 40, Mourinho had suddenly emerged as one of the most promising managers in Europe. His success, though, was not without controversy. Mourinho was pragmatic to the point of cynicism and, for all the conservatism of his upbringing, seemed to regard authority as an obstacle to be got around rather than something to be respected. Leading Lazio 4-1 in the first leg of the UEFA Cup semi-final, for instance, Mourinho physically prevented the opposition midfielder Lucas Castromán from taking a throw-in that might have led to a counter-attack, for which he was banned from the touchline for the second leg. Instead, he sat in the stand shouting instructions to two assistants (one of them André Villas-Boas) sitting near him, who would then text them to the bench. That was sufficient to circumvent UEFA's attention, but every text is reproduced in Lourenço's biography, a book in which Mourinho's guiding hand is clear. On the one hand, the list shows Mourinho's remarkable attention to detail; on the other it shows not only his willingness to play on the edge of the rules but his lack of compunction about doing so.

The final, played in ferocious heat in Seville – for which Mourinho, with typical meticulousness, had prepared by having his team start training at noon – was a minor classic, as they beat Celtic 3-2 after extra time. Martin O'Neill, the Celtic manager, with some justification complained about the 'poor sportsmanship' of Porto, 'the rolling over, the time-wasting'. There had been a cynicism about Porto but then, as Mourinho pointed out in a characteristic counter-attack, there had been times when Celtic's physicality could have led to a red card long before Bobo Baldé was finally sent off in extra time.

Mourinho had tended to favour a 4-3-3 in the league, switching to a 4-4-2 with a diamond in midfield for the tougher European

SPECIAL

games. For Jorge Costa that was not a sign of reactivity; it wasn't
that Mourinho's principal aim became to stop the opposition playing.
'He never changed tactics thinking about the opponents, but always
thinking about us, about his own side,' he said. 'He changed so we
could play along with his strategy. We would always stick to our
tactics, the 4-3-3 or the 4-4-2 diamond, but those formations didn't
mean we had to be offensive or defensive: it depended on the match,
it depended on what he wanted us to do on each night. More than
formations, our team lived off its dynamic, because despite changing
formations, we would never change our playing philosophy.'

Shape was less significant than style. 'He wanted us to press
very high,' said Maniche, who tended to operate on the right of the
diamond. 'He wants the team to react quickly when they lose the
ball, so we gain it in their midfield. This pressure would be done as
a team, and not only one or two players. He would prepare us for
each game throughout the week and work on that. If he knew that
one of the central defenders had trouble on the ball, he would tell us
to pressure the other defender, to force the weaker one to run with
the ball. It depended a bit on who we were facing; he liked to have
possession as well.'

That sounds very much like Cruyff's theory of press and possess, but
already Mourinho had begun to modify that approach. He was heavily
influenced by his director of methodology, Vítor Frade, a pioneer of
periodisation. 'It is not a method,' Vítor Frade insisted. 'It is a methodology. You have a methodology so that you don't need methods.'

Frade was 50 in 2004 and working as an academic at the University
of Porto. He has inspired not only Mourinho and other Portuguese
coaches such as André Villas-Boas and Vítor Pereira but also the
likes of Brendan Rodgers and the England rugby coach Eddie Jones.
Periodisation for him is not a footballing philosophy but a theory

of everything, which is why in explaining it he hops from theme to theme, from cell structure to quantum mechanics. 'Football is not a linear process,' Frade said in an interview with the *New York Times*. 'It is not a sum of things: if you do this, plus that, you will achieve this … the coach must consider every aspect, of the individual, of the team. Football is not two-dimensional. It is multidimensional.' Every action has an effect elsewhere.

Frade is opposed to specific drills to improve stamina or technique. Instead, he believes everything must replicate in-game scenarios; to put it in its simplest terms, he believes players will improve their fitness for playing football by running in game-related scenarios rather than slogging through a cross-country run. He wants players to be presented with problems they have to solve so that rather than, say, endlessly hitting 50-yard passes to get the technique right, they should be placed in situations in which a 50-yard pass is one possible solution.

Mourinho's studies in psychology had drawn him to many of the conclusions reached by the Portuguese neurologist António Damásio, who wrote the introduction to a study by four Portuguese researchers about Mourinho's methods. In his 1994 book *Descartes' Error*, Damásio had dismissed the Cartesian dualism to argue that neuro-anatomically and neuro-biologically there was no separation of emotional and rational processes and that therefore emotions are more rational than is commonly believed and decisions more influenced by emotional factors. He also outlined his concept of 'neuronal man': consciousness is conditioned not only by an awareness of the outside world but by a perception of the body within the outside world.

'For us, to say that this or that player is in great physical shape is a mistake,' Mourinho said. 'The player is either fit or not. And what do we mean by being fit? It is to be physically well and to be part of a game plan which a player knows inside out. With regard to the psychological side, which is essential to play at the highest level, a fit player feels confident, cooperates with and believes in his teammates, and shows solidarity towards them. All of this put together means a player is fit and it is reflected in playing well.'

What that means, as Sandro Modeo explains in his book *L'Alieno Mourinho*, a player becomes a 'functional unit' comprised of 'physical appearance, technique (relationship with the ball), tactics (his role in relation to space, his teammates and opponents) and psychology (the relationship … between his emotional narrative and team goals)'.

This is where the theory meshes with Frade's concept of periodisation. For him there is no point in training exercises that are not specifically created to replicate the game. The gym is for those recovering from injury. He does not believe in automisation. Valeriy Lobanovskyi and his great collaborator Anatoliy Zelentsov had players practise preset moves, believing that they could be adapted and used in a game situation in the manner of a chess grandmaster, a line of thought that has influenced a swathe of coaches from Joachim Löw to Antonio Conte. Mourinho, rather, sees the game as so complex that such pre-packaged solutions are inadequate. He tries instead to condition the mindset of a player, to imbue him with his principles, so he makes the correct decisions in any given situation. 'I'm not the kind of mechanic coach that says Player A pass to Player B, Player B pass to Player C, and Player C to Player D,' he explained. 'I'm much more a supporter of preparing the players to decide well and feel the game.'

There is much here that is counter-intuitive. Mourinho's football is often derided as grimly functional, as favouring a rigidity of structure, but at its best it is, at least conceptually, extremely plastic, versatile and spontaneous. The practice also places him squarely, in this one regard at least, in the Cruyffian tradition. The point of those *rondos*, the endless small-sided games focused on the retention of possession, is not merely to teach technique but also to condition a mental approach: for the player with the ball not to panic under pressure but to find a solution; for the players without the ball to offer one.

Mourinho's approach is 'guided discovery'. Players are not taught moves by rote which, for him, offers a false sense of virtuosity that unravels against a better organised or more aggressive opponent. They are essentially persuaded by example of the efficacy of the Mourinho level until they instinctively reach for a Mourinho solution. 'It is not easy to put this theory into practice, especially with top players who are not prepared to accept everything they are told just because it comes from you, the authority...' Mourinho said. 'I will arrange the training sessions to lead along a certain path, they will begin feeling it... all together, we reach a conclusion.' The players are made to feel they own the conclusions Mourinho wants them to reach. It's a form of brainwashing, which perhaps explains the air of cultishness that so often characterises his relationship with his squad. It is emotional as well as technical, Mourinho's understanding of the psychology of human relationships allowing him to secure a buy-in that, for instance, can persuade Samuel Eto'o to operate as an auxiliary full-back or Xabi Alonso to turn against his Spain teammates as he did during that sequence of four *Clásicos* in 18 days in 2011.

But there is a problem. Weber argued that instances of charismatic authority 'cannot remain stable; they will become either tradition-alised or rationalised, or a combination of both'. It is that, perhaps, that best explains why Mourinho has only ever been successful in short bursts; in time, the impact of his charisma wears off and players kick against an authority that has become habitual.

While much of the underlying theory isn't particularly different from the practice at Barça, where the influence of Juanma Lillo, another advocate of periodisation, remains strong, there were tactical differences. Particularly in the Champions League, Mourinho was prepared to employ a low block and sit deep to absorb pressure and strike on the break. What had been a necessity at Leiria became a useful option at Porto. Parallel to that, but perhaps more significant, was a growing scepticism about the value of possession. 'The more the ball circulates in midfield,' Mourinho said, 'the more likely it is that the other team will dispossess us.' That was the first expression of a theory that would later become notorious.

Still, even if Porto weren't playing in a classic Cruyffian way, it would be fair to say the style was broadly similar to that which Mourinho had experienced at the Camp Nou, something that is perhaps made most clear by his use of the goalkeeper Vítor Baía, who rates Mourinho as the best coach he worked under. 'I was very important in the defensive organisation and also in the first moment of transition,' he said. 'Mourinho liked the Dutch style, which meant the keeper had to know how to play with his feet, that he had to know how to start an attack. Our defensive line was mid-high on the pitch, so that tells you a lot about how we pressed, very high. This obviously was good for me, because I was more involved in the game: I loved to initiate attacks and be a part of the switching of the ball from one side to the other.'

Even if Mourinho didn't make huge changes for specific games, even if he wasn't as reactive as he would become, he did hand out dossiers on Porto's opponents in the days before the game. 'One of the most important aspects about José, which I support, is that the other team has to be the one making the changes; you have to keep your own identity,' said Costinha. 'Of course, he would give us detailed information about the team we were facing next at the start of the training week, and more precisely about the player that would be closest to our area of play. "What was the player like? Did he have a tendency to get many cards? What kind of movements did he make?" It was new for many of us back then, but it was very helpful and meant we were much better prepared for each match.'

Attention to detail was critical and where Mourinho excelled was in anticipating scenarios that might occur during the game. 'Sometimes it was as though he could see the future,' said Vítor Baía. 'I remember a specific incident against Benfica, when throughout the week he prepared us for what we should do after we scored a goal … he told us that [the Benfica coach José Antonio] Camacho would make a specific substitution and change his tactics, which was what happened. So we already knew what to do when he did it; we were completely prepared for it. For the same match, we also prepared to play with ten players, because José knew the referee would not be able to take the pressure and would show a red card along the way. That also happened, but we had already seen that movie during the week, so we knew what to do and got a narrow win.'*

That capacity for foresight carried on at Chelsea. Paulo Ferreira recalls his first goal for the club, in an FA Cup game at home to Colchester in February 2006. 'I normally never appeared in the box at the corners, as the other full-back and I stayed behind for the defensive transition,' he said. 'However, in this match, José came to me in the dressing room and said, "Paulo, I want you to go up to the box at the corners today. I want you to drift from the centre to the far post. Something tells me that you will score today." And so I did. We

---

* This, unfortunately, does not appear to fit any actual game. It may be that Vítor Baía is thinking of the league game played on 20 October 2002, when Porto survived the first-half dismissal of Jorge Costa to beat Benfica 2-1, but the opposition coach that day was not Camacho but Jesualdo Ferreira. It's possible that he has conflated the red card in that game with Porto's 1-0 win over Camacho's Benfica on 4 March 2003.

were down by one [an own goal by Ricardo Carvalho] and the first corner we had, I made the movement he had suggested, a ball was deflected off a defender and I pushed it in at the far post. Of course, I thought about that moment throughout the rest of the game and laughed about it – how did he know?'

Mourinho's other way of preparing for specific opponents and big games was psychological. 'The rivalries would do their work,' Maniche said, 'and the press conferences.' Playing the media has always been part of Mourinho's armoury, antagonising opponents and pressuring referees.

The other side of that is his relationship with his own squad, a capacity to create remarkably strong bonds. That, perhaps, is an aspect of Mourinho that is often overlooked, that while he can be grouchy in public, while he pursues feuds with rivals and can fall out with his own players, he is also capable of inspiring devotion. There are stories of players in tears as he hugged them goodbye on his first departure from Chelsea. 'He would fool around with us outside practice, but when the time to work arrived he would be ruthless,' said Vítor Baía. 'We only practised for one hour each day, yet those hours were the most intense I have ever seen.'

That is part of the periodisation programme, promoting fitness through game-based training, but Vítor Baía stresses how good Mourinho was at handling different personalities, what an astute man-manager he was. 'He knew everybody so deeply that he could control our emotions in every situation,' he said. 'In my case, he would just pat me on the back and I was ready to go. However, there were players who needed motivation, who needed to be praised, and he knew which ones needed what; that's what made him so good.'

That, though, is only part of the story. A more complete version of his relationship with Vítor Baía is revealing of Mourinho's

Machiavellian charm, of the sense he gives of planning out every interaction. In September 2002, Vítor Baía was banned from all club activities for a month after a training-ground row with Mourinho. 'That was the turning point in his career,' the goalkeeper said. 'He was very young and wanted to make a statement – and he did it. We had a great relationship, because we had been together at Porto with Bobby Robson, then for three years in Barcelona, with him always as assistant coach, but when he arrived at Porto he wanted to show everyone who was the boss: friends off the pitch, players on it. Performance was what counted, not relationships, so I was not in the best form and was chosen as an example: I was his statement. Of course, I was not pleased at the time. Today, after many conversations with him and the assistant coaches from that time and some players, I know that it was all a plan. Everyone knew how to react to me, how to speak to me, everyone was ready. After the month of suspension, José welcomed me back with a big hug and I was straight back into the first team.'

This was the psychology of which Van Gaal and Frade had spoken. Mourinho at Porto created a team that wasn't just tactically flexible but that was devoted to him – at times extraordinarily so. Even now those Porto players seem in awe of him, like initiates quite unable to believe their leader has moved on. And success begat success. The more Porto won, the more his players believed in Mourinho, and so the more they won. In 2003-04, Porto again lost only twice in the league and won the title by eight points from Benfica. They lost to Benfica in extra time in the Portuguese Cup final, but in the Champions League, having finished second to Real Madrid in the group, they squeezed by Manchester United 3-2 on aggregate as Costinha capitalised on Tim Howard's last-minute flap. Mourinho ran down the touchline and slid on his knees in celebration and United were left to ponder how different football might have been had Paul Scholes not had a goal wrongly ruled out for offside in first-half injury time. Lyon and Deportivo La Coruña then succumbed before Porto dismissed Monaco 3-0 in the final in Gelsenkirchen.

Even in that moment of triumph, Mourinho felt the need to make a point to Barcelona, observing that he had won the Champions League as often as his former club. The newspaper *AS*, although based in Madrid, responded with a punchy editorial. 'Although he has won many trophies in Portugal,' it noted, 'there were too many instances of poor behaviour towards opponents and too many dirty tricks.'

Not that Mourinho cared. By then, he was already on his way to Chelsea.

* * *

Mourinho had been a little subdued in Gelsenkirchen, seemingly unwilling to glory in his success while another, wealthier, club made clear their interest in him. But when he was appointed, he gave one of the most memorable press conferences the Premier League has known. Wearing an open-necked shirt under a well-cut charcoal suit, he was the image of continental sophistication, his heavily gelled hair just greying sufficiently at the temples to give an air of wisdom and authority. He was handsome and charismatic, delivering lines that would have seemed like absurd bombast in another mouth with enough of a twinkle that they added to the sense of charm: yes, he was self-confident and self-assured, but he had a lot to be self-confident and self-assured about. There was no false modesty, no lowering expectations. 'I have top players and I'm sorry, we have a top manager,' he said. 'Please do not call me arrogant because what I say is true. I'm European champion, I'm not one out of the bottle, I think I'm a special one.' He was, essentially, underlining his authority.

Just as he'd done on taking the Porto job, Mourinho wrote to his players, establishing behavioural rules in support of his vision and obtaining the group's buy-in to such an extent that they themselves enforced those behavioural rules. 'From here each practice, each game, each minute of your social life must centre on the aim of being champions,' he said in those letters. 'First-teamer will not be a correct word. I need all of you. You need each other. We are a TEAM... Motivation + Ambition + Team Spirit = SUCCESS.'

His impact was immediate. 'The press were saying how strict he was and how it was going to be like the army for us for the next few years,' the forward Eiður Guðjohnsen said in an interview with *The Times*. 'Instead he walked in and showed us a sort of map of what he expected of every individual and how we would work together as a group. A few of us looked at each other that day and said, "We're going to win the league this year" – and that was just one meeting. The first training session convinced us even more. The tempo went up straight away.'

It took a little while, though, for success to come. Chelsea's form in Mourinho's first weeks in charge was scratchy. He started with a midfield diamond, similar to the way he'd played with Porto in the Champions League. In his first match, a hard-fought 1-0 win over Manchester United, Claude Makélélé patrolled in front of the back four, while Frank Lampard was deployed behind a front two of Didier Drogba and Eiður Guðjohnsen with Geremi and Alexei Smertin at the sides of the diamond. Joe Cole and Tiago Mendes sometimes came in as the flanking players and Mateja Kežman sometimes played instead of Guðjohnsen, but that was the shape for the first six league games of the season. Chelsea conceded only one goal in that spell, and they picked up 14 points, but they only scored six goals. Lampard seemed uneasy as a number ten, struggling to play with his back to goal and lacking the tight technical skills or vision to operate as Deco had for Porto. Mourinho spoke about the importance of practising not only attacking and defending but also the transitions from attack to defence and defence to attack, and introduced to public conscious-ness the concept of 'resting on the ball', passing it around at the back to give players time to recuperate, but his football was scratchy and, frankly, at times a little dull.

Nonetheless, Mourinho had already begun to impose his methods. Discipline was strict: at least part of the reason Hernán Crespo was loaned to AC Milan was his late return after the summer break. Training, meanwhile, followed the meticulous, intense pattern it had at Porto. The move from the ramshackle training ground at Harlington to Cobham was already under way when Mourinho arrived, but he helped shape the new facility. Periodisation was central. 'A great pianist,' Mourinho observed at a lecture he gave in Tel Aviv, 'doesn't run around the piano or do push-ups with the tips of his fingers. To be great, he plays the piano.'

After successive goalless draws against Aston Villa and Tottenham, Mourinho switched to a 4-3-3 for an away game at Middlesbrough. Damien Duff came in on the left with Guðjohnsen pushing across to the right, while Lampard fell back into a shuttling midfield role in which he excelled, specialising in those late runs into the box that brought him 13 goals that season. They won that game 1-0 and then beat Liverpool at home by the same scoreline. A 1-0 defeat at Manchester City followed, their first defeat of the season and, it turned out, their last. From then on, Chelsea were remorseless. There were a couple of dabbles with a back three, and Arjen Robben some-times played on the wing, but 4-3-3 was the base with Makélélé at the back of midfield flanked by Lampard to his left and either Tiago Mendes or Alexei Smertin to the right. Mourinho was more cautious than he had been at Porto, most notably in the way the full-backs – Paulo Ferreira and Wayne Bridge in that first season – rarely advanced beyond the halfway line. His side didn't press anywhere near as high, in part because of the lack of pace of John Terry at centre-back. The shift away from the Cruyffian model had begun. Chelsea conceded only 15 goals in 38 games, a Premier League record, while scoring 72 goals and setting a Premier League record of 95 points.

There was also victory in the League Cup final, against Liverpool, a game in which Mourinho was sent from the touchline for apparently shushing Liverpool fans after Steven Gerrard had scored an own-goal equaliser. He claimed the gesture was aimed at the media, whom he accused of trying 'to disturb Chelsea' by their focus on the money they had spent – if so, his aim was roughly 180 degrees out – but even if that were true, it seems an odd way to celebrate. That detail also hints at how fractious Mourinho's relationship with the press was from the off, despite subsequent claims to the contrary.

For all the controversy, though, there were only two real wrinkles. The first, a major one, was frustration in the Champions League. Chelsea stormed through a last-16 tie against Barcelona and a quarter-final against Bayern Munich in a series of tense and brilliant games, winning both home legs 4-2 and losing by a single goal away. The defeat at the Camp Nou may have been overturned in an exhilarating second leg, in which Chelsea raced into a 3-0 lead in 18 minutes, but it was a game that had other, further-reaching consequences. Chelsea had been leading when Didier Drogba, having already been booked, was shown a second yellow card ten minutes after half-time for a challenge on Víctor Valdés that was neither as bad as the goalkeeper made it appear nor as blameless as Chelsea fans subsequently claimed. With a man advantage, Barça, who had seemed becalmed, went on to score twice.

Mourinho, at least in public, had no doubt who was at fault. He attacked the Swedish referee Anders Frisk, accusing him of having received the Barça coach Frank Rijkaard in his room at half-time, although when challenged he declined to provide evidence (as it turned out, Rijkaard had approached Frisk as the players left the field to complain that Damien Duff had been offside for Chelsea's goal but had not entered the referee's room). Was he perhaps, even then, too determined to beat Barcelona, to make a point to his former club? Patrick Barclay, in his generally positive biography of Mourinho, first published in 2005, long before he was overlooked for the Barcelona job, suggested there was 'unfinished business'.

The generous interpretation is to say that Mourinho had no idea what he was unleashing. Frisk, with his highlighted hair and extravagant gestures, had long been regarded as a popinjay and had been left bleeding from a head wound after being struck by a missile thrown by Roma fans earlier in the competition. Certain Chelsea fans gleefully took up the cause against him. For two and a half weeks, Frisk was subjected to abuse and threats before, at the age of 42, deciding to retire. 'I won't ever go out on a football pitch again,' he said. 'I am too scared. It is not worth it. I've had enough. I don't know if I even dare let my kids go to the post office.' This was the human consequence of Mourinho's constant machinating: he never seemed to learn or care that what he said in public had consequences beyond winning the next game. A few weeks later, in an interview on Portuguese television, Mourinho was asked about a refereeing decision. He couldn't give an opinion, he joked, in case the referee quit. If there were any contrition for ending Frisk's career, he hid it well.

The head of UEFA's referees committee, Volker Roth, described Mourinho as 'an enemy of football'. Mourinho was also banned from the touchline for the two games against Bayern, a sanction he reportedly circumvented by hiding in a laundry basket to give his pre-match address to players in the dressing room and then by communicating with Rui Faria via an earpiece hidden under his assistant's woollen hat. UEFA officials were so suspicious they made him remove his hat at half-time, but no evidence of wrongdoing was uncovered.

William Gaillard, UEFA's director of communications, accused Mourinho of 'using lies as a pre-match tactic ahead of the second leg'. That second leg was a spectacular game that Chelsea won 4-2 with John Terry's decisive fourth goal being headed in after Ricardo Carvalho had blocked Víctor Valdés at a corner. Pierluigi Collina was probably too good a referee to have been influenced by Mourinho's comments, but it was easy to understand why some thought the Chelsea manager had achieved exactly what he had set out to.

Mourinho, after all, was unapologetic, as he had been at Porto, about the importance of controlling the message. 'Talking to the media,' he said, 'is part of the game. When I go to the press conference before a game, in my mind the game has already started. When I go to a press conference after a game, the game hasn't finished yet. Or if the game has finished, the next one has already started.'

That insistence on control – something at which he was very successful during his first spell at Chelsea – perhaps explains his truculence when the media refuses to follow the trail he has set for them. Shortly before the publication of Joel Neto's 2004 biography, for instance, he rang the author and berated him for most of a phone conversation lasting 40 minutes before seeking an injunction against four sections of the book that, as he saw it, portrayed him in a bad light. A judge dismissed his claims.

In the semi-final, Chelsea faced Liverpool. They had beaten Rafa Benítez's side in both league games as well as in the League Cup, but at Stamford Bridge they were thwarted as Liverpool secured a 0-0 draw. The decisive moment of the second leg at Anfield came after four minutes as Milan Baroš ran on to Steven Gerrard's flick and poked the ball past Petr Čech, who cleaned him out. John Terry dithered, allowing Luis García to steal in and prod the ball goalwards. William Gallas hacked it clear but the referee Ľuboš Micheľ deemed it had crossed the line. For 86 minutes, Chelsea probed and got nowhere, leaving Mourinho to rage at the 'ghost goal', conveniently ignoring the fact that had it not been given, Micheľ would have had little option but to give a penalty and send Čech off.

The other wrinkle was an issue of style. After the cavalier success of Manchester United in the Champions League in 1999 and the feast of high-class attacking technical football of Euro 2000, it felt, following Greece's improbable success at Euro 2004, that football was moving into an age of astringency with Mourinho in the vanguard. Given those games against Barça and Bayern and the fact they'd averaged almost two goals a game in the league, that might not have been entirely fair, but they certainly weren't as obviously easy on the eye as the side they'd succeeded as champions, Arsenal's Invincibles.

That was a particular issue given the suspicion Roman Abramovich felt that having invested as much as he had, he might be due a little more entertainment. Michael Essien and Shaun Wright-Phillips arrived in the summer of 2005 while Hernán Crespo returned from his loan spell in Milan and there were experiments with a front two again in the first two games of the season, against Wigan and Arsenal, both won 1-0. But the 4-3-3 soon returned and so did the sense of Chelsea as a remorseless winning machine. They conceded seven goals more and won four points fewer, but they still took the title by eight points from Manchester United.

But it seemed that wasn't quite enough for Abramovich. Chelsea had gone out of the League Cup on penalties to Charlton and had been beaten 2-1 by Benítez's Liverpool in the FA Cup semi-final. Their Champions League campaign had ended against Barcelona in the last 16, the course of the tie shaped by the dismissal of Asier del Horno for a foul on Lionel Messi in the first half of the first leg at Stamford Bridge. 'It was top-quality play-acting,' Mourinho said. 'Besides, I've lived with you, in Barcelona, and I know all about your taste for the theatre.' The relationship between Mourinho and the club that had formed him was becoming increasingly fraught.

Cruyff presciently observed in a column in *La Vanguardia* between the two legs that Mourinho's approach was a risk; everything was predicated on results and if they didn't follow there was nothing else to fall back on. 'There are two ways to approach football,' he said, explicitly comparing Chelsea to Greece's European champions. 'One is purely for the results. The other is to prioritise the quality of football. I will always defend that second way. The state of happiness is not determined by the number of titles, but by the way you have chosen to try to win them. As a pure spectator, one team left me feeling fulfilled, and the other disappointed me. If Chelsea do not translate this miserly style of football into titles, Mourinho will not last for four days. I cannot stand that style.'

Nor, it seemed, could Abramovich. He had decided to buy a football club after watching Manchester United's 4-3 victory over Real Madrid at Old Trafford in March 2003: he didn't just want success; he wanted football like that (although his excitement at that game perhaps suggests a lack of understanding: Real Madrid were 3-1 up from the first leg and never in serious danger). So he bought more stars: Andriy Shevchenko, Ashley Cole, Michael Ballack, Salomon Kalou and, after a protracted tussle with United, Mikel John Obi.

Mourinho was unimpressed. There were awkward attempts to squeeze Shevchenko into a 4-4-2, or to play a narrow 4-3-3 with Shevchenko on the flank, but none really worked. Shevchenko, who had just turned 30, seemed not to have recovered fully from a knee injury from which he had rushed back to play in the World Cup; there were times when Mourinho seemed openly to despair of his form, laughing ruefully on the bench at another bungled first touch. Chelsea were still essentially defensively solid, but they lacked anything approaching fluency. They only lost three times that season but, ending the season with five successive draws, they surrendered the title to United having scored 19 goals fewer than the champions.

The relationship between Mourinho and Abramovich soured as the season went on, reaching crisis point in a League Cup semi-final first leg at Wycombe. Injuries meant Mourinho fielded Essien and Paulo Ferreira at centre-back and, after a 1-1 draw against the League Two side, Mourinho erupted. In a small room off the tunnel at Adams Park, as a tea urn belched steam into the freezing January air, Mourinho bemoaned a recruitment policy that had left him over-burdened with attacking players but bereft of defensive cover. It was a mesmerising incident, partly because of the incongruity of the sophisticated manager and the parochial surroundings and partly because the player Mourinho was so desperate to sign was Tal Ben Haim. The Israel international did arrive that summer but played just 13 league games before being offloaded.

Chelsea won both Cups that season, but in the competition that might have redeemed the season, the Champions League, Liverpool and Benítez again stood in the way in the semi-final. Joe Cole slid in a Drogba cross to give Chelsea a 1-0 win at Stamford Bridge but they went down 1-0 at Anfield to a Daniel Agger goal and, with Benítez sitting cross-legged on the touchline in a pose of exaggerated calm, lost on penalties. By then questions of style had become an international matter. 'Put a shit hanging from a stick in the middle of this passionate, crazy stadium and there are people who will tell you it's a work of art,' the former Argentina striker Jorge Valdano wrote in *Marca*. 'It's not: it's a shit hanging from a stick.

'Chelsea and Liverpool are the clearest, most exaggerated example of the way football is going: very intense, very collective, very tactical, very physical and very direct. But, a short pass? Noooo. A feint? Noooo. A change of pace? Noooo. A one-two? A nutmeg? A backheel? Don't be ridiculous. None of that. The extreme control and seriousness with which both teams played the semi-final neutralised any creative licence, any moments of exquisite skill.

'If Didier Drogba was the best player in the first match, it was purely because he was the one who ran the fastest, jumped the highest and crashed into people the hardest. Such extreme intensity wipes away talent, even leaving a player of Joe Cole's class disoriented. If football is going the way Chelsea and Liverpool are taking it, we had better be ready to wave goodbye to any expression of the cleverness and talent we have enjoyed for a century.'

Mourinho lingered a further eight months after the rant in the steam, but as Abramovich appointed Avram Grant as technical director, the atmosphere became increasingly rancorous. In September 2007, Chelsea lost 2-0 at Aston Villa and drew 0-0 at home to Blackburn, meaning they faced Rosenborg in their opening Champions League group game in an atmosphere of extraordinary pressure. They drew 1-1. After the final whistle, Mourinho and Abramovich passed each other in a corridor. The owner said he was disappointed and expressed a hope that Chelsea 'could do better'. Mourinho, bridling, said that if he didn't like how the team was playing he could always sack him. Abramovich told Mourinho he could go if he wanted and so, in the space of a conversation lasting less than a minute, a form of the 'mutual consent' to which club statements later referred was reached.

Mourinho had been the most successful manager in Chelsea's history, winning five major trophies in three completed seasons and twice reached the last four of the Champions League, and yet by the time he left, after almost a year of brewing unrest, his departure had come to seem inevitable.

CHAPTER FOUR

# OUT OF DUTCH

During the winter break in 2003-04, Ajax went to a training camp in Portugal. It was there that the first signs emerged of tension between the manager, Ronald Koeman, and his technical director, Louis van Gaal, who had been appointed a month earlier. During a practice match, Van Gaal took a plastic chair, approached the pitch, placed it by the touchline and, as *Voetbal International* put it, took up 'a pontifical position'. He might not have been on the pitch with a whistle, directing operations, but nobody could doubt he was overseeing everything, judging. When photographs of the incident were published in the Dutch press, Koeman's brother Erwin sent him a text message. 'Good luck with your new technical director,' it said.

Van Gaal then asked if he could join in the performance review discussions with players. 'I said that I assumed he would not speak,' Koeman said. Van Gaal insisted that would not be a problem. 'He kept that promise,' Koeman went on, 'until the discussion with Zlatan Ibrahimović. Suddenly, he told him that he never moves towards the near post. I could have sunk into the ground. I was white-hot livid.'

During training the following day, Ibrahimović made a run to the near post. Van Gaal, sitting on his plastic chair, began to applaud. 'Very embarrassing,' said Koeman. 'The players also became increasingly annoyed with his behaviour.'

As so often in Dutch football, personalities and political wrangling undermined what had been an extremely successful team. Koeman and

Van Gaal had worked together well at Barcelona, and their reunion at Ajax seemed a way of carrying Barcelona's post-Cruyffian principles back to their origin. What happened at Ajax, though, prompted a frostiness that still hadn't thawed when they met as managers of Southampton and Manchester United in the Premier League more than a decade later.

* * *

After two years as his assistant, Koeman had been the first major figure to break away from Van Gaal's Barcelona, leaving in November 1999 after being offered the manager's job at Vitesse. He led them to fourth and although they fell back the following season to sixth, that could be blamed on the club's difficult financial situation as the chairman Karel Aalbers, who had appointed him, was forced to quit after sponsors threatened to withdraw their support from the club. In December 2001, when Co Adriaanse was sacked by Ajax, Koeman, then 38, was the obvious man to replace him.

Koeman had been born in Zaandam in North Holland, son of the Netherlands international defender Martin Koeman. He had learned the game playing in the streets with his elder brother Erwin. The pair were devoted to football, so much so that their mother Marijke despaired of them ever coming home for meals and took to tossing peanut butter sandwiches into the street for them. 'I was afraid people would think we were an anti-social family,' Marijke said in the book *Koeman & Koeman*, 'but the boys didn't want to miss out on playing football.'

The elder Koeman was quiet and introverted; the younger was determined, strong-willed and well aware of his own potential, pushing through a move from his club Helpman to their local rivals GRC Groningen and securing, it was rumoured, a set of red training kit and a new colour television as part of the deal. 'I was much more a fanatic than Erwin,' Ronald said. 'If we had lost, Erwin shrugged and thought, "Next time, we'll do better." But I would be in a very bad state after a defeat. I would sulk and get really angry.'

Koeman was given his first-team debut at Groningen in 1980 as a 17-year-old by the former Den Haag centre-back Theo Verlangen, and took to turning up at training in a second-hand Porsche. He was widely praised for his early displays, but Verlangen soon dropped him, suggesting Koeman played 'too much at one pace'. Koeman hit back and was suspended for a game. Long before he got to Ajax, the classic traits of self-belief and an inability to keep tactfully quiet were there. 'I must have the ball because I can always play a good game if I have a lot of the ball,' he explained. 'Your teammates see it soon enough. If you always do something good with the ball, the ball will come to you naturally.'

The young Koeman, *VI* said in 2003, was 'rebellious and impatient, stubborn and self-confident'. The magazine was comparing him to his young Ajax playmaker Rafael van der Vaart, but the echo of Cruyff – or indeed a host of talented young Dutch players – is hard to miss. 'I thought I was important,' Koeman said in 1990, reflecting on how he had been a decade earlier, 'which of course, as a 17-year-old, you cannot be at all. You can play a bit of football, but beyond that, you have experienced nothing yet.'

Yet Koeman largely lived up to his self-image. 'Mr [Walter] Waalderbos [a Groningen defender] and his associates kicked me all over the field, but I kicked back just as hard,' he said. 'If you do not [respond] after their first bite at you, you never will. And of course, I knew myself that I could play football well.'

Well enough that, in 1983, he moved to Ajax. Initially, under Aad de Mos, he found the atmosphere cold. 'I learned,' he said, 'to think about myself and only about myself. I soon found that you are an individual at Ajax; nobody thinks for you and nobody thinks about you.'

That meant that he felt emboldened to criticise those around him, particularly when his own form was questioned – not that he needed much encouragement. 'The problem is that my play in the current Ajax side does not totally live up to its potential,' Koeman said in the autumn of 1984. 'There are no players whom you can send deep. Rob de Wit comes inside, Gerald Vanenburg comes in and Marco van Basten is difficult to launch from the centre. Ajax play very much to the ball.'

Ajax ended up regaining the title that season but De Mos was sacked shortly before the end of the campaign after a run of poor form. In the summer he was replaced by Johan Cruyff, who changed the style to one based more on control of space. It was only then that Koeman became a fixture in the side, used more as a libero than as a central midfielder. Previous attempts to deploy him in the role had failed, but Koeman was again able to find others to blame. 'I played with Jan Mølby just in front of the defence, and I can assure you that it's hard,' he said.* 'Then you will occasionally be passed by on all sides. There must be defensive discipline. Let me play libero with the [Feyenoord] trio of Troost, Wijnstekers and Nielsen, and then there's nobody who would sound a critical note.'

Not that Koeman found Cruyff easy to work for. 'At a training session or in a game, you could feel his eyes burning on your back,' he said. 'I wasn't used to it, being shouted at as much as he did. Often you thought, "Man, just for once keep your mouth shut!" Then you'd come home and be reluctant to go train again the next day. You would have the idea that he was targeting you but everyone got their turn.

---

* While nobody doubted Mølby's technical ability, he was neither quick nor mobile.

Actually, every footballer must go through something like this, especially if you've had it relatively easy previously, as I had. You become stronger from it – if, at least, you are not broken easily.'

Koeman spent only a year under Cruyff at Ajax before controversially moving to Hans Kraay's champions, PSV. Kraay resigned towards the end of 1986-87 to be replaced by Guus Hiddink, under whose leadership PSV overhauled Ajax to defend the title. They won it the following two seasons as well and also claimed the European Cup in 1988. Koeman, and his brother, who was by then at Mechelen, were also key members of the Netherlands side that, under Rinus Michels, won the European Championship in 1988.

His relationship with Cruyff might not always have been straightforward but, in 1989, Koeman rejoined him at Barça, eventually winning four league titles and becoming the second player – after Miodrag Belodedici – to win the European Cup with two different clubs. He wound down his career with two seasons back in the Netherlands with Feyenoord before, in 1997, retiring to become assistant to Hiddink with the Dutch national side. He then accepted Van Gaal's offer to take up a similar position at Barcelona.

Koeman, like Cruyff, could be extremely strict as a coach. If a player wasn't following his instructions, he would take him off, as he did once to the Egyptian striker Mido before half-time at a match in Groningen. 'If anybody after a good game thinks he can afford to train less hard, he will catch my attention,' he said. 'If I have to be, I will be *keihard*.'*

In terms of style, Koeman the young manager described himself as a believer in the traditional ideals of Dutch football. 'I want a team that takes the initiative,' he said, 'that utilises the freedom they have

---

* Literally, as hard as a rock.

to change positions, that independently probes for the shortest route to victory.'

He was never, though, a fundamentalist. 'I have experienced all sides,' Koeman explained. 'The Ajax system, for example, but also PSV who won the title three consecutive seasons with a 4-4-2 [between 1986-87 and 1988-89]. Then we also had people on the flanks who could be decisive: [Gerald] Vanenburg and [Frank] Arnesen. Barcelona were the most attacking of the clubs I have played for. Sometimes I thought myself that we took too many risks. At Feyenoord sometimes I thought, can we not play more attacking? I know after all these years that there is no monolithic truth or one right way in football. It is about winning; the result is the primary barometer of happiness. If I make an adjustment, it is purely to be better. Sometimes as a trainer, you must transform things, in the hope that you win matches.'

Still, Cruyff's influence over him was clear and Koeman was dropped from the national team for a game in 1990 for criticising the then national coach Rinus Michels for being too defensive in a defeat to Italy. 'With these tactics,' he said, 'we do not achieve anything. You cannot expect Marco van Basten and other strikers to affect the game with passing moves from the back. So they always end up with their back to the goal, and before they can do something there is already a defender on them. Playing with two real wingers, as we do at Barcelona, proves to be the most effective way of playing football.'

By 2003, he perhaps wasn't quite so certain, clearly troubled by the balance between defence and attack and wondering whether the traditional Ajax focus on the Cruyff philosophy were too tilted towards the offensive side of the game. 'In Holland most of the players who develop to the top are offensive players,' he said. 'Defensive players are difficult to find because most Dutch players are offensive technical players. Now we are pushing defence as an important factor. We are looking more to the results and not just the need to play attractive football. Ten years ago, attack was everything. We are changing that but it used to be that a good defence was the defence that could play in an offensive way. Now you always have to respect the quality of the opponent. We cannot say, "Oh we are the best in Europe, it doesn't matter about the opponent." Sometimes you have to accept the opponent is better and do everything you can to get a good result.'

Whether it were true Ajax or some less idealistic version, whether Koeman inclined more to Cruyff or to Van Gaal, the new coach had an immediate impact. Ajax may have been on a sticky run when he took over, but the squad he inherited was extraordinarily talented, featuring the likes of Mido, Zlatan Ibrahimović, Rafael van der Vaart, Tomáš Galásek, Cristian Chivu, Johnny Heitinga, Hatem Trabelsi and Maxwell. By May they had won a league and Cup double.

* * *

Having left Barcelona, Van Gaal succeeded Rijkaard as coach of the Netherlands. Although there are those who credit the 'Masterplan' he devised and implemented as being responsible for the upturn in Dutch youth football in the years that followed, his reign was hugely disappointing. The Netherlands had lost in the semi-finals of both the 1998 World Cup and Euro 2000, but under Van Gaal they failed to qualify for the 2002 World Cup.

Barcelona, though, had not thrived without him. Preferring, as ever, to promote from within, Barça had replaced Van Gaal with Llorenç Serra Ferrer, who had had success with Real Mallorca and Real Betis before joining Barça in a directorial role in 1997. He couldn't reinvigorate the side and was sacked shortly before the end of a season in which Barça finished fourth.

That summer, after 22 years as president, Núñez resigned, wearied by the criticism that had also brought down Van Gaal. Elections were held in July, and he was replaced by his former deputy Joan Gaspart. Almost immediately came a profound shock, the after-effects of which would undermine the club for years. Whatever issues there may have been in terms of results, playing style or the make-up of the squad, the event that did most damage to Barcelona could hardly have been foreseen.

The Portuguese winger Luís Figo had spent five seasons at Barcelona, winning two league titles and a Cup Winners' Cup. He was hugely popular and had no great desire to leave but contract talks had been put on hold until Gaspart won the election. At the same time, he was approached by the construction magnate Florentino Pérez who offered him €1m to say he would join Real Madrid if Pérez defeated the incumbent Lorenzo Sanz in the club's presidential election. Given Sanz had led the club to two Champions Leagues in three years, nobody thought that was likely, so Figo accepted what appeared to be essentially free money. But Pérez did win, Madrid met Figo's buyout clause of £36.2m and Serra Ferrer was suddenly taking over a side that had lost its biggest star, a fact highlighted when Figo won the Ballon d'Or that December. That was the beginning of Pérez's *galácticos* policy, which never really paid off, but it spooked Gaspart enough that he signed up Barça's other stars to huge contracts to try to ensure nothing as embarrassing as the sale of Figo ever happened again. That largesse, though, was the first indication of a spirit of free spending that undermined both the club's economics and its sense of self.

That summer Barcelona spent €39.6m on Marc Overmars, €21.6m on Gerard López, €15m on Alfonso Pérez and €9m on Emmanuel Petit. They finished fourth, 17 points behind the champions, Real

Madrid. Even worse, they were eliminated from the Champions League in the first group stage and then lost to Liverpool in the semi-final of the UEFA Cup. When Barça had three men sent off and lost 3-1 to Osasuna towards the end of April, Serra Ferrer's fate was sealed.

He was succeeded by his assistant, Charly Rexach, who had also been Cruyff's assistant and for whom it was a third caretaker stint at the club. Seven games of the season remained and his task was clear: get Barça from fifth to fourth and into the Champions League. It was a struggle, but qualification was secured on the final day as Rivaldo completed his hat-trick with an 88th-minute overhead kick to give Barça a 3-2 win against Valencia. That was enough to earn Rexach a permanent contract.

The appointment of a figure so steeped in Barcelona, somebody who had played alongside Cruyff as they had won the league in 1974, could not disguise a general sense of decline about the Camp Nou. Guardiola left that summer, his final game a Copa del Rey semi-final as Barça failed to overturn a first-leg deficit against Celta Vigo at home. He had missed the 1998 World Cup with a calf problem that eventually required surgery and, constantly battling injuries, he was ruled out for the last three months of 1999-2000 after an operation on his ankle. Frustrated with Barça's underperformance and with what he saw as the growing physicality of football, the 30-year-old, after 17 years at the club, decided he had to move on. As Guardiola saw it, the drift away from the Dutch style risked repeating the problems of the past. 'Barça also had the best players before Cruyff to try and win competitions and prizes,' he wrote in *La meva gent, el meu fútbol*, 'but the club never had a consistent or distinctive playing style. With a German trainer they played the German way, with an Argentinian, the Argentinian way and under a Brit, the English way.' The result had been a lack of continuity and only fitful spells of success. Guardiola diagnosed a similar problem, even with Rexach's return. There was no consistency of thought, little sense the manager had been appointed with any sense of the players the board wanted to bring in.

Guardiola's pessimism was soon justified. Javier Saviola, Fábio Rochemback, Geovanni, Patrik Andersson, Philippe Christanval, Francesco Coco and Roberto Bonano arrived in another wave of spending that summer; none lived up to expectations. Barça did get themselves to second by the beginning of November, but defeat to Real Madrid prompted a slump from which, in the league, they never really recovered. Long before Madrid had beaten them over two legs in the Champions League semi-final, it was clear that Rexach would be gone at the end of the season. The only question was who would replace him. After Deportivo had beaten Madrid in the Copa del Rey, they looked like going for their manager, Javier Irureta, but then Depor's league form collapsed. Hector Cúper was next but then his Inter blew the *scudetto*. So they turned to Celta Vigo's Víctor Fernández, at which his side stuttered and missed out on qualification for the Champions League. Which brought them, implausibly, to the last man to lead them to a league title: Louis van Gaal. The news of his return was broken when he was tricked into revealing he was about to sign a contract by an impressionist working for a radio station.

It was a frankly staggering move. By the time he had left after his first stint, Van Gaal had been at war with the press and unpopular with a number of players. The arrival of such a divisive figure in an environment that already roiled with conflict was only ever likely to provoke further discord.

Rivaldo left immediately and others must have wished they could have followed him. Again the lack of any sort of coherent planning was clear. The goalkeeper Robert Enke was signed from Benfica and found himself being asked to play the ball out from the back in a way he never had before. Juan Román Riquelme joined from Boca Juniors for €11m that November. Van Gaal described him as 'a political signing' and treated him with open disdain.

So why go back? 'Because Gaspart was the president and I liked him very much,' Van Gaal explained. 'He promised me that I could buy two players of my own desire but he bought Riquelme and that was exactly the player who was difficult to fit into the team.'

To nobody's great surprise, other than perhaps Van Gaal's, pretty much everything went rapidly wrong. Barça did go through their Champions League group with a 100 per cent record, but the only long-term positive from Van Gaal's second spell in charge was the emergence of Andrés Iniesta, who was described by his manager as 'the player I wanted to be, but wasn't'.

Iniesta himself seems to have relished the opportunity without questioning Van Gaal's methods. 'He was more demanding, tougher than anyone,' he said, 'but he treated all the players the same way. It didn't matter if you were 18 or 28.' That might have been good for youth development, but everything else was a shambles.

In the *Clásico* at the end of November, a 0-0 draw, fans threw a pig's head at Figo. When Barça then lost to Real Sociedad at the beginning of December, they lay tenth, six points off the relegation zone after their worst start in 31 years. They lost their next two matches as well, defeats to Rayo Vallecano and Sevilla leaving them two points off relegation. Out came the white handkerchiefs as Barça fans called on the president, Joan Gaspart, to resign.

He and Van Gaal clung on a little longer – long enough for Van Gaal to be cast as a *Caganer*, the traditional figures of an unpopular celebrity on the toilet produced by a local confectioner every Christmas – but defeats to Valencia and Celta Vigo at the end of

January brought the end for the manager. Two weeks later, Gaspart announced his own resignation. During his two-and-a-half-year reign, Barça spent £150m on 16 players and won nothing, not even the Copa Catalunya.

\* \* \*

In November 2003, Leo Beenhakker stood down as Ajax's technical director for personal reasons. He was replaced, ten months after the departure from Barcelona, by Louis van Gaal. Cruyff was consulted about Van Gaal's appointment but later came to suspect the decision had been made long before he was asked. Not surprisingly, he felt Van Gaal was the wrong man at the wrong time. 'There wasn't a single reason to change Koeman's working situation because he was doing brilliantly,' he said, seeing a similarity with how the Ajax board had treated him in 1987. 'Something that was good was broken from above.'

It was soon broken from within as well. Van Gaal arrived announcing his career as a coach was at an end, almost as though he saw his return to Ajax as the completion of a cycle. At his first press conference, he read out a poem declaring his love for the club, but the club itself never seemed entirely to reciprocate.

Ajax had gone trophyless in 2002-03, but in 2003-04 Koeman won the Eredivisie. Mido had gone, but Steven Pienaar, Wesley Sneijder and Maarten Stekelenburg had emerged from a youth set-up that for a decade had been the envy of Europe (Pienaar, admittedly, having moved from Ajax's sister club in Cape Town). Despite their on-field success, though, there was tension, of which Van Gaal's habit of sitting disapprovingly on the touchline as Koeman took training was only the most obvious manifestation. What Van Gaal saw as useful advice to help a young coach, Koeman felt undermined him.

The parallels to what Cruyff had done to Beenhakker 23 years earlier are clear.

Every Monday, Van Gaal would meet first with Marco van Basten and John van 't Schip, who coached Jong Ajax, and then with Koeman. One particular day stood out. 'When we ran into each other on the stairs,' Koeman recalled, 'Marco and Johnny were already shaking their heads. Then I went in and Van Gaal had prepared a "Topcoach" booklet in which he had constructed a team and made some notes. We discussed that. On many points we agreed but I was increasingly getting the impression that he was sitting in my chair.'

That summer, Ajax went to England for pre-season training. 'Louis came to me then with the news that he was going to evaluate my performance,' Koeman said. 'I responded, "I don't know if you have read my contract but the fact is that I'm only accountable to the general director." From that moment, it was a real race between us. Van Gaal no longer defended me nor I him.'

Crisis point was reached in August 2004, triggered by a friendly between the Netherlands and Sweden. The Dutch had eliminated Sweden from the Euros earlier that summer and there had been talk in the build-up of revenge. Three minutes in, Ibrahimović set up Mattias Jonson for the opener. In doing so, he stretched for a loose ball and caught Van der Vaart just above the ankle. Ajax's captain was stretchered off and accused Ibrahimović of having caused the injury deliberately. Ibrahimović denied the claim – and while only he can be sure of the level of intent, the challenge certainly didn't look vicious – and telephoned Van der Vaart to apologise.

Van der Vaart wouldn't accept his explanations and demanded a meeting with Koeman. Ibrahimović was furious. 'I didn't injure you on purpose, and you know that,' he told his clubmate. 'If you accuse me again I'll break both your legs, and this time it will be on purpose.'

That didn't resolve matters. The dressing room was divided, with Van der Vaart refusing to back down and Ibrahimović refusing to play in the same side as him until he did. Van Gaal, rarely a man to attempt diplomacy when he could make a blunt assertion of will, ordered Ibrahimović to change his mind, at which Ibrahimović told Koeman he wanted to go to Juventus.

On 31 August, transfer deadline day, Van Gaal decided there was no point hanging on to a disaffected player, so allowed Ibrahimović to leave for €16m. The deal, though, was done too late for Ajax to complete the signing of the forward they'd lined up as a replacement, the Ivorian Arouna Koné. Ajax were left with just Wesley Sonck and Yannis Anastasiou as strikers for 2004-05 and a furious Koeman, feeling both marginalised and undermined, protested to the board. Most of the players seem largely to have sympathised with Koeman, who was accorded respect because of his status as a great player and because he wasn't Van Gaal, whose schoolmasterly approach rankled.

Ajax's league form remained decent but they began the Champions League campaign with a home defeat to Juventus and then a 4-0 reverse away to Bayern. 'For the last few weeks I've not been having fun at work,' Koeman said in Munich. 'There is, from inside Ajax, too much expected of the XI and that is not right. Between what I myself view as a real ambition and what the club expects, there is a big difference. I want to talk about it soon.'

The board arranged a meeting: 'a matter of bells being synchronised' the director Arie van Eijden said, optimistically. 'And we're going to do it all in peace.' Koeman was angered that Van Gaal had publicly made reaching the Champions League semi-final a target for the season and started dropping hints about his future. He was stubborn, but so too was Van Gaal and, as the columnist Johan Derksen put it in *VI*, 'The presence of technical director Van Gaal is a guarantee of unrest in the ArenA. It should have been possible for the Ajax leadership … to know that in advance. Van Gaal has a fascinating view of football, but is so convinced of his own vision that he wants to put the whole organisation in his own hands… Van Gaal is too dominant a personality to lead a club in a modern way, especially where most members of the technical staff are Johan Cruyff followers. Ruud Krol, Tonny Bruins Slot, Arnold Mühren, Bryan Roy, Sonny Silooy, Gerrie Mühren and everybody's friend Danny Blind share Cruyff's vision of football.' Van Basten could have been added to that list; he and Van Gaal never got on.

The final straw was a speech Van Gaal gave at a meeting of Ajax Business Associates. There he presented his policy but also said that, at the moment, there was no longer an Ajax philosophy, a clear criticism of Koeman. 'After that,' Koeman said, 'I could tolerate it no longer.'

He effectively issued the board with an ultimatum: him or Van Gaal. The general director Arie van Eijden and the president John Jaakke deliberated for a while but decided Van Gaal had to go. On 19 October, Van Gaal resigned. 'Compromise,' he said, 'does not go well with my character and I foresee more differences of opinion. In view of this, I decided to make room. I sincerely hope that by doing this, I serve the interests of Ajax. I would have liked to have grown old at Ajax but it unfortunately cannot be so.'

Results, though, didn't improve and, gradually, the public mood turned against Koeman: perhaps Van Gaal hadn't been the problem, or at least not the only problem. There was much mockery of the decision to have the number one embroidered onto club ties when Ajax were lying sixth in the table, while Koeman's decision to sell a property in Barcelona to buy one in the Algarve was subjected to profound scrutiny. Was that, Bert Wagendorp asked in *de Volkskrant*, a sign he had given up his ambitions of managing Barcelona to play golf with his neighbour John de Mol, the founder of the media company Endemol? And in turn, was that a sign of a general diminution of ambition at Ajax after Van Gaal's departure? He would soon have another neighbour; seemingly to make a point, Van Gaal built his own holiday home, slightly larger than Koeman's, on the same street.

When Auxerre put Ajax out of the UEFA Cup in February 2005, Koeman also resigned. What had seemed so promising when the league was won the previous year lay in ruins, the dream of a gifted young squad ripped apart by egos and off-field machinations; the Ajax way, perhaps, isn't only about pressing, possession football and the use of wingers. John Jaakke, in a confusing interview in *Het Parool*, said that Van Gaal had been right but that the board had backed Koeman to give him courage to speak up. 'You often see that the atmosphere in distributing inheritance among family members is so bad that there are heated discussions about who grandmother's bedside table actually belongs to,' Jaakke said. In *VI*, Bas Heijt was scathing of Van Gaal for being 'irritating and too intrusive', of Koeman for being 'a spoilt child', of the Ajax board for 'prioritising packaging over the contents'.

And yet, what seems ridiculous in retrospect, amid all the talk of philosophy, is how similar their ideas were. 'Van Gaal was very fond of the vision of Van Basten,' said Jaakke. 'He thought that if a man could implement the Ajax culture, it was Van Basten. The fact that those two did not get along as individuals is another story. The ideas of Van Gaal on the one hand and Van Basten and Cruyff on the other hand are very close together. The annoying thing is that they cannot get along with each other.'

\* \* \*

The election to replace Gaspart as Barcelona president was won by the 40-year-old Joan Laporta. Backed by Johan Cruyff and various young local businessmen, he was fresh and energetic and promised renewal on Cruyffian lines, something manifested in his appointment of the Dream Team winger Txiki Begiristain as sporting director. Yet Laporta's reign did not begin auspiciously. He had promised to sign David Beckham but that had never really seemed likely and the England captain joined the *galácticos* at Real Madrid.

Then there was the issue of the manager. Radomir Antić, the affable Serbian who had replaced Van Gaal on a temporary basis, had done a fine job in steadying the ship, taking Barça from 15th when he took over to sixth and leading them through the second group phase of the Champions League only to lose to Juventus in the quarter-final. He also gave more game-time to Víctor Valdés and Iniesta and moved Xavi higher up the field, freeing him from some of the defensive responsibility he had found inhibitive under Van Gaal. But Antić was not Laporta's man and, as part of a general overhaul of the coaching set-up, his contract was not renewed when it expired that summer.

Laporta turned first to Guus Hiddink and then to Ronald Koeman and after failing to land either of them, to Frank Rijkaard. He was 40 and neither of his previous managerial jobs had gone particularly well. His Netherlands side had been beaten on penalties by a nine-man Italy in the semi-final of Euro 2000 and he'd then led Sparta Rotterdam to the first relegation in their history. He and his assistant Henk ten Cate had been on the verge of accepting an offer to coach the Netherlands Antilles when the call had come.

Rijkaard and Cruyff had fallen out in September 1987, the midfielder storming off the training pitch and vowing never to play for Cruyff again, before signing for Sporting (although, as it turned out, he never played for them; having joined too late to register he was loaned out to Real Zaragoza, joining AC Milan at the end of the season). 'Fuck you and your eternal whining!' he shouted at Cruyff before using a Dutch idiom in which he wished cholera upon him. A little over two years later, though, Rijkaard was among a group of players calling for Cruyff to replace Leo Beenhakker as national coach for the 1990 World Cup finals. 'Johan intrigues me immensely,' Rijkaard said. 'Especially that double person in him. There's the football genius but also that frail man who rarely forgives and forgets and even holds little grudges.'

But Cruyff was sure Rijkaard was the right choice: this was a chance to re-establish the Ajax principles, Cruyffian principles. 'Johan wanted that thread to be picked up,' said Eusebio Sacristán, who came in as an assistant coach. 'Txiki knows Cruyff's philosophy … he's another of the faithful, someone who deciphered the greatness of that side … he wanted that to return, wanted us to take up the thread again. So, you have Johan, Txiki, Rijkaard as coach, a disciple of the past, even though not at Barcelona.'

The style of play was everything. 'It is an ideology that has turned Barcelona into an institution,' Cruyff said. 'A club that symbolises a unique philosophy in football.' There's a certain irony, of course, in the fact that Cruyff was better able to shape Barcelona, ostensibly the bigger club, than Ajax, where he ran constantly into the obstreperousness of other Dutchmen.

Although Dutch, Rijkaard was not particularly obstreperous. He was, though, successful – eventually. He endured a difficult start as Barça won just two of their first seven games. They lost 5-1 at Malaga. They were beaten at home in the league by Madrid for the first time in 20 years, a game in which Rijkaard's team selection drew allegations of cowardice. When they lost 3-0 at Racing Santander in the first game back after the winter break, they lay 12th in the table. Things were so bad that Sandro Rosell, at the time a board member but later a president of Barcelona, plotted to replace him with Luiz Felipe Scolari who had won the World Cup with Brazil, but whose methods could hardly have been further removed from the Cruyffian ideal.

Everything was transformed by the arrival of Edgar Davids on loan from Juventus. Davids had been part of the Ajax side that had won the Champions League under Louis van Gaal in 1995 and he brought a new combativeness. His example, Xavi said, had a profound effect, making clear the level of commitment necessary to have success. It was then, he said, that he understood Barcelona were 'fighting a battle for the soul of football'.

Incorporating Davids meant a change of shape, from 4-2-3-1 to the more obviously Cruyffian 4-3-3. 'From that system,' Eusebio said, 'everything starts to fall into place, the development of the idea and the philosophy is easier to impose. There's no double *pivote*, there are more lines of pass, more vertical lines, Ronaldinho comes inside, creates almost a diamond, we open the wing up, especially with the left-back, where Ronnie goes inside. From that change to the system, all these possibilities appear.'

Barça went on a run of nine league wins in a row, then won a league game at the Bernabéu for the first time in seven years. Had they not lost two of their final three matches of the season, they would have won an implausible title. As it was, they finished second, which was enough. With his man in charge, Cruyff's influence was strong again. 'I have conversations with Cruyff, in which Johan brings up many sensible things about the team,' Rijkaard said. His mindset was overtly Cruyffian: Barça were playing attacking football, pushing high up the pitch, focusing on maintaining possession and using the wings to stretch the play.

But had the switch to 4-3-3 been Rijkaard's idea? Eusebio was reluctant to say, almost embarrassed by the question. 'I don't know if it's something to talk about,' he said, leaving long pauses. 'Well... Well, I've answered, I think: there were some of us there who were disciples of Johan and he was there.'

Rijkaard wasn't as outspoken or such a political character as Cruyff, clearly, but he did have a similar understated calm on the touchline, trying always to keep things simple. His preparation for the Champions League tie against Chelsea in 2005 was typical. He gave his players the Sunday off and on the Monday they performed just simple physical exercises. Only on the Tuesday was there serious preparation for the game and even then the key words Rijkaard jotted down suggest how succinct his instructions were: 'Positional Play. Look for the free man in [Demetrio] Albertini. Game-changing subs. Shoot from the edge of the box.'

That tie, lost 5-4 on aggregate, was just about the only disappointment of the season. Barça went unbeaten through their first ten games, taking top spot, a position they never looked like surrendering as they won the title by four points. The championship was won at Valencia and as the squad entered the departure lounge at the airport on the journey home, Laporta took Rijkaard's arm and raised it in the air: this, he was saying, this is the champion. But Rijkaard, forever undemonstrative, simply pulled his arm down and looked confused. On the triumphal bus parade through Barcelona, with his players celebrating on the top deck, he sat below, smoking. 'The key to our success is the calmness Rijkaard transmits to everyone,' Laporta said.

The following season, 2005-06, was even better. Ronaldinho was given a standing ovation by the Bernabéu after orchestrating Barça's 3-0 win in the *Clásico*. This time the gap to a self-destructing Madrid was 12 points and there was, at last, a second European title. Mourinho's Chelsea were beaten in the last 16 and Benfica and Milan seen off in the quarters and semis before a 2-1 victory over Arsenal in the final in Paris. Pep Guardiola, writing in *El País*, called the team 'a manifesto', describing Rijkaard's side as the best Barcelona since the Dream Team.

The return to a Cruyffian manager and the return to Cruyffian principles had brought a Cruyffian level of success.

# CHAPTER FIVE

# THE RETURN
# OF THE KING

There is a photograph taken in the aftermath of Barcelona's dramatic victory over IFK Gothenburg in the 1986 European Cup semi-final that shows the midfielder Víctor Muñoz, having scored the decisive penalty in the shoot-out, battling his way through a knot of people on the pitch. His eyes are fixed on some point in the middle distance and his mouth is half-open, whether in joy or determination to get off the pitch it is hard to say. The collar is stretched tight, exposing a square of upper chest, his sleeve pulled down by a 15-year-old ballboy who clings to his left arm, asking for his shirt. That ballboy is Pep Guardiola.

There is perhaps nobody so steeped in the modern Barcelona as Guardiola. He was born six months before Rinus Michels arrived and grew up with the club, as a fan and a player. He was the embodiment of the Cruyffian philosophy, neither quick nor powerful, but technically gifted and hugely intelligent. He had won the European Cup under Cruyff, left the club as disillusionment set in and returned to reimpose those Cruyffian values. 'Johan built the cathedral,' Guardiola said. 'Our job is to renovate it.'

'Our model was imposed by Cruyff,' said Xavi.* 'It's an Ajax model. It's all about *rondos* [the piggy in the middle exercise in which

---

* In an interview with Sid Lowe in the *Guardian*.

a circle of players pass the ball around one or two interceptors]. *Rondo, rondo, rondo.* Every. Single. Day. It's the best exercise there is. You learn responsibility and not to lose the ball. If you lose the ball, you go in the middle. *Pum-pum-pum-pum*, always one touch. If you go in the middle, it's humiliating. The others applaud and laugh at you.'

Yet what sounds so simple produced extraordinary results. By the time Guardiola left Barcelona in 2012 after four years as manager, he had not merely won three league titles and two Champions Leagues, he had redefined the boundaries of how football could be played. He had taken the Cruyffian ideas, revised and refined them, and the result had been one of the greatest teams ever to have played the game. 'If we continue this religious idea,' Eusebio said, 'Guardiola is … the Messiah, no?'

\* \* \*

After leaving Barcelona in 2001, Guardiola joined Brescia, playing alongside Roberto Baggio under the management of Carlo Mazzone, a passionate eccentric who employed a press-and-possess style that would also have a significant influence over Antonio Conte. He had a four-game stint at Roma as well, but generally his two years in Italy were unspectacular, overshadowed by a four-month ban after he tested positive for nandrolone. Guardiola always protested his innocence, appealed and, although he had served the suspension, was subsequently cleared.

He moved on in 2003 to Al Ahli in Qatar but seemingly remained gloomy about the future of the game. In March 2004, he gave a striking interview to Gabriele Marcotti in *The Times*. 'Players like me,' he said, 'have become extinct because the game has become more tactical and physical. There is less time to think. At most clubs, players are given specific roles and their creativity can only exist within those parameters.' What followed later that year, as Mourinho's Porto won the Champions League, Greece won the Euros and a functional Brazil beat Argentina in the final of the Copa América, confirmed Guardiola's outlook: football, after the flurry of excitement around Euro 2000 as the coming of 4-2-3-1 began to liberate dribblers again, had become once more a game of caution and muscularity.

By 2006, Guardiola was on the verge of retirement when he decided to spend six months in Mexico playing under Juanma Lillo at Dorados de Sinaloa while studying management in Atlixco. In terms of the manager he subsequently became it was Lillo who became the most significant influence and the pair would sit up long into the night discussing theory. Lillo stood in opposition to the prevailing pragmatism; he is a romantic, far more concerned by process than by results.

'The objective is the journey,' he said.* 'In a race you can be first, miles and miles ahead of anyone else, and then, metres from the line, fall over. And? Are you going to write that race off? You ran brilliantly ... what enriches you is the game, not the result. The result is a piece of data. The birth rate goes up. Is that enriching? No. But the process that led to that? Now *that's* enriching. Fulfilment comes from the process. You debate the game not the results. Results are not debatable, they *are*. Do you buy a paper on a Monday morning for a euro and the only thing in it is list after list of results? Do you go into a football stadium, in the last minute of a game, have a look at the scoreboard and leave? You watch 90 minutes, which is the process. You can't validate the process through the results. Human beings tend to venerate what finished well, not what was done well. We attack what ended up badly, not what was done badly.'

---

* To Sid Lowe in Issue One of *The Blizzard*.

In November 2006, Guardiola retired. He was clear in his desire to be a coach, and clear what sort of coach he wanted to be. He continued his education in Argentina, speaking to César Luis Menotti, the coach who had led Argentina to the World Cup in 1978, and to two others who believed in what might perhaps best be termed proactive football, Ricardo La Volpe and Marcelo Bielsa. To say all three share a common philosophy would be misleading but all three prefer high-energy, high-tempo football and all prefer to play in the opponent's half. Menotti is probably the most traditional and has the greatest focus on possession. La Volpe became a controversial figure in Argentina with his dismissal of the number ten position. Bielsa represented a third way between the idealism of Menotti (although that has often seemed overstated) and the repetitive training and drive of Menotti's supposed polar opposite, Carlos Bilardo.* The meeting with Bielsa was particularly productive. The two spent 11 hours over an *asado* at Bielsa's house in Rosario, becoming so animated that at one point Guardiola's assistant was asked to demonstrate man-marking a chair.

All three of the men Guardiola visited, it might be noted, had reputations as great theorists rather than coaches who actually won trophies: apart from the World Cup, Menotti won only a Metropolitano title with Huracán and the Copa del Rey and League Cup with Barcelona; La Volpe won just a CONCACAF Gold Cup with Mexico and a Mexican league title with Atlante; while Bielsa's trophies amount to only two league titles with Newell's Old Boys and one with Vélez Sarsfield.† Lillo, similarly, has never won a major trophy as a manager.

\* \* \*

---

\* For more on this, see my book *Angels with Dirty Faces*.
† Although he did also lead Argentina to Olympic gold in 2004.

While Guardiola was on his voyage of self-exploration in Latin America, Barcelona were slowly sliding into decadence. At the 2006 UEFA awards, held in August in Monte Carlo on the night before the European Super Cup against Sevilla, Carles Puyol was named best defender, Deco was named best midfielder and Ronaldinho was named best forward. Back at the hotel after the event, Rijkaard had a Dutch pop group join him at his table for dinner and imposed no curfew on his squad. Certain players took advantage. On the morning of the match, Ronaldinho was allowed to pose in a photo shoot for his sponsors. Everything seemed a little slack, a little unprofessional, and Barcelona were beaten 3-0. It was only the Super Cup, but it was the first hint of a deeper malaise. Ronaldinho failed to turn up for a training session the following day and was dropped for the opening game of the season, a 3-2 win over Celta Vigo.

Henk ten Cate, Rijkaard's assistant and enforcer, had left for Ajax in the summer and had been replaced by Johan Neeskens, who was far less hard on the players. Ronaldinho was a particular issue, putting on weight, frequenting a club in Castelldefels and losing form. Eto'o suffered a knee injury and was allowed to recover away from the club. Rijkaard indulged his players and seemed himself to ease off. Before the final of the Club World Cup in Yokohama that December, he didn't even watch a video of Barça's opponents, the Brazilian side Internacional. Barça lost, 1-0. Márquez, Deco and Ronaldinho were all given time off over Christmas to visit family in Latin America. All returned late. None were sanctioned.

When Eto'o returned he was appalled by the atmosphere of laxity and told Laporta. That led to public sniping between Rijkaard and Eto'o, who also made a series of pointed comments to the press that clearly referred to Ronaldinho. As ever, the club's politics inflamed the situation. Ronaldinho was a friend of Sandro Rosell, who had just resigned from the board saying Laporta had become authoritarian.

On the pitch, 2006-07 was a season of near misses. As well as defeat in the European Super Cup and Club World Cup finals, Barça went out in the Copa del Rey semi-final to Getafe despite winning the first leg 5-2 (the game in which Messi scored his replica of Diego Maradona's second goal against England in 1986). Although their Champions League campaign featured a win over Mourinho's Chelsea at the Camp Nou and a draw at Stamford Bridge, it ended in the last 16 with defeat to Liverpool. The league was all but won heading into injury time of the penultimate round of games, with Barça 2-1 up on Espanyol and Madrid trailing by the same score against Real Zaragoza. But then, in the space of 18 seconds, came two equalisers, one from Ruud van Nistelrooy and one from Raúl Tamudo. Suddenly, rather than there being a three-point gap, Barça and Madrid were level at the top, but Madrid had the better head-to-head record. Both sides won on the final day and the title was Madrid's. Crises are never far away at the Camp Nou and there was a clear sense of one brewing. That they had come so close to winning the league, that their Copa del Rey exit had been so careless, only made it worse. When the margins were that slight, every small loss of discipline or moment of laxity was potentially decisive.

That summer, six years after he'd left, Guardiola returned to Barcelona. Initially the plan had been for him to take on a directorial role and for Luis Enrique to take over the B-side, but Guardiola was adamant he wanted to be a coach and so got the job of managing the reserves, who had just been relegated to the third flight. First, though, there was some making up to be done, particularly with Cruyff.

Their relationship had begun to break down shortly after Van Gaal's arrival. When the new manager offloaded a number of home-grown players, Cruyff felt Guardiola, as captain, should have intervened. Then, in 2003, Guardiola had broken a tacit agreement between various Dream Team players not to become involved in the club's presidential elections to announce that he would become director of football if Lluís Bassat beat Laporta. His support for Bassat, the defeated candidate, also made Laporta sceptical.

Bridges mended, Guardiola set about reforming the B-side. He disbanded the C-team to increase competition for places and allowed the Bs to select three senior players rather than being restricted to under-21s. He demanded professionalism, treating the Bs like the first team and imposing a ruthless discipline. One of his captains, Marc Valiente, for instance, was dropped for leaving a weights session five minutes early. Guardiola's intensity, though, caused problems and he was sent from the touchline three times that season for protesting at refereeing decisions, an issue he resolved by taking to swearing in Italian. Lillo watched every game and would meet with Guardiola to discuss it afterwards.

His managerial approach was a logical extension of the player he had been. 'He was very faithful to [Cruyff's ideas] as a player, being a number four, an organiser; all that information was good for him,' said Eusebio. 'He has the capacity to analyse, to take in information, to organise and to put it into practice... And those qualities allow him to be at the heart of the moment when the club decided to put that idea back into practice ... first with the *filial*, then... "Now I'm going to impose this, perfect it, think about it, apply it."'

The season began poorly and Guardiola was troubled by two rebels who didn't seem to take him seriously. He went to Cruyff for advice and was told to get rid of them: no individual could be bigger than the unit. The problem resolved, Barça's B-team won promotion back to the second flight. Just as importantly, two talents emerged who would have a huge part to play in the first team's future: Sergio Busquets and Pedro.

As Guardiola's second string was thriving, the senior side was sliding from bad to worse. Some of it was misfortune, much of it was not. Ronaldinho was becoming increasingly ill-disciplined. Rafael Márquez was regularly travelling to see his partner in Madrid. Thiago Motta went missing for a day after an evening out slipped into the following morning. Deco often turned up at training having not slept the previous night because he had been at the hospital with his sick child. In total, ten of that first-team squad went through the break-up of a relationship.

At the end of November, as Barça drew 2-2 with Lyon to secure their place in the knockout phase of the Champions League, Rijkaard was sent from the touchline for the first time in his career, which many took as an indication that the pressure was beginning to get to him. Earlier that month, Guardiola had for the first time begun to be spoken of as a possible replacement as the football department of the club accepted the reality that Rijkaard's reign was coming to an end. 'Rijkaard,' Cruyff said, 'was true to himself throughout the five years. Unfortunately the same cannot be said of the players.'

They had lost faith in him and lost their hunger and that had profound consequences, no matter how good the theory that under-pinned them. 'A five per cent drop in commitment at the highest level creates difficulty,' Ferran Soriano, at the time vice president with responsibility for economic affairs, wrote in his book *Goal: The Ball Doesn't Go in by Chance*, 'and Frank didn't know how to re-energise the group.'

The club drew up a profile of what they were looking for in their new manager. Each candidate was to be assessed according to nine criteria:

1. Respect for the sports management model and the role of the technical director.
2. Playing style.
3. Promoting the right values in the first team and paying. special attention to the development of young talent.
4. Training and performance.
5. Proactive management of the dressing room.
6. Other responsibilities with, and commitment to, the club, including maintaining a conservative profile and avoiding overuse of the media.
7. Experience as a player and a coach at the highest level
8. Support for the good governance of the club.
9. Knowledge of the Spanish league, the club and European competition.

A longlist was drawn up but Manuel Pellegrini, Arsène Wenger and Michael Laudrup were quickly scrubbed from it. When it became apparent that he lacked support in the boardroom, so was Ernesto Valverde, a bit-part player in Cruyff's first two seasons at the club who at the time was managing Espanyol. That left two candidates: Guardiola and Mourinho. Another vice president, Marc Ingla, and the director of football Txiki Begiristain arranged to meet Mourinho and his agent, Jorge Mendes, at a bank in Lisbon. Mourinho offered a memory stick on which he outlined how he would develop Barça's familiar 4-3-3 to a more physical version similar to that which he had used at Chelsea. The rancour of those various Champions League meetings between Barça and his Chelsea he explained away as being simply part of the psychological warfare necessary to win a game.

For all his charm, though, that remained a point of concern. Ingla acknowledged that he came out of the meeting feeling 'uncomfortable', while Cruyff and Begiristain were ideologically more attuned to Guardiola. In terms of the checklist, both candidates fell down on point nine, but Mourinho also fell down on points two, three, six and eight. 'It was clear that Mourinho was a great coach but we thought Guardiola would be even better,' said Soriano. 'There was the important issue of knowledge of the club. Mourinho had it, but Guardiola had more of it and he enjoyed a greater affinity with the club. Mourinho is a winner, but in order to win he guarantees a level of tension that becomes a problem.' When news of the Lisbon meeting leaked, it confirmed certain minds that had been wavering: when it came down to it, Mourinho would do what was right for him which might not necessarily be what was best for the club.

From January 2008, Laporta had taken to watching the B-team, sizing up Guardiola. The following month, he took him to dinner at the Drolma restaurant in the Hotel Majestic and told him that if Barcelona didn't reach the Champions League final, he would be appointed. Rijkaard was so amenable that he offered to allow Guardiola to join the coaching staff until the end of the season. Guardiola refused, but negotiations began to sign Seydou Keita, Dani Alves, Aliaksandr Hleb, Gerard Piqué and Martín Cáceres on the assumption he would be taking over.

When Barça drew 0-0 at home against Getafe at the beginning of April, fans jeered and waved white handkerchiefs. They called for Laporta to resign and condemned their players as 'lazy', chanting, 'less millions, more *cojones*'. The widespread suspicion was that Ronaldinho and Deco had been left out of the side for reasons other than the injuries the club insisted they had. Thierry Henry, the big summer signing, was generally regarded as being past his best.

Barça lost 1-0 on aggregate to Manchester United in the Champions League semi-final and, on 6 May 2008, Laporta visited

Guardiola at the Dexeus clinic where his third child had just been born and offered him the job. For Van Gaal, the appointment was a natural progression. 'Cruyff started it,' he said. 'I continued it, Rijkaard continued it… Guardiola was Johan's player and my player too. For the board of Barcelona it was logical that they take coaches with that style. I was selected only because of the style and the way I was educated.'

The following day, Barça were humiliatingly beaten 4-1 by Madrid. Mourinho, eager to press his case, rang Laporta, only to find the decision had already been taken. The club, he told the president, had made a terrible mistake. Mourinho has never forgiven Barcelona. All those doubts came rushing back. Even when he worked for Robson and Van Gaal, had they really accepted him? Or was he always the outsider, doomed by his lack of playing career to exist beyond the club's heart, never anything more than 'the translator'? Is it too much to suggest that at that moment, like Milton's Satan, he resolved to set himself against the heavens, to fight their dominance and their doctrine with every tool he had, even if, like another Miltonian hero, he ended up pulling the temple down on his own head?

'He is,' Mark Ingla observed, 'a bit poisoned by the fact he was rejected.'

* * *

Barça had finished 18 points behind Real Madrid in the league in 2007 and with both the handball and basketball sections of the club faring poorly, a motion of censure was enacted against Laporta. Sixty per cent voted against him but as it required the support of two-thirds of the membership for him to be ousted, he survived. Guardiola arrived like Cruyff, an icon of the club appointed by a president desperate to restore faith.

It was his overt intention to be like Cruyff. 'We are a bit like disciples of the essence that Cruyff brought here,' Guardiola wrote in his 2001 autobiography. 'Cruyff wanted to play that way, on the wings and using the wingers, and I apply that whole theory ahead of everything. It was he, Johan, who imposed the criteria for quick movement of the ball, the obligation to open up the field in order to find space. To fill the centre of the pitch in order to play having numerical superiority ... so that everybody knew how Barça played and, above all, so it would be known how to do it in the future.' He had become that future.

Before there could be any reimposition of those principles, though, there had first to be discipline. Ronaldinho was offloaded to Milan and Deco to Chelsea. Eto'o, promising to knuckle down, earned himself an additional year. Determined to eradicate the decadence of Rijkaard's final two seasons, Guardiola insisted the squad sat down to eat together, denied the media access to training and, following one of Bielsa's principles, refused to give any one-on-one interviews or privilege any media outlet over another. The suggestion is that Guardiola was over-strict in those first weeks, telling off Éric Abidal, for instance, for speaking to Thierry Henry in French rather than Spanish.

Guardiola also promoted Busquets and Pedro from the B-team. Another 20 players would follow them in Guardiola's four years at the club. At a pre-season meeting in St Andrews, he outlined his vision to his players, explained his vision of restoring the Cruyffian ideal.

They started the season with a 4-1 victory over Wisła Kraków in a Champions League qualifier. The league campaign started at Numancia, newly promoted, about to begin only their fourth season in the top flight and with an annual budget 26 times smaller than Barça's. Guardiola's side had 20 shots to Numancia's three and hit the woodwork twice, but lost 1-0.

Barça probably could have done with another game straight away to find their rhythm and dispel the doubts, but there followed an international break during which they faced a Copa Catalunya game away on an artificial pitch against Sant Andreu, a fifth-flight side based in the north of the city. Guardiola opted not to send the three first-teamers who hadn't joined up with their countries – Dani Alves, Eto'o and Sylvinho – and Barça lost 3-1. The few dozen fans who made the trip jeered Guardiola and Laporta.

That increased the pressure yet further on the first home league game, against Racing Santander. Messi, having played for Argentina in Peru, was left on the bench as Barça again dominated and again failed to win, drawing 1-1. Guardiola was assailed by doubts. Fail to beat Sporting de Gijón in his third game and he might have become the first Barça manager ever to lead his side to the bottom of the table. Andrés Iniesta went to see him in his office to tell him he had the backing of the players and that he should keep going on the course he had set. In *El Periódico*, Cruyff said this was 'the best Barça side ... in many years.' As he had the previous season, Guardiola went to see the *éminence grise*. Cruyff told him to persevere: the philosophy would prevail. Barça beat Sporting 6-1. Many of the features that would come to characterise Guardiola's Barça were already present: Busquets was there at the back of midfield, dropping between the central defenders, while Eto'o kept moving to the right, creating space for Messi to cut in from the flank.

Barça won their next 12 games in a row in all competitions and didn't lose again until they went down 3-2 at home to Shakhtar in their final Champions League group game, by which time their progress to the last 16 was already secure. That game fell amid a run of league fixtures against Sevilla, Valencia, Madrid and Villarreal. Barça won all four by an aggregate of 11-1, including a 2-0 home victory in the *Clásico* in Juande Ramos's first league game as Madrid manager after replacing Bernd Schuster. The German had been sacked after admitting that following a run of three defeats in four games, it was impossible for Madrid to beat Barcelona at the Camp Nou.

The imprint of Guardiola was clear: this was a discernible shift in style. 'In the world of football,' he said, 'there is only one secret: I've got the ball or I haven't. Barcelona have opted for having the ball... And when we haven't got the ball ... we have to get it back.'

The method was based in technical virtuosity, relying not on over-powering or outrunning teams but on outplaying them, teasing them out of position by making them think they had the opportunity to make a tackle or interception. After the 2011 Champions League final, for instance, Wayne Rooney noted how Xavi would wait for an opponent to get close before playing a pass, taking him out of the game to the greatest possible extent.

There was minute attention to detail. 'It was often about the philosophy, but also about little things – about how we can create space against this opponent, where we can create superiority,' said Eiður Guðjohnsen, who described the feeling when Guardiola took over as being similar to that he'd experienced under Mourinho at Chelsea; there was a sense that success was now inevitable. 'It's all about creating superiority all the way up the pitch – how to move in a way that creates freedom for the man on the ball, how to get the full-backs as far up the pitch as possible, how to get the players to move around the man with the ball so that it gives us an extra man in a certain area of the pitch at a certain time.'

The approach, though, isn't to attack at all costs. Pressing is central to the Guardiola ethos. When he spoke at a coaching conference in 2009, the title of his lecture was 'Recovering Possession'. His first training session with Barça had been based on winning the ball back.

He'd even blamed that early defeat to Numancia on the failure of his players to push high. 'You're the best player in the world with the ball,' he told Messi. 'You have to be the best without it.' Having forwards who could begin the process of regaining possession was vital. 'Our defenders are our attackers,' Dani Alves explained.* 'Pressure is the key... The closer we are to the opposition's goal when we win the ball, the easier it is to score. There's less distance to cover, fewer players to beat and normally the other team's out of position.'

A player, Guardiola reasoned, was never more vulnerable than when he had just won possession. He would have just expended energy in making the tackle or interception, might be off balance and would probably, in focusing on the ball, have lost sight of where everybody else was on the pitch. It would take a second or two to reset, to work out where he might be going to play the ball. That meant the press was best if it was rapid, which in turn meant it was usually led by the player who had just lost the ball. If the ball wasn't won back quickly, though, Barça would abandon the press, and drop back into defensive formation, allowing the opposition the ball and challenging them to pass their way through a set defence. The key was co-ordination.

'While we attack,' Guardiola said, 'the idea is to always keep your position, always being in the place you have to be. There is dynamism, mobility, but the position has always got to be filled by someone. So if we lose the ball it will be difficult for the rival to get us on the counter-attack – if we attack in order it becomes easier then to hunt down the opposition player with the ball when we lose possession.' In that, which is perhaps the essence of *juego de posición*, Guardiola sounds rather less like Cruyff than he does like Van Gaal, whom he has always acknowledged as a huge influence.

---

* In an interview with Sid Lowe in the *Guardian*.

To acknowledge influence, though, is not to deny the radicalism of what Guardiola was doing. He was taking what had gone before and developing it further, pushing new boundaries. In that, he was aided by a change in the environment. His gloom when talking to Gabriele Marcotti in Qatar had not been misplaced: his type of player *had* been falling into obsolescence. But by the time he became Barcelona coach, the game had changed. Referees became stricter and stricter on the tackle from behind, making it harder to intimidate creative players, while the offside law had been significantly amended. That was an ongoing process that had begun in the aftermath of the 1990 World Cup and had a far greater impact than was perhaps initially intended. First it was ruled that players who were level with the penultimate defensive player were to be considered onside, then the nature of what it was to be interfering with play was reinterpreted, making it impossible for sides to maintain a flat line and push out with impunity, confident that anybody behind them would be ruled offside. That meant that defences tended to play deeper – the number of offsides per game almost halved across major European leagues in the decade from 1997 to 1998 – which in turn increased the effective playing area as the space between the base position of the two defensive lines stretched from roughly 40 yards to nearer 70. That in turn meant there was more space in which technical players could operate. Paradoxically, Barça's passing game was facilitated by a development that made their pressing game harder to implement.

In Guardiola's first season, Barça developed a habit of winning games that seemed to have gone against them, finding a late winner against Betis after losing a 2-0 lead, coming from 1-0 down to beat Espanyol with a late Messi free kick and, most implausibly of all, winning 2-1 away at Shakhtar having trailed 1-0 with seven minutes remaining. There was a bristling self-belief about them, rooted in a profound team spirit. In part, that was a natural result of having so many players who had grown up in the youth ranks together but it was also something Guardiola fostered: the day before a Champions League game away to Basel he had the whole squad travel to Pamplona for the funeral of the father of the goalkeeping coach Juan Carlos Unzué. The message was clear: they were all in this together. 'There is order and discipline now,' said Xavi. 'It's all for one; there is solidarity again. Pep has restored order.'

By the time Barça played Madrid in the fourth-last game of the season, they were four points clear at the top of the table and had reached the Champions League semi-final after beating Bayern 4-0 at home in the first leg of the quarter-final. Barça had won the *Clásico* at the Camp Nou 2-0 but since then Madrid had found form, taking 52 points from their previous 18 games – and Barça had just been held to a draw by Valencia and, at home, by Chelsea in the first leg of their Champions League semi-final. Realistically, Barça knew that if they avoided defeat at the Bernabéu, they would win the title. Playing for a draw, though, is not Guardiola's way and, having had to give a guard of honour to Madrid the previous season before a 4-1 defeat in which Xavi was sent off, there was an urge for payback.

Guardiola decided to deploy Messi as a false nine, reasoning that if he dropped back to join Xavi and Iniesta in midfield, they would dance around Madrid's two holding players, Fernando Gago and Lassana Diarra. Gonzalo Higuaín put Madrid ahead but Henry equalised and then, having pretended he was leaving the field for treatment to distract the defence, Puyol headed in a Xavi free kick. It was Messi, though, who was the key. Fabio Cannavaro and Christoph Metzelder were trapped in the classic bind of the central defender against a deeply-lying forward. Follow him and they left space for Henry and Eto'o to dart into. Leave him and he ran the game. Despite missing four one-on-one opportunities, Barça went on to win 6-2, Piqué scoring the last, the fact that a centre-back was charging forward on the counter when his side already led 5-2 a neat encapsulation of the spirit in which Guardiola wanted the game played. *El Mundo Deportivo* called it 'the best performance Barcelona have ever produced', while on Canal+, Michael Robinson described Barcelona as 'the best team I have ever seen'.

Four days later, Barça went to Stamford Bridge for the second leg of their Champions League semi, having drawn the first leg 0-0. That stalemate at the Camp Nou, which brought to an end a run of 51 consecutive games in which Barça had scored, raised doubts about Guardiola's side for the first time since the beginning of the season. Guus Hiddink opted for an extremely defensive approach, so much so that Petr Čech, the goalkeeper, attempted more passes than any other away player that night. Michael Ballack was extremely fortunate not to be sent off for a foul on Iniesta when he was clean through, particularly given he had already been booked, but while protests about that incident were understandable, the general tone of Barça's players struck an uncomfortable note. 'We know referees allow more in European competition than they do in the Spanish league,' said Iniesta, 'but there is a difference between that and simply letting teams do whatever they want – which is what happened.'

It all sounded a little entitled, a team used to getting its own way whingeing that an opponent had taken a physical approach against them. 'The referee was very poor,' Xavi said. 'All that talk about fair play – it's a shame that they don't put that into practice on the pitch. There was no fair play from Chelsea at all. We played football; they did not play anything at all.'

At Stamford Bridge, Iniesta struck in the final minute to cancel out Michael Essien's ninth-minute strike and put Barça through on away goals but that night was about far more than the result. Chelsea fans remember that game now as a scandal, the night on which they were denied four penalties by the Norwegian referee Tom Henning Øvrebø. The less stable end of the anti-Barcelona lobby has seized on that game as well, using it as evidence of a pro-Barcelona conspiracy. It is, of course, nonsense unless we're seriously being asked to believe that the red card shown, extremely harshly, to Abidal after a tangle with Nicolas Anelka as both chased a flick-on from Didier Drogba was all part of the plan, a disguise of profound ingenuity. The full-back probably did catch the forward's heel, although it's hard to be absolutely sure, but it requires an imaginative stretch to construe the incident as a deliberate attempt to prevent a goalscoring opportunity. Certainly there was enough doubt for Øvrebø not to have sent Abidal off had his intention been to favour Barça. And even if those decisions are considered subterfuge, what sort of plot involves waiting until injury time and then relying on Barcelona winning the game by having Iniesta pick out the top corner from 25 yards?

Then take the four penalty appeals. Dani Alves's tug on Malouda happened outside the box and Øvrebø accordingly gave a free kick. Perhaps there's a case that the infringement continued into the box but it's far from clear either that it did or that Øvrebø hadn't already blown. Abidal did then pull Drogba's shirt in the box but it was momentary and Øvrebø's view was obstructed by the full-back: it probably should have been a penalty but it's easy to see why it wasn't given. Piqué's handball was clear, even allowing for the fact that he was very close to Anelka when the ball was flicked at him but, again, his body probably blocked Øvrebø's view. The Eto'o handball was far less clear-cut: although his arm was raised, in an unnatural position, the ball was driven first into his upper ribs, before deflecting up. It's readily understandable that Øvrebø might have been uncertain precisely where the ball struck the Cameroonian or might have deemed the offence accidental given the deflection. Any (or all) of the four could have been given, but only the Piqué handball was really obvious and even then it was possible to see why Øvrebø turned the appeal down. Øvrebø had a difficult night, but his performance wasn't even a particularly bad one, never mind a corrupt one.

In *AS*, Alfredo Relaño quoted St Teresa of Avila, observing that 'God writes straight with crooked lines'. Ramón Besa, in *El País*, similarly saw the game in quasi-religious terms: 'Sometimes,' he wrote, 'football is generous towards the virtuous and cruel to the evil; sometimes redemption comes.' Generally, though, it was a game that showed up Spanish journalism at its parochial worst. The back page of *AS* carried a cartoon in which a boy asked his mother for a Barça shirt. 'Which one?' she asked. 'Goalkeeper, home or ref?'

There hadn't been much in the semi-final to suggest just how good Barcelona were and many expected them to be overpowered by a more experienced Manchester United in the final in Rome, particularly given the slightly patched-up nature of their back four. With Abidal and Dani Alves suspended and Márquez injured, Barça fielded Sylvinho at left-back, with Puyol on the right and Piqué and Touré in the middle.

Before kick-off, Guardiola showed the players a video he had commissioned, a montage of clips of them in action set to the *Gladiator* theme. It may sound saccharine but those who were there insist it was very moving – perhaps too moving. In the first ten minutes, United were almost entirely dominant and Cristiano Ronaldo drew an awkward save from Víctor Valdés with a free kick that dipped in front of him. All the pre-match predictions that United would overwhelm Barça physically seemed to be coming true, but Guardiola's players stuck to the blueprint. Eto'o and Messi, as had been planned, swapped positions so the Argentinian operated as a false nine and the Cameroonian went out to the right. Almost immediately, Iniesta surged forward on the break and pushed a ball out to Eto'o, who checked inside, beat Nemanja Vidić and poked a shot past Edwin van der Sar.

What followed was remarkable, a demonstration of the impact of Guardiola's method on opponents. United, to Alex Ferguson's fury, became so dispirited as they vainly chased the ball that they stopped pressing and when they did have possession they were unable to do anything with it, disarmed both by Barça's pressing and by an awareness of the consequences of losing the ball. Ferguson, needing to change something, brought on Dimitar Berbatov for Park Ji-Sung after 65 minutes but that merely confirmed Barcelona's domination of midfield. Eventually Patrice Evra was dispossessed, leading to Xavi crossing for Messi to confirm Barça's victory with a rare header. 'Barcelona,' Relaño wrote, 'have shown that perfection is possible. There is no antidote to their exquisite football.'

Three years after Rijkaard's side had triumphed in Paris, Barça had their third Champions League. More than that, they had made an ideological point: Guardiola's way, Cruyff's way, not merely still had a place in the game but could elevate a side to dominate Europe.

# CHAPTER SIX

# ERUPTION

At the final whistle, José Mourinho leapt from the bench, bounded over the touchline and ran, right arm raised, finger extended, across the pitch, his mouth open in a roar of emotional release. There was a slight arc to the run, an opening of the chest, making himself the centre of attention. He looked less a manager delighted with a game plan well executed than a striker glorying in having scored the winning goal. He didn't shake hands with anybody, he didn't go to any of his players, he just ran towards the section, high in the corner of the Camp Nou, where the Inter fans were gathered. Víctor Valdés, for reasons best known to himself, tried to head Mourinho off. There was some brief grappling, before Mourinho shrugged him off to stand, both arms aloft, both fingers up, soaking in the congratulations of his players and the adulation of the fans. This, he was making clear to any who might possibly have doubted it, was his triumph.

His Inter had just lost 1-0 to Barcelona to progress to the final of the 2010 Champions League by a 3-2 aggregate. But it wasn't just a victory in a Champions League semi-final. It wasn't even just a victory against all odds, playing a man down against the European champions for more than an hour. It was a victory for Mourinho and his style, a victory over Barcelona, Guardiola and their philosophy, his nemesis downed in their own cathedral. Even better, as Sulley Muntari and then the rest of Inter's players joined their manager in celebration, Barça turned the sprinklers on. Mourinho, as he saw it, had not merely demonstrated the limitations of the way they played, he had exposed the sanctimony of their *més que un club* self-image. It was, as he put it, 'the most beautiful defeat of my life'. He had taken conscious aim at Barça's halo and had dislodged it.

\* \* \*

Mourinho's time at Inter was successful but bloody. When, in 2008, he was appointed to succeed Roberto Mancini, who had won three successive *scudetti* (the first of them awarded after Juventus had been stripped of the title following the *calciopoli* scandal), Mourinho struck a more humble note than he had at his Chelsea unveiling. He was not special, he insisted, he was normal. 'I don't change,' he said, 'I am the same person I was before.'

It didn't take long for Italy to find out what that meant. Inter began the season with a draw and three wins but then lost to Milan, at which Mourinho embarked on a classic diversion, berating the media and then launching an unprovoked ad hominem attack on the manager who had preceded him at Chelsea and was then in charge of Juventus, Claudio Ranieri. He couldn't speak English properly, Mourinho scoffed, while pointing out that he himself had spent five hours a day getting his Italian up to speed before taking over at Inter.

Generally, though, that first season went well. As at Porto and Chelsea, Mourinho was hugely popular with a core of players, who appreciated his focus on training with the ball, his distaste for gym work or building stamina by running. 'The secret,' he had said at his first training session, 'is to think. You will be strengthened by thinking. You will think about the schemes that I am telling you; you will play ball while thinking. A player who does not think cannot play football.' Provided, of course, that they were thinking in the way he wanted them to.

The focus on thinking, though, did not mean that Mourinho's football was complicated. On the contrary, he kept his instructions as simple as possible. 'As a coach,' Javier Zanetti wrote in his autobiography, 'he reads matches in a simple and straightforward way. The tremendous amount of study and data he grinds through on the computer are distilled into a few lines of analysis.'

There was a 4-0 win at Roma and then, in November, a hugely impressive 1-0 home win over Juventus that consolidated Inter's position at the top. 'You didn't see Juve,' said Mourinho, 'but only because we were so good.' He had, surprisingly, recalled Adriano for that game, playing him up front with Ibrahimović in a 4-3-1-2. 'I needed an animal to go up against [the Juve defenders Giorgio] Chiellini and [Nicola] Legrottaglie,' Mourinho explained. This was avowedly not a Cruyffian approach but it was Mourinho at his best, designing a specific tactic for a specific game and seeing it pay off: it had been Adriano's run that had drawn two defenders out of position to create room for Ibrahimović and the goalscorer, Sulley Muntari. Already it was clear that a profound team spirit had been generated, the sort of togetherness and hunger for success that can lift a team far beyond its notional ability. The Argentinian midfielder Esteban Cambiasso, who would emerge as a key Mourinho lieutenant, had played superbly despite having been up all night as his wife gave birth.

There were the familiar complaints about referees, but the title was wrapped up in mid-May when Milan, the only team that could still have caught Inter, were beaten 2-1 by Udinese. Mourinho allowed his players to celebrate that night but they still came back to beat Siena 3-0 the following day. Ibrahimović seemingly asked to come off in the second half but Mourinho kept him on and he scored. Three more goals in the two games that remained meant that Ibrahimović was, by one, Serie A's top scorer for the season – an example of Mourinho at times seeming to know players better than they knew themselves. 'When I look at him,' Mourinho said, 'I see myself – a person with the same winning mentality.'

Although the title had been won with three games still remaining, it was, perhaps, slightly underwhelming. Inter had gone out of the Champions League in the last 16, beaten 2-0 by Manchester United and, with no Italian side making it to the quarter-final, there were legitimate questions about the strength of Serie A. With the Bundesliga closing fast in the UEFA coefficient table and likely to take Serie A's fourth Champions League qualification slot, and Ibrahimović and Kaká leaving the league for Spain, that was a summer of introspection. So great were the doubts about quality that *Gazzetta dello Sport* dubbed the 2009-10 season 'Year Zero' for Serie A.

One star, though, did come the other way. Wesley Sneijder joined Inter from Real Madrid, landed in Milan on the Friday and then orchestrated a 4-0 victory in the Milan derby two days later on the second weekend of the season. A 3-1 win over Napoli in their fifth game took Inter top and they remained there despite defeats to Sampdoria and Juventus.

For Zanetti, the real mark of Mourinho's calibre as a coach had come away to Dynamo Kyiv in the Champions League. Inter had drawn their first three games in the group – and had gone eight European games without a win – when they went to Ukraine. They fell behind to an Andriy Shevchenko goal and at half-time looked to be in serious danger of another early exit. Mourinho took off Cambiasso and Cristian Chivu and replaced them with Thiago Motta and Mario Balotelli, telling Balotelli and Eto'o to pull wide to create space for Diego Milito and Wesley Sneijder through the middle. Inter probed, without success until, with 11 minutes remaining, Mourinho brought on Muntari for Walter Samuel, adding a midfielder for a defender to allow Sneijder to play closer to Milito. With four minutes remaining, Milito equalised. With two minutes to go, Sneijder got the winner. Mourinho had gradually increased the pressure while sticking to the same basic plan and, at the last, had been rewarded. A defeat in Barcelona and a win over Rubin Kazan saw them through.

But all was not quite as serene as results may have suggested. Mourinho raged regularly about referees and the media, finally erupting in January after the second Milan derby of the season. Diego Milito put Inter ahead after ten minutes but 17 minutes later Sneijder was sent off for sarcastically applauding the referee Gianluca Rocchi as he booked Lucio for diving when it appeared he had been caught by Massimo Ambrosini. Mourinho did not have his side simply sit back but, maintaining a 4-3-2 shape, kept attacking and was rewarded with a second goal midway through the second half from Goran Pandev. Lucio was then sent off in injury time, collecting a second yellow card for handling in the box. Ronaldinho missed the resulting penalty and Inter, who also hit the woodwork in both halves, won 2-0. 'We understood as time went on that it was not a coincidence that the referee gave Sneijder that red card,' Mourinho said. 'I have already understood that they won't let us tie up the title quickly. Today they did everything to stop us from winning.'

Why, he asked, had Bari's Leonardo Bonucci not been sent off in his side's 2-2 draw against Inter the previous week? Why did Milan keep getting soft penalties? Why had Milan's Coppa Italia quarter-final been postponed, giving them a full week to prepare for the derby? If Ronaldinho had scored that injury-time penalty, he insisted, the game would have gone on for another 'eight minutes'.

'I leave here,' Mourinho said, 'with a strange taste in my mouth. But this is your country, your championship. I will move on sooner or later and the problem will remain yours.' The reference to the *calciopoli* affair and Juventus's manipulation of referees was oblique but unmissable. 'I believe we will succeed in winning this title one way or another. Now everyone can shut their mouths. This match was an embarrassment.'

But of course, this was just part of the Mourinho method. 'He always needs an enemy in front of him to attack so he can defend his squad,' said Milito, explaining how Mourinho motivated players 'to perform to their maximum'. Did that mean that he sometimes invented an enemy? 'Clearly,' he said. 'He does it on purpose. He puts himself out front to be hit and the squad is calm.'

Inter beat Cagliari and then drew with Parma and Napoli. Juventus won a penalty against Genoa for a foul that was committed outside the box. 'I don't stick my head in the sand,' said Mourinho. 'I know there is only one team that has a penalty area that is 25 yards long.' Juventus at the time were seventh, 18 points adrift.

Walter Samuel and Iván Córdoba were sent off in a 0-0 draw against Sampdoria, prompting Mourinho to raise his hands as though handcuffed towards the television cameras. He also directed 'offensive expressions' as the Italian federation afterwards termed them, towards the referee. With officials threatening to boycott games, he was given his fourth touchline ban in Italy, this one for three games. Muntari and Cambiasso, meanwhile, were suspended for two games each for, respectively, insulting the match officials and becoming involved in a fracas in the tunnel. Mourinho, of course, refused to take responsibility and decided the only solution was to stop speaking to the media. 'Many hoped he would bring some maturity and culture to our football,' said *La Repubblica*, 'but instead we are going back to the Borgias.'

Three successive draws had ended the sense that Inter were essentially on a coronation march. Was Mourinho just deflecting, or was the pressure beginning to get to him? After all, the game after that Sampdoria draw was against Chelsea in the last 16 of the Champions League.

At San Siro, Inter won 2-1. Their league stutter continued: a win at Udinese, a draw at home to Genoa, a defeat at Catania. Mourinho's return to Stamford Bridge in the middle of March felt like a crisis point. Lose that and the whole season could have collapsed. That was a game Mourinho simply could not lose.

But with a lead to protect, he attacked.

To describe Mourinho as a defensive coach is inadequate. It's a little more complicated too than saying he is a pragmatist, although that is the term he frequently uses of himself. But at that point of his career, he was pragmatic. He did what was needed to win. Just because he gave little thought to the spectacle or any sense of the aesthetic, rejecting that part of the Cruyffian philosophy that demanded a team entertain, does not mean his instinct was always to retreat. Rather if what was necessary was to go on the front foot, that was what he did. Pragmatism is not a synonym for defensiveness. Against Chelsea, he fielded three forwards – Pandev, Milito and Eto'o – with Sneijder behind them. It's true that after a bright opening, the game became attritional, but it's also true that Inter ended up controlling the ball. They won, 1-0. 'In football,' Luigi Garlando wrote in *Gazzetta dello Sport*, 'courage doesn't come from the heart but from the feet: keeping hold of the ball makes you feel strong... Inter had more possession than Chelsea, who needed to attack. A revolution.'

But the domestic strife continued and when Ranieri's Roma beat Inter 2-1 at the end of March, the gap between them, which had been 14 points when Inter had hammered them in November, was down to one. Mourinho was still maintaining his media silence, which meant he was unable to explain exactly how the fact his side's goal should have been ruled out for offside fitted into the national conspiracy against him.

Later that week, though, Inter faced CSKA Moscow in the Champions League quarter-final and, compelled by UEFA rules, Mourinho had to face the press. 'Not speaking about Italy or the Italian league allows me to sit on the bench,' he explained, as though it were unreasonable that the Italian authorities should take action when he made wild allegations that undermined the integrity and image of the competition. 'I am very happy at Inter but not in Italian football,' he added. 'I don't like it and it doesn't like me.'

Inter won both legs against CSKA 1-0, setting up the semi-final against Barça. The weekend after the second leg, they were held to a 2-2 draw by Fiorentina. When Roma then beat Atalanta, Ranieri's side were top. Roma's subsequent defeat at home to Sampdoria, when they were denied a penalty for handball – another fact it's hard to square with Mourinho's protestations and might, in fact, have been the result of them – handed the initiative back to Inter, who surged to the title with a run of five wins in their final five league games of the season.

After all the talk of conspiracy, the title was sealed at the beginning of May with what may as well have been a walkover against Roma's great rivals Lazio. Federico Peluso's equaliser for Bologna against Atalanta earlier in the day had eased Lazio's relegation fears and there is no doubt that their fans, at least, saw hindering Roma's title push as the most important aspect of the game. 'If you win we'll beat you up,' the ultras chanted, while unfurling a banner reading 'Get out of their way'. Inter won 2-0 and it would have been far, far more had it not been for the heroics in the Lazio goal of Fernando

Muslera who played, as Garlando put it in *Gazzetta*, 'like the Japanese man in the forest who doesn't realise the war is over'.

* * *

Guardiola's response to an extraordinarily successful first season was further revolution. There was no sense of simply keeping the machine running as Eiður Guðjohnsen, Aliaksandr Hleb and Samuel Eto'o all left in the summer of 2009. Guardiola had very nearly offloaded the Cameroonian the previous year and although he had largely played well – and scored in the Champions League final – he was seen as a disruptive presence. At times he was too competitive, berating team-mates in training for, as he saw it, not giving their all, something that caused problems because Guardiola's aversion to confrontation meant he wouldn't step in, even if he knew there was a good reason for a player being under the weather. A row over the lack of seriousness with which Eto'o was performing his stretches at a training session before the Copa del Rey quarter-final against Espanyol seems to have come as the final straw. For Eto'o plus €46m, Barça landed Zlatan Ibrahimović. They also signed the Ukrainian defender Dmytro Chygrinskiy from Shakhtar Donetsk and the Brazilians Maxwell and Keirrison. It soon became apparent that outsiders – or at least these outsiders – could not easily be integrated into the Barcelona ecosystem. 'Ours is a complex game,' Guardiola said. 'Before a new player comes in I tell them it will take time and hard work to learn, but a player from the *cantera* already knows how to do it.'

Ibrahimović had said that a major factor in his decision to move was the fact that Barça played 'the most beautiful football' but almost immediately Guardiola, 'with his grey suits and brooding expressions', managed to rile Ibrahimović by telling him repeatedly that at Barcelona, players kept their feet on the ground and came to training in their club car rather than in a Ferrari or a Porsche. In his autobi-ography, Ibrahimović suggests he found the instruction ridiculous: he drove flash cars because he liked cars, not, he insisted, because they made him look good. But his autobiography is a curious document: for all the praise it received, for its wit and its candour, it is also remark-ably self-serving (if, that is, we take it at face value; it's not entirely clear to what extent it is an autobiography rather than an imaginative biography written in the first person). Almost nothing is ever Ibra-himović's fault; if people don't understand him, that is their problem, but he rarely takes time to consider anybody else's point of view or to see how things may look to outsiders. At the same time, a persistent insecurity glints through the bluster: he is the kid from Rosengård, a working-class district of Malmö with a large immigrant population; he is suspicious of blond middle-class Swedes with 'names like Bosse Larsson, who said nice, refined things' and, for all his self-assertive-ness, he seems constantly worried they may be mocking him. (That he ended up getting on so well with Mourinho, another self-styled rebel, albeit one from a very different background, is perhaps no surprise). The implication is that he thinks Guardiola, born into a working-class family in Santpedor but by then thoroughly absorbed into the Barce-lona establishment, saw the ghetto in his love of fast cars and was warning him to leave that part of himself outside the club.

That's not to say that Ibrahimović's account is entirely without merit. There clearly is some truth to his observation that in offloading Ronaldinho, Deco and Eto'o, Guardiola ensured 'all the big personal-ities were chased out'. Whether you consider that a bad thing probably depends on whether you happen to be a big personality. Guardio-la's comment about cars confirmed the impression Ibrahimović had already formed that Barcelona was 'like a school ... the best footbal-lers in the world stood there with their heads bowed ... they were like schoolboys.' And perhaps that too is an apposite criticism: there was something institutional about Barça at that time. They were resistant to outsiders. There was something unnervingly automatic about the way they played, as though they were not individuals but had somehow been assimilated into a greater whole. That was what allowed them to pass and move with such rapidity but it was also why some observers were left cold by them.

Systems were not for Ibrahimović. He was scornful of those who theorised about football – Van Gaal he dismissed as 'a pompous arse', Guardiola as 'the philosopher' – and responded best to hard men who allowed him to be an individual. It was at Juventus that he first really prospered as Fabio Capello vowed to 'knock Ajax out of your body… I don't need that Dutch style. One, two, one, two, play the wall,* play nice and technical… I can get by without that. I need goals.'

That attitude raises an obvious question: if Ibrahimović thrived after having the Ajax knocked out of him, why did anybody think he would be a good fit for Barça, even if he did give them a more physical attacking option? And, what, after all, did Ibrahimović expect? It was absurd for him to speak of the beauty of Barcelona's football, to seek to be part of it, and then to refuse to accept the sacrifices necessary to be assimilated into that system. 'Ibra was a very good player,' said Hristo Stoichkov, another big ego with a tempestuous personality but one who had thrived at Cruyff's Barça. 'But he came and wanted to be the number one and forgot that Messi was already there. That's the big problem. Villa played for the team, Eto'o the same: so much pressure on the defenders, he activates other players. He makes them run. He activates: I'm going, you come too. Ibra is different.'

---

* That is, a one-two.

That Christmas, Ibrahimović was fined by the club for driving a snowmobile as he took a break back in Sweden. He played that for its symbolism, the Barça establishment pettily curtailing the freedom he required, but the fact is that it was a pointless act of disobedience and most players at a certain level have clauses in their contracts forbidding them from activities that might cause injury.

Whatever tensions there were in the background, though, Barça's results remained extremely good. Although they went out of the Copa del Rey on away goals to Sevilla in the last 16, Barça didn't lose in the league until Atlético beat them on Valentine's Day, their 22nd fixture.

They also won the Club World Cup, Pedro equalising in the last minute of the final against the Argentinian side Estudiantes before Messi's winner in extra time. Before the game, Guardiola had struck a maudlin note, as though aware that the magnitude of his team's success, winning every competition they had entered while playing a style of football that redefined what was possible in terms of the maintenance of possession, was unlikely ever to be repeated. 'The future,' he said, 'is bleak because there is no way we can improve on what we have achieved so far.'

On the touchline, Guardiola sobbed, seemingly overwhelmed. Ibrahimović went and embraced him, whispering something in his ear, and, as Graham Hunter points out in his book *Barça*, there was something very strange, very abrupt, about Guardiola's reaction. Quite what was said remains unknown, but it seems reasonable to wonder if some crass comment from the Swede at that moment helped set Guardiola's mind against him.

In the Champions League, there was the first meeting as coaches of Guardiola and Mourinho, the Messiah of post-Cruyffianism against the fallen angel. Barça went to the San Siro for their first game in the group stage and, despite having the better of the game, drew

0-0. Back at Camp Nou, Barça won 2-0, with both Ibrahimović and Messi left on the bench. Barça fans taunted Mourinho throughout, telling him to 'go to the theatre', a reference to his complaints when Chelsea coach about Messi 'acting'. 'Imperious Barcelona demolish impotent Inter,' said the headline in the *Guardian*. Both sides, though, went through.

Ibrahimović claims he tried to fit in at Barça, tried to behave. Until the February, everything went relatively well. He scored 15 goals but was feeling increasingly bored. Then Messi, who had been playing on the right, was moved to play centrally, behind Ibrahimović. According to Ibrahimović, that was Messi's decision: 'Guardiola sacrificed me.' He wasn't the only forward to be irritated by the way Guardiola at times seemed to indulge Messi, the one individual who perhaps was bigger than the system, nor the only forward, either for Barcelona or for Argentina, who found it difficult to accommodate their own talent to his genius. Ibrahimović approached Guardiola and told him he felt the new shape restricted him. Guardiola, he said, promised to sort it out, but 'then came the cold shoulder'.

Barça beat Stuttgart in the last 16 of the Champions League to set up a quarter-final meeting with Arsenal. Ibrahimović scored twice at the Emirates as Barça took a 2-0 lead in the first leg. He was taken off with 13 minutes remaining; Arsenal scored twice. Ibrahimović suffered a calf injury and was out for a couple of weeks; during that time, Guardiola didn't speak to him. Nicklas Bendtner gave Arsenal a surprise lead in the Camp Nou, but then Messi scored four. However Ibrahimović subsequently tried to spin it in his book, Barça could clearly cope without him.

Ibrahimović came off the bench against Espanyol and played the final eight minutes. That was enough to prove his fitness and he was selected to start the away leg of the Champions League semi-final against Internazionale. But that tie became about far more than Ibra-himović. Those two games came to define an era.

\* \* \*

Barça had developed a habit of failing to win Champions League away games but still, the question seemed to be, what could possibly stop them defending their title? The answer turned out to be the sulphuric partnership of an Icelandic volcano and José Mourinho. The explosion of Eyjafjallajökull sent an ash cloud spewing over Europe that prevented plane travel for two crucial days. Barcelona travelled to Milan by bus. 'The journey was a disaster,' said Ibrahi-mović. It took 16 hours.

That wasn't the only problem. 'Guardiola,' Ibrahimović said, 'had a hang-up about Mourinho.' Perhaps he did; Mourinho certainly had a hang-up about Barcelona, and perhaps about Guardiola. That said, Milito suggested he thought Mourinho had generated their enmity: 'I think so,' he said. 'He's a very smart guy, he knows what he wants.'

But for Ibrahimović none of that mattered. For him, Mourinho was the more charismatic man, the better manager. 'He's the leader of his army,' Ibrahimović said. 'But he cares, too. He would text me all the time at Inter, wondering how I was doing. He's the exact opposite of Guardiola. If Mourinho lights up a room, Guardiola draws the curtains.' Increasingly, they were becoming exact opposites in terms of football.

Zanetti saw the game as a matter of avoiding temptation, describing Barça as sirens. 'Like Ulysses,' he wrote in his autobiog-raphy, 'we had to let their song be only for the ears and not allow possession of the ball to become a goal. We had to leave it sterile in midfield and then strike, while the midfield line protected and shielded the defence.'

Barça went ahead when Pedro steered in a Maxwell cutback, but Wesley Sneijder levelled before half-time. Mourinho was so convinced he had got his tactics right that he told his side at the break that if they kept their discipline they would win 4-1. He was nearly right. Maicon, charging on to a Diego Milito lay-off, put Inter ahead three minutes into the second half. Milito was just offside as he nodded a third and Dani Alves probably should have had a penalty when he was caught by Sneijder, which allowed Barça to think they had been unfortunate, but at the same time Inter had ruthlessly exploited the vulnerability of their defence to players running at them with pace.

Three days later, Barça played away at Villarreal. Ibrahimović was left on the bench, coming on only in the 83rd minute. He seems to have been scapegoated for the Inter defeat and all his frustrations came to a head. He went into the dressing room screaming at Guardiola and kicked a metal skip that was used to transport kit. Saying nothing, Guardiola picked it up and walked out 'like a little caretaker'. The next day, finally casting off the advice about what car to drive to training, Ibrahimović arrived in his Ferrari and parked as close as he could to the door. Guardiola, he concluded, was a 'frightened little over-thinker who couldn't even look me in the eye … the man has no natural authority, no proper charisma'. He left at the end of the season, sold to AC Milan at an enormous loss, while Barça signed David Villa to replace him.

Before the second leg, Mourinho stirred the pot with practised charm. 'We are,' he said, 'used to seeing these Barça players throw themselves to the floor a lot.' This was a mind game beyond a mind game. His words weren't necessarily aimed at the Belgian referee Frank De Bleeckere; they were designed to goad Barcelona, to hint at a deviousness and cunning behind the beauty of their football, to make them seem hypocritical. And what made it worse for Barça was that by full time he had been proved right.

Guardiola had another inspirational video made. This one was a little over four minutes long and showed various sports stars and teams mounting successful comebacks from difficult positions. At the last, though, sensing his side was already dangerously hyped, he decided not to show it.

The initial team sheet Mourinho submitted suggested he would field the same line-up that had begun the first leg, but Pandev was mysteriously injured shortly before kick-off and replaced on the left side of midfield by the Romanian full-back Cristian Chivu. Inter, as had always seemed inevitable, sat deep and they had been absorbing the Barça pressure well when, with 27 minutes played, Thiago Motta was sent off. It's an incident that seems over time to have developed a quality of myth, as though the decision were manifestly ridiculous. It was not.

Motta, in shielding the ball from Busquets, raised his right arm and flexed his fingers to give the Barça midfielder a slight shove. Busquets collapsed, clutching his face and, as he rolled on the grass, he parted his hands to steal a glance at the referee and make sure the contact had been seen. His feigning of injury was, without question, disgraceful and it is clear that his reaction got Motta sent off. But he was pushed in the face and there's no reason to believe his initial fall was manufactured. Was the incident enough to warrant a red card? No, clearly not. Was it an offence? Possibly. This wasn't just a protective arm, there was a clear and conscious effect to push Busquets away and, while that probably wouldn't be penalised had it been directed to the chest, it was directed to the head. And when hands go to faces, yellow cards often result. It was almost certainly a mistake for De Bleeckere to show a straight red, but had he shown a second yellow – Motta had already been booked for a foul on Dani Alves – it's doubtful any neutral would really have complained. Equally, had no card been shown at all, the incident would have been instantly forgotten. So Motta was unfortunate and Busquets's behaviour was shameful but it wasn't the indisputable scandal Mourinho would later have the world believe.

On the touchline, Mourinho grinned his 'look how blatant this is' grin. But if anything his side were galvanised. They dropped to a 4-4-1 and defended and defended and defended. Eto'o ended up playing as an auxiliary full-back, Milito as a midfielder. 'We had a team that trusted a lot in itself, from the first to the last minute,' said Cambiasso. 'In any circumstance, but especially if it was unfavourable. There were many nationalities in that dressing room, and many had been discards from other clubs, but we were all very close... We felt invincible even if we were not.'

Inter had just 19 per cent possession but they held their shape and Barça struggled to create chances. Ibrahimović was taken off for Bojan and then Piqué was sent forward as an emergency striker. It was he who, finally, broke through with six minutes remaining, meaning one goal would have taken Barça through on away goals. It seemed that they'd got it a minute into injury time as Bojan swept the ball into the roof of the net, but De Bleeckere disallowed it for a handball by Yaya Touré in the build-up. The ball did clearly strike the Ivorian's arm but it was driven into him from close range by Samuel and his hand was in front of his body. It was easy to understand why De Bleeckere had penalised it but at the same time no neutral could really have argued had he decided there was no intent. The grand UEFA conspiracy against Mourinho had the chance to click into action but oddly failed to grasp the opportunity, almost as though it didn't exist. The goal was ruled out, Inter held on, and Mourinho embarked on his delighted charge across the pitch.

He was, understandably, exultant about how his team had resisted, conceding just four shots on target. 'It is a style of blood not skill,' Mourinho said. 'When the moment of leaving everything on the pitch arrives, you don't leave the skill, you leave the blood. We were a team of heroes. We sweated blood. It's a pity I could not play because I have got the same blood.' In the emotional aftermath of the game, a strange truth had slipped out, one that was understandably lost in the general excitement of the evening.

There was always a sense that Mourinho hadn't ever quite got over his failure to make it as a player, a feeling that, certainly in his early career, he wanted to enjoy the camaraderie of the dressing room. His run across the pitch, finger raised, that night wasn't the only time he had celebrated as a player. There was, famously, his touchline dash at Old Trafford after Porto's win there or the occasion, after Chelsea had beaten Barça at Stamford Bridge, when he leapt on John Terry's back. Later still, there was another touchline sprint after Demba Ba's late winner against Paris Saint-Germain, although on that occasion Mourinho was sufficiently abashed by his outburst of glee to claim that he was merely urging his players to reorganise and refocus. There were numerous knee slides, repeated shushing of his critics, a constant desire to insert himself into the narrative of the game, a trait high-lighted by Jorge Valdano in his 'shit on a stick' article in *Marca* about the Champions League semi-final in 2007. If Mourinho could not be one of the players, if he remained forever a player *manqué*, he could at least control the players, become the player of players.

'I have already won a Champions League but today was even better,' Mourinho went on. 'We made huge sacrifices. We played to win at home and here we played as we could. They had the ball more but I did not say to my players "give them the ball, we don't want it". It is Barça that take the ball from you and don't give it back. When you play against a team of this quality for an hour with ten men it is something historic, something really incredible.'

After his press conference, Mourinho went to the stadium chapel to give thanks.

\* \* \*

In the final, Mourinho faced a Bayern side managed by the man who had been his boss at the Camp Nou, Louis van Gaal, who after his departure from Ajax had undergone a remarkable renaissance at AZ. Before the game, Van Gaal seemed vaguely amused by how his former protégé had found a way past Barça. 'I would not have done what Mourinho did at the Camp Nou,' he said. 'I wouldn't have behaved in a provocative way. His analysis was good. Even [working for Van Gaal at Barcelona] you could see he understood football. But at that time he was very humble and it's great to see how he has evolved. He gradually became a personality. He trains to win. So do I, but I also choose to express good football. My way is more difficult.'

So it proved. Bayern had 68 per cent possession and almost twice as many shots as Inter, but Inter had more shots on target and in truth never looked like losing once Diego Milito had finished off a Sneijder through ball after 35 minutes. The Argentinian added a second on the counter with 20 minutes remaining, twisting and turning past Daniel Van Buyten to seal the victory.

'You must not forget that we chose a very difficult playing style …' Van Gaal said. 'You have to be in superb form against a team like Inter if you want to play an attacking game… Defending is so much easier than attacking.' It's a familiar enough complaint; after a defeat it's very easy to redefine the parameters of what constitutes success to include an appeal to a subjective quality like aesthetics or 'attacking', but it's also an intriguing criticism for what it suggests about Mourinho. When he worked for Van Gaal, presumably he was encouraged to play the 'right' sort of football. This was, in essence, Van Gaal accusing Mourinho of apostasy. Not that that would have bothered Mourinho, who had just become only the third manager to win the European Cup with two different sides.

At the end of the season, though, even if they had surrendered their Copa del Rey and Champions League titles, Barça were still clearly the best team in Europe. But 2009-10 had not been as good as 2008-09 and there was a sense within the club that forces, not necessarily direct footballing ones, were rising against them. 'Sometimes we felt scorned,' Guardiola said in his final press conference of the season, a fairly clear thrust at the Madrid press. 'Sometimes we were ashamed to celebrate titles.'

That was indicative of a changing atmosphere. Madrid had once insisted it was a gentlemanly club. Even in the first *galácticos* period, players had been given a handbook explaining how they were expected to behave. But crisis point had been reached. Madrid hadn't won a Champions League knockout game in six years, their failings highlighted by the brilliance of Guardiola's Barcelona, and the dire sense that La Masia was producing an endless stream of technically brilliant players who could hold on to the ball for ever. It wasn't just that they were no longer winning, it was that they were being made to look foolish, spending millions and millions of pounds on celebrity players round whom Barcelona's diminutive maestros twisted mocking skeins of passes. So pervasive was their style that when Spain won the World Cup that summer, Laporta was able to claim, without fear of ridicule, that it was Barcelona's triumph. 'Madrid buy European Footballers of the Year,' he said. 'We make them.'

Barça had to be stopped, whatever it took, and that meant only one thing. Whatever quibbles the president Florentino Pérez had over

Mourinho's style of play were pushed to one side. Inter's success at the Camp Nou had persuaded him that Mourinho was the man to topple Guardiola. He was appointed Real Madrid manager, their 11th in nine seasons, on a four-year contract at the end of May 2010.

For Mourinho, Inter had only ever seemed a position of convenience. While his time there helped reinforce parallels with Helenio Herrera, the high priest of *catenaccio* who had won two European Cups in the sixties, the sense was always that Mourinho was eyeing a return to either England or Spain. That's where the money was and that's where the real power was – which of course made the fact that he has won Champions Leagues with clubs from outside the very elite all the more impressive.

And, perhaps most importantly, Spain was where Barcelona and Guardiola were. 'Having enemies in order to give your all isn't necessary,' Mourinho said. 'But it is better.'

Johan Cruyff in action for Barcelona against Aston Villa in 1978.
© Colorsport/REX/Shutterstock

Ronald Koeman hammers in the free-kick that gives Barcelona victory over Sampdoria in the 1992 Champions League final at Wembley.

Pep Guardiola crouches behind the trophy as Barcelona celebrate their first European Cup triumph. Cruyff is directly behind him, with Charly Rexach to his right.

*Above:* Guardiola, the player, chats with José Mourinho, the assistant coach. © Offside/Marca

*Right:* A 14-year-old Guardiola, working as a ball boy, looks on as Terry Venables is chaired from the pitch having led Barcelona to the 1985 league title.

*Left:* Bobby Robson with Mourinho during Barcelona's victory over Paris Saint-Germain in the 1997 Cup Winners' Cup final. © Colorsport/REX/Shutterstock

*Below right:* Luis Enrique runs away in glee after scoring for Barcelona against Galatasaray in the 2002 Champions League. © Shaun Botterill/Staff/Getty

Mourinho celebrates Porto's late winner against Manchester United in the Champions League at Old Trafford in 2004. © REUTERS/Ian Hodgson IH/MD/JV

Mourinho is suspended for Chelsea's Champions League tie against Bayern Munich in 2005, but he has the support of the fans.
© Matthias Schrader/picture-alliance/dpa/AP Images

*Above:* Barcelona players throw Guardiola in the air to celebrate beating Manchester United in the Champions League final in 2009.
© Nick Potts/PA Archive/PA Images

*Left:* Guardiola passes on instructions to Lionel Messi at the Camp Nou in April 2010.
© Lluis Gene/AFP/Getty Images

*Below:* Xavi evades Ryan Giggs during the 2011 Champions League final at Wembley.
© Laurence Griffiths/Staff/Getty Images

Mourinho charges across the Camp Nou pitch after Inter eliminate Barcelona in the Champions League semi-final in 2011.
© PA IMAGES

Cristiano Ronaldo squares up to Andrés Iniesta during Barcelona's 5–0 win over Real Madrid in November 2010, the first Guardiola-Mourinho clásico.
© JAVIER SORIANO/AFP/ GETTY IMAGES

Cristiano Ronaldo and Messi during the Champions League semi-final second leg in 2011.
© SIU WU/AFP/GETTY IMAGES

Guardiola takes the Manchester City job in July 2016. © OLI SCARFF/AFP/GETTY IMAGES

Mourinho and Guardiola on the touchline in Manchester. © RYAN BROWNE/ BPI/REX/SHUTTERSTOCK

Guardiola celebrates City's Premier League title win after victory over Huddersfield in 2018. © Matt McNulty - Manchester City/Man City/ Getty

# CHAPTER SEVEN

# AS TWO TWINS TOGETHER

For Real Madrid, José Mourinho was the manager of last resort, a *galáctico* manager to go with the *galáctico* players. Madrid's director-general José Ángel Sánchez had been in contact with him since 2007 when they'd signed Pepe, a fellow client of the super-agent Jorge Mendes. The then Madrid president Ramón Calderón had decided against turning to Mourinho at that point, deeming him too cautious – he described him as 'a young Capello' – and recognising that he would try to seize power. By 2010, only one thing mattered: toppling Guardiola. Manuel Pellegrini had never had the full support of the board and, as his reign drifted to its conclusion, Inter's victory over Barcelona suggested Mourinho was the man who could do that. So pivotal had the semi-final at the Camp Nou become in the Mourinho mythos that he installed in his office in Madrid a life-size cardboard cutout of himself running across the pitch at the final whistle, arm outstretched, finger pointed in celebration.

Style was only one aspect of a grander problem. There have been exceptions – Helenio Herrera's Inter, the grandmasters of *catenaccio*, most notably – but there has historically been a sense that the biggest clubs must play in a manner that befits that status, which is to say not merely to win, but to win stylishly, with a swagger. When, in the late 1940s, the small Russian side Krylia Sovetov first began dropping an additional player behind the defensive line to offer extra protection, the football writer Lev Filatov, in an influential article, dismissed criticism of their caution by insisting it was 'the right of the weak'. The biggest clubs are not afforded such an option; indeed, it's arguably a waste of their resources not to invest in the most exciting attacking players and give them, within reason, licence to play. What sort of football, after all, will draw the most neutral fans? And what sort of football do most players want to play? Football tends to respect reactivity in a manager only when it is successful.

Mourinho had, until that point, always been able to portray himself as the underdog. Porto were taking on the might of the Lisbon clubs and, beyond them, the plutocrats of Europe. Chelsea might have been rich, but with only one league title to their name when he arrived they were not the establishment. Inter had lived in the shadow of Milan and Juventus for long enough and Italian football had fallen far enough behind Spain and England, that a similar shtick was just about justifiable. At Madrid it was not.

In an interview with the *Jornal de Notícias* in January 2004, Mourinho said that his ideal were players with 'titles, zero; money, little'. He wanted hunger, players with a point to prove – 'discards', as Cambiasso had described the Inter squad. The way Mourinho inspired the likes of Deco, Maniche, Didier Drogba, Frank Lampard, Samuel Eto'o and Wesley Sneijder, gifted players who had previously not quite delivered on their talent, demonstrates how effective he was at that. But Madrid were the richest club in the world. His resources there were multi-millionaire superstars. Even with Barcelona in their pomp, it was difficult if not impossible to generate the siege mentality and underdog spirit that had previously driven his best sides. That summer, the Mendes clients Ricardo Carvalho and Ángel Di María were signed, as were the Germany internationals Mesut Özil and Sami Khedira as part of €89m worth of expenditure.

Diego Torres's biography of Mourinho is fairly obviously written from a critical standpoint and with the aid of figures within the dressing room who didn't like their coach, so its judgements must always be treated with a degree of caution, but it's intriguing nonetheless how quickly he identifies warning signs. The season was less than a month old when Mourinho revealed that the club had prevented him from managing Portugal through the World Cup qualifiers, making it clear he thought he could have done both jobs. That, though, is extraordinary. There may be isolated examples scattered through history of coaches leading a club and national side simultaneously – Leonid Slutsky did it briefly with CSKA Moscow and Russia – but only in exceptional circumstances and never with a club of Madrid's stature. Surely he must have known that, so what game was he playing? Was he simply chafing at restrictions the job placed on him, reminding Madrid, even at that stage, that he was a man in demand?

Mind games had always been a key part of Mourinho's strategy, both internally and externally. He stepped up his campaign against Barça that September when he tore into Guardiola at a coaching conference in Nyon. 'Barcelona,' he said, 'draw you into the trap of thinking they are all likeable, nice, friendly people from a perfect world. They try to make you think they don't buy players, that they develop them all in their youth teams … and some people today believe that.'

On the pitch, Mourinho started out conventionally enough, deploying a 4-2-3-1 with Cristiano Ronaldo, Özil and Di María behind Gonzalo Higuaín. The season began relatively well, although there were goalless draws away to Mallorca and then Levante in mid-September, hinting at a difficulty in breaking down packed defences that would become a recurrent problem. The issue had first emerged in pre-season, during a friendly away to Alicante. Mourinho had told his players then to improvise in possession and at half-time they trailed 1-0. He raged at their 'anarchy' and the second half brought an improvement as it finished 2-2 but the problem had not gone away: Mourinho, it was felt, was good at organising a defence, good at organising counter-attacks, but rather less good at organising static attacking, equipping a side to break down a massed, deep-lying rearguard. This, perhaps, was a problem of his approach of avoiding automisations: without them, his team at times lacked the pace of interaction to pick its way through a packed defence.

Levante, the lowest-paid team in the league with a budget 27 times smaller than that of Madrid, became a particular sore point for Mourinho. Madrid had only two shots on target in that game and Mourinho was so frustrated that from the touchline he berated the Levante left-back Asier del Horno, who had played for him at Chelsea, with remarks about his private life. After the game, Mourinho picked a fight with the apparently blameless young winger Pedro León. That was the first time Madrid's players had really seen the nastier side of Mourinho's will to win and some reportedly found it a little distasteful: they were, after all, not merely the richest team in the league but a club that had traditionally prided itself on its gentlemanly conduct.

Still, when Madrid went to the Camp Nou at the end of November, they'd won every other game and were a point clear at the top of the table, the best start ever enjoyed by a Madrid manager. This was the moment Madrid had been waiting for, the moment at which Mourinho was supposed to show he could bring down Guardiola, that his method was a match for the Barcelona philosophy.

Because of Catalan elections, the game was played on a Monday. It was set apart, isolated so the whole world could watch. This was a game of games, not just a *Clásico*, but a clash of proactive and reactive, thesis against antithesis, the best side in the world against the manager who had downed them six months earlier. Mourinho's plan was to do what he had done with Inter, to operate a low block and look to frustrate Barça. The previous season, though, Barça had had Ibrahimović at centre-forward: their front three of Pedro, Messi and David Villa presented a different, more mobile threat. Within 14 minutes, Barça were 2-0 up. Mourinho switched to a high press and then at half-time brought on Lassana Diarra for Özil, the first sighting of what became known as the *trivote* of Diarra, Khedira and Xabi Alonso – the term suggesting three *pivotes*, or holding players. It didn't work, and Barça won 5-0. Wayne Rooney, watching on television at his house in Manchester, was so enraptured that he stood up and began applauding. 'We played very, very badly,' said Mourinho, 'and they were fantastic.'

Madrid only lost another three games that season, but that wasn't enough as Barcelona finished four points clear. Faced with the implacable pass-and-move rhythms, the endless possession-based victories of Barcelona, all Mourinho could do was cry foul. He may not have been able to win the battle on the pitch, but he could sour the atmosphere and unsettle Barça off it while strengthening his own hand within Madrid – although that was a high-risk strategy. A week before Christmas, Madrid won 1-0 at home to Sevilla, Di María getting the winner after Ricardo Carvalho, a loyalist who had also played for Mourinho at Porto and Chelsea, had been sent off. There was a scuffle between officials from the two sides in the tunnel after the game, but that was only the beginning of the controversy. In the post-match press conference, Mourinho brandished a folder that, he said, contained a list drawn up by his staff of 13 'serious mistakes' made by Carlos Clos Gómez, the referee. It was a classic Mourinho deflection, but it had a secondary effect, allowing him to suggest that he wasn't being supported by Jorge Valdano, the club's sporting director, who seemed to regard the complaints as vaguely ridiculous.

By January 2011, their relationship had broken down to the point that Valdano was banned from the training ground and official club flights. Perhaps that was just an internal power struggle, the sort many managers face to try to ensure they have control over transfer activity, but it was a move that seemed to have symbolic connotations. Valdano, after all, was a World Cup winner with Argentina, a successful former Real Madrid striker, La Liga's Foreign Player of the Year in 1985-86. He was urbane and intelligent; he exemplified the *señorío*, the code of gentlemanly behaviour to which Madrid liked to believe they aspired. And, of course, he had been the author, in 2007, of the 'shit hanging from a stick' column after watching Mourinho's Chelsea lose a Champions League semi-final to Liverpool at Anfield.

Perhaps most hurtfully of all, he had drawn attention in that article to the fact that had haunted Mourinho since the Barcelona hierarchy had dismissed him as 'the translator' a decade earlier: 'Neither Mourinho nor Benítez made it as a player. That has made them channel all their vanity into coaching. Those who did not have the talent to make it as players do not believe in the talent of players, they do not believe in the ability to improvise in order to win football matches. In short, Benítez and Mourinho are exactly the kind of coaches that Benítez and Mourinho would have needed to have made it as players.' With that in mind, getting rid of Valdano, the great establishment figure, comes to look like the outsider's revenge.

Yet whatever was going on off the pitch, results on it were good, even if Madrid were overshadowed by Barça. By the end of February, when they went to La Coruña to take on Deportivo, Madrid were five points adrift. Mourinho urged caution, releasing the players only for the final quarter of the game. It wasn't enough and Madrid drew 0-0, their fourth frustrating away draw of the season. Mourinho instructed his players to blame the schedule, saying it favoured Barça, but Casillas broke rank, making the fairly obvious point that Madrid needed to be more aggressive.

In March came a provocation too far, as Manuel Pellegrini, Mourinho's predecessor at Madrid, brought his Malaga side to the Bernabéu. Mourinho was asked, reasonably enough given he too was trailing Barça while racking up a points tally that would have won the league in most seasons, whether their situations were comparable. They were not, Mourinho replied: when he left Madrid he would go to a big club in England or Italy, not to Malaga. His scorn for Pellegrini was obvious, but it was the subtext that was really problematic: Malaga, he seemed to be saying, were a club not worth bothering with. The Madrid director Fernando Fernández Tapias, appalled by such a breach of the *señorío* code, demanded that Mourinho be sacked. With public opinion turning against him, certain players believed Mourinho wanted to go.

But abruptly, there came a change of tone, as though Florentino Pérez had considered his options and decided that, having taken the Mourinho route, he had no option but to keep following it. At a ceremony to hand over medals to Madrid's oldest members, he publicly endorsed Mourinho's way of doing things. 'Defending Real Madrid from whatever we think is unfair, irregular and arbitrary,' he said, 'is also *Madrileño*.' That wasn't just an acknowledgement that there were times when *señorío* wasn't enough; it was tacit approval for Mourinho to maintain his campaign against officials, referees and Barcelona. On 15 March, Mourinho had dinner with Pérez and the political future was clear; four days later he gave the players an ultimatum to back him or Valdano.

There were other issues. The attention to detail that had characterised Mourinho's management at Porto and Chelsea and that had drawn such praise came at Madrid to seem like paranoia. In the winter of his first season, he complained about the meat being served in the canteen, saying it contained a 'very high percentage of nerve tissue', demanding that either the suppliers be changed or the chefs sacked. It was part of a general atmosphere of tension which Mourinho seemed to encourage by being overtly friendly to certain players and distant towards others. Yet at the same time, Mourinho himself seemed insecure, something that manifested in his office, which contained not merely the cutout of his on-field celebration at the Camp Nou but also his FIFA Coach of the Year award for 2009-10 and a photograph of himself lifting the Champions League trophy. There were those who felt he needed reminders about him that he belonged at this level. Here, though, Mourinho was not in control, distrust gnawing at him as he sought out the informers he believed (with good reason if Torres's book is anything to go by) were briefing against him.

In March 2011 there came a flurry of players insisting everybody was united, something lapped up by the Madrid-inclined media. Three targets were attacked: the television companies, referees and Barcelona. Players were banned from giving interviews or individual press conferences unless the contents were agreed in advance. Some players were embarrassed by what was a fairly unsophisticated propaganda campaign, but Mourinho demanded control. So paranoid was he that, according to Torres, the following season he twice had the Sheraton Mirasierra, where Madrid stayed before home games, swept for bugs. Yet Mourinho could never control the narrative in Spain as he had elsewhere and it was even rumoured he went so far as to check the phone records of players and officials, trying to find out who was leaking information to the press.

Barcelona, meanwhile, went from strength to strength. They suffered an early-season defeat at home to Hércules, but then began winning relentlessly. By the time they suffered their next defeat, losing 3-1 to Real Betis in the second leg of the quarter-final of the Copa del Rey having already won the first leg 5-0, 28 games had gone by, 23 of them won.

They seemed invincible but it wasn't just that they were winning, it was the way in which they were doing so, highlighted by Xavi in a revealing interview with Sid Lowe in the *Guardian*. 'I like the fact,' he said, 'that talent, technical ability, is valued above physical condition now. I'm glad that's the priority; if it wasn't, there wouldn't be the same spectacle. Football is played to win but our satisfaction is double. Other teams win and they're happy, but it is not the same. The identity is lacking. The result is an impostor in football. You can do things really, really well – last year we were better than Inter – but not win. There's something greater than the result, more lasting.' Xavi was always an evangelist for the Barça way, for the belief that winning was only part of the game and that style had a moral dimension. But while his words are clearly heartfelt, admirable even, it's understandable that opponents might detect in them an element of smugness or sanctimony.

That, perhaps, is why refereeing decisions that went Barça's way stood out more, seemed somehow more galling. Take the moral high ground and when you get a break from the officials, when, to use Relaño's phrase, God starts writing straight with crooked lines, it seems not merely fortunate but hypocritical. Amid all the bluster from the anti-Barcelona press about refereeing, much of it tendentious or inconsequential, one decision stands out as inexplicable.

It came in the last 16 of the Champions League in March 2011. Barça had lost 2-1 at Arsenal in the first leg, their first defeat (other than the meaningless Copa del Rey reverse against Betis) since the second weekend of the league season. At the Camp Nou, Messi put Barça ahead, but Arsenal levelled to take a 3-2 aggregate lead through a 53rd minute Busquets own goal. Three minutes later, the Arsenal forward Robin van Persie, who had been booked in the first half for a foul on Dani Alves, chased on to a through pass, was called offside and lashed the ball past Víctor Valdés into the net. It seemed an instinctive action, as though he hadn't quite processed the whistle. Certainly there was no hint of dissent or any sense he was trying to waste time. It may even be that he hadn't heard the whistle. But the Swiss referee Massimo Busacca showed a second yellow card and Van Persie was sent off. In a technical sense, the decision was correct, but it's the sort of incident that happens hundreds of times a season without punishment. Arsenal, understandably, were furious and, equally understandably, conceded twice more to lose 4-3 on aggregate. While the red card was controversial, though, it's not clear it was decisive; Barça pummelled them over the two legs and probably would have won anyway. They went on to see off Shakhtar 6-1 on aggregate in the quarter-final.

But whatever the problems at Madrid and however well things appeared to be going at Barça, Mourinho was beginning to have an impact on Guardiola. His intensity and the nature of Barcelona perhaps would have ground him down anyway, but Guardiola had serious doubts as to whether he should continue for a fourth season. On 18 January, the night of his 40th birthday, he and his wife went to see the Catalan indie group Manel. At the end, the band and the 600 members of the audience sang 'Happy Birthday' to him and begged him to sign a new contract. The next day he went to see Laporta and offered to extend his deal for another year, although he didn't actually sign the deal until the summer, after Sandro Rosell had been elected as president.

* * *

The struggle between Guardiola and Mourinho, Barcelona and anti-Barcelona, the two most extreme manifestations of post-Cruyff-ianism, would have been intense enough anyway, but it was made exhausting by a quirk of the calendar. They were scheduled to meet on 16 April in the league, but then both progressed to the Copa del Rey final, to be staged on 20 April. Two derbies in four days became four in 18 as they were also drawn against each other in the semi-finals of the Champions League. Relations between any sides playing each other that often in such a short space of time would become frayed; given the history between both the clubs and the managers, this was apocalyptic.

The first, in the league at the Bernabéu, was drawn 1-1. Messi put Barcelona ahead from the penalty spot after Raul Albiol had been sent off for bringing down David Villa, and Ronaldo then equalised with another penalty after a foul by Dani Alves on Marcelo. 'I would like to play one day against Barcelona with 11 men,' said Mourinho, not that there was much disputing the red card. 'I would really like to but I know that in Spain and in Europe that is mission impossible. They are a team that controls every situation that surrounds the club.'

There was talk in the Madrid press of a moral victory – which suggested just how low expectations had fallen – but the point meant Barça were eight points clear with six matches remaining and the title was all but theirs. And there was criticism from the most potent of all sources, Alfredo Di Stéfano, the winner of five European Cups and as close as Madrid came to an equivalent to Cruyff as the conscience of the club. 'Barcelona's football was simply brilliant,' he said. 'Their superiority was there for the whole planet to see... To see this team in action is a delight... Madrid are a side with no personality. They just run back and forth constantly, tiring themselves out... Barcelona were a lion, Madrid a mouse.'

Perhaps, but they were an aggressive mouse, with Messi irritated enough by the tight marking to which Pepe subjected him that he belted the ball into the crowd near the end, provoking a minor controversy as the Madrid-based media asked why the referee César Muñiz Fernández hadn't taken action against him. There was nothing especially untoward about the game, although there were reports of low-key scuffles in the tunnel afterwards in which Pepe was a central figure.

But there was much that was untoward about what happened in the Madrid dressing room. Around four hours before kick-off, three hours before the teams were officially released, *Marca* had published Madrid's line-up on its website. Mourinho was furious, seeing this as proof of a mole in the squad operating against him. After the game, he raged. Casillas, whether because he felt accused or because he had tired of the rant, walked off for a shower, at which Mourinho picked up a can of Red Bull and hurled it against the wall. It burst and as players ducked to avoid the spray, the meeting broke up.

Perhaps his outburst helped to clear the air. At last, in the Copa del Rey final at the Mestalla, there came some succour for Madrid with a 1-0 win. It may have been the least important of their five meetings with Barcelona that season but it was something. Mourinho again fielded his *trivote*, this time composed of Pepe playing slightly in front of Xabi Alonso and Khedira, but perhaps most significant was his decision to move Sergio Ramos from right-back into the centre of defence, the position in which he would excel over the following seasons.

Casillas made three excellent saves, Pedro had a goal ruled out for a marginal offside following a characteristic dribble from Messi, before Cristiano Ronaldo scored the winner 13 minutes into extra time. Madrid were more aggressive and forward-thinking than they had been in previous Guardiola–Mourinho meetings and Barça struggled to get to grips with the deployment of Mesut Özil as a false nine later in the game. With Mourinho instructing his players not to acknowledge their international teammates, the level of hostility was a touch higher: Busquets clattered Xabi Alonso and Alvaro Arbeloa trod on David Villa, then accused the forward of play-acting.

From a rare position of strength, Mourinho turned on his critics. First he responded to Cruyff, who had described him as a 'titles coach' rather than a 'football coach'. 'I like that,' he said. 'All of us here work hard so we can win titles, so I'll take that as a compliment.'

Then he took aim at the press. 'If I'd gone along with the newspapers,' he said, 'I would have chosen a formation with six forwards but I didn't change my mind and I think it went just fine… Here people think that good football is just about having possession. They're limited thinkers. I believe there are many other ways of playing well, like defensive organisation, solidarity, the ability to withstand pressure and to close down space while preparing a counter-attack at the same time.' It was a classic Mourinho explanation: it contained large elements of truth – who could deny the value of all those humble virtues? – but it omitted any sense of context.

Guardiola, meanwhile, was characteristically restrained, doing little more in his post-match press conference than acknowledge what a tight game it had been. 'A two-centimetre decision from a linesman with a good view ruled out a goal for Pedro,' he said, words most took as a statement of fact: Pedro had been close, but not quite close enough. Not Mourinho, though, who saw an opportunity.

As the Champions League games approached, the tension was increased. The Madrid-based press made the usual allegations that

Barcelona were favoured by referees and the football authorities and then a radio station claimed, without anything approaching concrete evidence, that Barcelona were engaged in systematic doping. The intention was clear: to distract and destabilise Barça. For relief, Guardiola and his wife went to the theatre. They sneaked in after the lights had gone down to try to avoid drawing attention, but as soon as they had taken their seats, the lights came back on and the rest of the audience applauded him. However under siege he may have felt, there was no doubt that Barcelona generally supported him.

Before the first leg of the semi-final, Barça laboured to a 2-0 win over Osasuna while Madrid put six past Valencia. The gap was eight points with five games to play. But those matches felt almost like a distraction and the day before the Champions League meeting at the Bernabéu, Mourinho stirred the pot again, suggesting Barcelona had used their influence to ensure the first leg would not be refereed by the Portuguese official Pedro Proença. Guardiola, it was true, had said Madrid would be 'super happy' if Proença were appointed – the suggestion presumably being that one Portuguese would help another – a strange and needless comment that offers a reminder that Guardiola was not entirely innocent in the souring of the mood, even if his fault was a fraction of Mourinho's. That he even bothered to mention the referee, particularly one who was never in contention to take charge of the game, was perhaps an indication that Mourinho had got to him.

Mourinho, of course, had issues with the referee who was appointed, Wolfgang Stark. The German had reportedly asked for Messi's shirt after Argentina's win over Nigeria at the World Cup the previous year, while he had denied Madrid a penalty for handball in the last-16 win over Lyon. 'If he doesn't make a mistake in his favour,' Mourinho said, 'then Pep won't be happy.'

It was then that Mourinho detonated his main weapon. 'Until now,' he said, 'managers could be divided into two groups. The small one comprises those who don't talk about referees at all and the other, huge one, in which I figure, is made up of those who only criticise referees if they make important errors. But now there is a third group with only one member – Pep! It's a new one, never seen in world football, somebody who criticises a referee for getting it right.'

The explanation, Mourinho went on, was the 'scandalous refereeing' at Stamford Bridge in 2009: 'Since then, he's never happy when a referee gets it right.'

It was an approach that was somewhere between petty and Machiavellian, but it was also well directed. The suggestion that referees favoured Barcelona had had plenty of traction in the Madrid press and beyond, and the accusation chimed with those who saw something holier-than-thou, something entitled and crybabyish in the way Barça players so often protested to referees about supposed rough play from opponents.

How, the world wondered, would Guardiola respond? Preceding him in the preview press conference was Mascherano, his performance typically reserved and uneventful. Then came Guardiola. The first question, inevitably, was about Mourinho's comments. Guardiola was expecting it and gave an answer that lasted two minutes and 23 seconds. 'Off the pitch,' Guardiola said, 'he has already won. He's been winning all year, all season and he'll continue to do so in the future. I'm happy to award him his personal Champions League trophy off the pitch… As for us, we'll just play… We will settle for our "smaller" victories which seem to inspire admiration all around the world… We always try to compete in the best way we know how, which is by playing good football. He knows this. He learned it here because we helped develop him into a coach.'

Guardiola went on to talk about the 'working relationship' he and Mourinho had had for four years a decade earlier, and to mock the fact that Mourinho apparently had staff to compile lists of grievances. He then turned his attack on 'the journalists who suckle on the teat of Florentino Pérez … in this particular press room [that is, at the Bernabéu], he's the fucking boss, the big fucking chief.'

It was a significant moment, not necessarily for the content of what was said but for the tone. Mourinho had made complaints all season about referees, about the fixture list, about opponents going to the Camp Nou and doing nothing but trying to minimise defeats, about all manner of baroque conspiracies that supposedly favoured Barça. Barça's players had wanted to bite back but Guardiola had restrained them. His outburst came as a tremendous release of tension. When he met his squad that night, they gave him a standing ovation. To lighten the mood, they were then shown a video of Víctor Valdés doing impressions of various Spanish football personalities.

In that semi-final first leg, Mourinho left the grass at a length of 3cm, 1cm more than Barça prefer, and managed, despite a prior agreement, to ensure it wasn't watered an hour before kick-off. He fielded a *trivote* of Diarra, Xabi Alonso and Pepe, who this time was deployed to the left to try to combat Xavi. As a disavowal of Cruyffian principles, that selection could hardly have been more pointed. All three of Madrid's centre-forwards, plus Kaká, were left on the bench as Mourinho fielded a front three of Özil on the right, Di María on the left and Ronaldo drifting.

Madrid, though, never had any real sense of control, in part because Xavi played higher than he had in the Copa del Rey final, a move balanced by the fact that Seydou Keita, who had come in for Iniesta, played deeper on the left of the midfield three.

As the players left the pitch at half-time, Pinto, Barça's reserve goalkeeper, aggressively approached Arbeloa, apparently for obstructing Pedro just before the whistle. In the confrontation that followed, Pinto shoved Miguel Porlán, 'Chendo', Madrid's match day delegate, and was shown a red card.

Adebayor was brought on at half-time for Özil, who had been largely ineffective, which meant Cristiano Ronaldo moving to the flank. That did little to alter the flow of the game, though, and Barcelona remained on top. Eight minutes into the second half, Sergio Ramos was booked for a foul on Messi, meaning he would be suspended for the second leg. Mourinho was furious, but at the time his anger appeared to be directed at the defender. Madrid were playing with great aggression; Barcelona reacting with great animation. Every decision led to protests with Stark surrounded by players pushing and shoving.

To nobody's great surprise, just after the hour Pepe was sent off by Stark for a dangerous challenge on Dani Alves. On the bench, Mourinho let his jaw drop as though amazed, although nobody could realistically have been shocked by the decision. Madrid subsequently released footage that supposedly showed there had been no contact, a protest that was both staggeringly petty and utterly irrelevant: a dangerous challenge doesn't have to make contact to be dangerous. But that's not to say either that he didn't make contact or that Pepe wasn't a touch unfortunate. Modern discourse in football has a revulsion to grey areas but this was one: often players would get away with a yellow for a challenge like that. The ball was bouncing between the players and Pepe probably was making a genuine attempt to win it, although he turned away as Dani Alves got his foot to the ball first. Neither was Pepe off the ground, out of control or using excessive force. But his foot was high, he did go in studs first and, although footage is inconclusive, it did appear that his boot caught the Brazilian just below the knee. Certainly a case could be made for it being a red and there was no clear argument that Stark had made a mistake, but equally nobody would have been too outraged had he shown a yellow. Just as certainly, it changed the game.

As Madrid were reduced to belting long balls towards Ronaldo and Adebayor, Barça tightened their grip. With 13 minutes remaining, Xavi created space for Ibrahim Afellay, who had come on for Pedro, and he beat Marcelo before crossing for Messi to score. Ten minutes later, Messi had a second, a goal out of keeping with the game. It had begun with a one-two with Busquets in the middle of the pitch, creating room for him to accelerate past Lassana Diarra and Xabi Alonso, and then past Raul Albiol before clipping a finish back across Casillas. 'With Pepe, Madrid refused to play,' José Sámano wrote in *El País*. 'Without him, they couldn't play.'

Piqué took up a similar theme, pointing out that the red card had not created Barça's superiority but had magnified it, had in part been caused by it. 'It wasn't as if they stopped playing once they went down to ten men,' the defender said. 'They weren't playing before that. The red card? It's always the same argument: when you play with fire in your blood, you end up getting burned.'

As the players left the pitch at the final whistle, Rui Faria shouted to Barça's players that they should be going to change in the referee's room. Another brawl broke out in the tunnel. A lot of relationships were damaged that night – Casillas and Xavi, Piqué and Ramos, Arbeloa and everybody.

At the press conference, Mourinho took his protests further than he had ever dared before, listing the officials who had, to his mind, favoured Barcelona over the years, going back to Anders Frisk, sentence after sentence beginning with *'por qué?'* – why? – a trope that, in his slightly high-pitched Portuguese pronunciation, came to be widely ridiculed.

'They killed us once again,' he said. 'Again it's been demonstrated that we have no chance at all. We had a game plan which the referee wouldn't let us use...' Given it largely seemed to consist of kicking Barcelona, that perhaps wasn't unduly surprising, but Mourinho was furious. 'This football world,' he said, 'sometimes makes me feel sullied.' His side had had 26 per cent possession. 'Madrid took a chance,' said Xavi. 'They kept everyone back and played dirty as they were instructed to by their coach. We were far superior, and we were superior on the pitch. Football won tonight.'

Dramatic as the evening had been, Mourinho probably wasn't the only one feeling sullied. It had been a horrible match. Both sides had reacted to innocuous bumps and challenges as though they'd been the victims of brutal assaults and both sides had repeatedly pressured Stark. It had demanded the attention but until Messi got going, not for the right reasons. Barcelona could reasonably claim that Mourinho had started it, but they were far from innocent.

Mourinho's words, though, went way beyond what is usually considered acceptable, even in the slightly childish, one-eyed world of manager quotes. 'Winning must taste different when you win like that,' he said. 'You would have to be an awful person not to sense a difference between winning normally and winning in the last minute with a handball.' Perhaps so, but when had Barcelona ever done that?

'I've won two Champions Leagues, both on the pitch,' Mourinho said, 'and with two teams that weren't Barcelona...' The implication was clear: Barcelona had advantages other teams didn't and that, to Mourinho, diminished what Guardiola had achieved.

'In both cases,' he went on, 'we won it with a lot of hard work, a lot of effort, a lot of difficulty and a lot of pride. Josep Guardiola is a fantastic coach, as I've said before, but I would be ashamed of the Champions League he won, because he won it with the scandal of Stamford Bridge.' Mourinho, it might have been pointed out, won the Champions League with Porto in 2004 after Paul Scholes had had a goal wrongly ruled out at Old Trafford and with Inter in 2010 after Bojan had had a goal controversially disallowed for Barcelona, but very few sides ever win anything without at least some refereeing decisions that might have gone the other way. When Mourinho won the UEFA Cup with Porto, it might have been added, he was banned from the touchline for the second leg of the semi-final because he had intervened to stop a Lazio break in the first leg, while Martin O'Neill has never forgiven him for Porto's conduct in the final victory over Celtic. Whatever the other rights and wrongs of what happened at the Bernabéu that night, Mourinho was in no position to start pontificating about clean victories or doing it the right way.

'If he wins it again this year,' Mourinho continued, 'it will be with the scandal of the Bernabéu. So I hope and wish that one day, he gets the chance of winning a proper Champions League, because Guardiola deserves it.'

Barça reported Mourinho to UEFA for his allegations and Madrid retaliated by asserting that Guardiola, Dani Alves, Pedro, Busquets, Piqué, Mascherano, Valdés and Keita pursued a 'preconceived tactic' by which they 'persistently simulated aggression with the sole purpose of misleading the referee, which led to the manifestly unjust decision to send off Pepe'. Mourinho was banned from the touchline for five games, reduced on appeal to three. Pepe was given a one-game suspension while José Pinto was given a three-game ban.

There were accusations that Busquets had racially abused Marcelo. Confusingly, it's not clear whether a UEFA investigation was triggered by a complaint from Madrid or their own delegate, although Madrid released a video of the alleged incident which shows Busquets covering his mouth and saying something to Marcelo. He was cleared.

Even as Mourinho was protesting and most of his players were following the prepared script, his biggest star was querying his approach. Ronaldo was initially compliant – 'I don't understand,' he said, 'why in all Champions League knockout games, Barça end up playing against ten men' – but then couldn't help himself: 'I don't like our defensive style but I have to adapt because that's the coach's choice. Nil-nil wouldn't have been a bad result – it would have allowed us to play on the counter-attack in the Camp Nou.'

Although there were some who felt it was about time Ronaldo sacrificed at least a little of himself for the team – there was a theory that one of the reasons Mourinho preferred a counter-attacking approach was so that Ronaldo had space to accelerate into – the wider reaction was of shock: if even Ronaldo was prepared to express such discontent, what were others saying in the dressing room?

Mourinho reacted by leaving Ronaldo out of the league game at Real Zaragoza the following weekend. Given Ronaldo was two goals behind Messi in the top scorer's chart and given how much Ronaldo valued that award, that was a significant statement; it certainly wasn't a case of him being rested. A clash between the two huge Portuguese egos had always been a concern. Paolo Condo, in his book *The Duellists*, suggests that Jorge Mendes was aware of the potential dangers of having his two highest-profile clients at the same club and had actively sought to keep them apart until Guardiola's rise had made Mourinho's gravitation to Madrid inexorable.

Barça rested a number of players that weekend and lost 2-1 at Real Sociedad. Some have claimed that by leaving out Ronaldo and losing 3-2, Mourinho missed the opportunity to apply pressure to the leaders, but the fact is that even if Madrid had won that game, Barça would have been five points clear with five games to play. It's entirely understandable for both sides that focus dipped between the two legs of the semi-final.

Before the second leg, it rained heavily. With Mourinho watching on television in the Hotel Rey Juan Carlos, a kilometre to the west of the Camp Nou, Madrid were far more ambitious but also far more aggressive and Diarra, Sergio Ramos and Marcelo could all have been sent off. Pedro put Barcelona ahead, Marcelo equalised and Gonzalo Higuaín then had a goal mystifyingly ruled out for a supposed foul by Ronaldo on Mascherano. The tie, though, had effectively been ended by Messi's second goal in the Bernabéu, which took some – but not all – the heat out of the occasion.

The whole semi-final was played out in a sulphurous atmosphere, largely of Mourinho's making, a smokescreen effective enough that Messi's brilliant second goal in the first leg, an act of genius under the most intense pressure which should be the defining memory of the game, is largely forgotten. Madrid did little but spoil: even if Barça did dive and whinge, the wider perception was that at its heart the rivalry had become about one team passing and dribbling, the other kicking and brawling; good against evil, football against anti-football. In the 17 *Clásicos* Mourinho was involved in in his time as Madrid manager, his side committed 346 fouls to Barcelona's 220.

That Champions League semi-final was probably the highest-profile, most watched *Clásico* in history. Barcelona prevailed but it was a victory from which Guardiola's reign at Barcelona never recovered. 'These aren't games that I will remember fondly, regardless of the result,' Guardiola said, 'because they were accompanied by too many incidents that are incomprehensible to me. I think, ultimately, Mourinho won the war.'

Barça wrapped up the league title, their third in a row and Guardiola's third in three seasons as a manager, but since the draw at the Bernabéu the focus had been the Champions League. In the week leading up to the final against Manchester United at Wembley, there were disturbing echoes of the previous season as another Icelandic volcano erupted, this time Grímsvötn. Not wishing to be forced into another lengthy bus journey by an ash cloud, Barcelona set off for London on the Tuesday, two days earlier than planned. The decision had added bonuses. Not only could Barça travel in comfort, but they were able to relax away from the frenzy of the build-up in Catalonia.

Perceptions had changed since 2009 and this time United were clear underdogs. Ferguson had devised a more defensive plan, despite the absence of Darren Fletcher, which meant Ryan Giggs and Michael Carrick ended up playing together in central midfield. He looked to press high but then to drop off once the first line had been broken. With United physically a much larger side than Barça, Ferguson sought to play narrow, surrendering the flanks, effectively gambling that Rio Ferdinand and Nemanja Vidić would win any balls crossed into the box. From an attacking point of view, he sought merely to get the ball forward quickly, to try to exploit the pace of Javier Hernández behind Barça's high line.

None of it mattered. Barça were just much better. Xavi, delaying his pass to draw defenders to him, laid in Pedro to score the first after 27 minutes and although Wayne Rooney levelled seven minutes later, Barça always seemed in control. They wrapped up the win with second-half goals from Messi and David Villa. By the end, Abidal said, the United players were begging Barça to 'Stop fucking about. We're finished.'

Ferguson had spent the second half rocking back and forth on the bench, looking as though he wanted to be sick. There were no excuses, just a frank admission that his side had been well beaten. 'Nobody's given us a hiding like that…' said Ferguson. 'In my time as manager, it's the best team we've played. They mesmerise you with their passing.'

Barça had won a third Champions League but, more than that, they had established themselves as one of the greatest teams, perhaps the greatest team, of all time. Arrigo Sacchi, who had managed the AC Milan side that won the European Cup in 1989 and 1990, welcomed Guardiola onto the highest level of the pantheon. 'Football,' he said, 'is a sport for teams that are in harmony. Very often teams aren't teams at all, they are just groups. And they struggle to move together. This is the difference between a very organic team, a team with great understanding, and a team that has a collective … many teams have soloists, and these break the harmony. Barcelona didn't have soloists, we didn't have soloists, Ajax [in the early seventies] didn't have soloists. We had people who played with the team, for the team, all over the pitch, for the whole game.'

They weren't just dominant; they seemed at times that season to be playing a different sport from everybody else. They weren't just brilliant, they were revolutionary.

Perhaps the Copa del Rey had been some consolation for Mourinho – and it did prove to be an indicator of brighter times to come – but there was no doubt who had come out on top in his first season in Spain. Doubts about Mourinho's methods were already beginning to take root in Madrid. The *trivote* was seen more and more against high-class opposition, despite opposition from various players – or at least that's what Diego Torres claimed in his biography. He suggests that at Madrid, Mourinho was not motivated merely by winning – which had been almost his sole objective elsewhere – but by the desire to do so in his way, to establish himself as a tactical pioneer. Mourinho spoke repeatedly of the *trivote*, his triangle of aggressive, hard-tackling midfielders who could press high and, in theory, either win the ball back high up the pitch or offer an impenetrable block in front of the back four. What was baffling to Torres's sources was partly that Mourinho seemed to portray himself as the inventor of the system when the term had been coined by Santiago Segurola in *El País* during the 1998 World Cup to describe Italy's midfield three of Dino Baggio, Luigi Di Biagio and Gianluca Pessotto. More worrying was that he played it at times when, as the sources saw it, it was of limited benefit and meant playing players out of position. It was as though, the implication was, he was determined above all else to promote his own legend. Maybe that's true, maybe it isn't – Torres's book isn't the most disinterested resource – but what is true is that Mourinho's record in big games as Real Madrid coach, particularly away from home, was poor.

According to Torres, Mourinho laid out a seven-point plan for winning big games:

1. The game is won by the team that commits fewer errors.
2. Football favours whoever provokes more errors in the opposition.
3. Away from home, instead of trying to be superior to the opposition, it's better to encourage their mistakes.
4. Whoever has the ball is more likely to make a mistake.
5. Whoever renounces possession reduces the possibility of making a mistake.

6. Whoever has the ball has fear.
7. Whoever does not have it is thereby stronger.

Mourinho may have been moulded as a manager by his time at the Camp Nou in the late nineties and thus be a post-Cruyffian, but this is the antithesis of the Cruyffian ideal, a categorical rejection of the possession-based, proactive approach of Guardiola and his ilk. It was precisely how Inter had played in that Champions League semi-final second leg but there was always a sense at Madrid that it was somehow unworthy of the club.

In the summer of 2011, as Valdano was ousted, Madrid signed Raphaël Varane and José Callejón, but they also brought in Hamit Altıntop, Nuri Şahin and Fábio Coentrão. Those last three signings raised eyebrows: Coentrão was a Jorge Mendes client while Altıntop and Şahin were represented by Reza Fazeli, a director of the Düsseldorf-based agency ISM, who was a close business associate of Mendes and also represented Mesut Özil. Mourinho also tried to land another Mendes client in the Portuguese striker Hugo Almeida. There's nothing necessarily wrong with that: it's natural that managers should work through agents they trust, using their networks of contacts to source and sign players. But Torres describes widespread concerns among non-Gestifute players at Madrid about the influence wielded by Mendes. What is clearly true is that, whether by design or not, packing the squad with players who shared an agent with him strengthened Mourinho's power base within Madrid.

The new season began with another pair of *Clásicos* in the Spanish Super Cup. The first leg at the Bernabéu was drawn 2-2. Barça won the second leg 3-2 with a Messi goal two minutes from time. In terms of the quality of the football and the drama, these had probably been the best pair of games between Mourinho and Guardiola teams, but what tends to be remembered is what followed Messi's winner. In injury time, Marcelo, who had come off the bench at half-time as Coentrão was moved into midfield to replace Khedira, kicked Fàbregas in front of the benches. A little pushing and posturing soon escalated into a full-scale melée involving players, coaches and officials from both sides. Marcelo and Özil were both sent off, but far, far more significant were Mourinho's actions.

His bodyguard alongside him, Mourinho walked up behind Tito Vilanova and hooked a finger in his eye. Vilanova turned and aimed a slap at him, at which the bodyguard intervened. Rather than take responsibility for what was manifestly a disgraceful act, Madrid sent videos to the Competitions Committee to claim provocation. The judge, Alfredo Flórez, a regular in the directors' box at the Bernabéu, somehow decided that the offences were of almost comparable severity and banned Vilanova for one game and Mourinho for two.

For Casillas, this was the tipping point. He had berated Fàbregas for play-acting and had rowed with his close friend Xavi and felt he had been left looking rather foolish, defending what had become indefensible. He apologised, privately and then publicly, to Xavi and Puyol. Mourinho responded with a statement in which, exercising the tactics of authoritarian leaders through the ages, he attacked '*pseudomadridistas*' and denounced those who opposed him as 'hypocrites'. Casillas was left out for the next game, a friendly against Galatasaray in which the La Clásica supporters group unveiled a 100-foot banner reading '*Mou, tu dedo nos señala el camino*' – Mou, your finger shows us the way. It's hard to believe a banner that large could have been arranged without at least the tacit consent of the club.

Madrid began the league season with thumping victories over Zaragoza and Getafe but then visited Levante, with whom Mourinho had contrived an entirely needless rivalry. Madrid had paid them back for their league victory the previous season by beating them 8-0 in a Copa del Rey fixture, a demolition in which Levante felt Madrid had taken undue delight. Mourinho knew his side would face a battle and warned them they had to be prepared to defend themselves – which, in his mind, meant making sure the referee was aware of any attempt at physical intimidation and sticking up for their teammates. Five minutes before half-time, Di María went down under a challenge from the notorious hard man and wind-up merchant Sergio Balles-teros, who stood over the Argentinian, accusing him of having dived. Khedira, who had already been booked, charged over and shoved Ballesteros, who collapsed. Khedira was shown a second yellow and Levante went on to win 1-0. Mourinho, to the amazement of his players given his instructions to them, blamed Khedira for the defeat. As discontent grew, Ramos asked for an explanation, for which he was dropped for a 0-0 draw against Racing Santander three days later.

At that moment, everything could have spun out of control. The first season had been a failure, Casillas was in open revolt, with Ramos seemingly on the verge of joining him, and four games in the second season had brought just seven points. There were long discus-sions in which grievances were outlined and, at least to an extent, the air cleared. Ramos moved permanently into the centre from right-back and Madrid, pushing far higher up the pitch, embarked on an extraordinary run of form, winning ten league games in a row and scoring 39 goals in the process.

Madrid went into the *Clásico* in December three points clear at the top of the table and with a game in hand on Barça, who had developed a habit of drawing games they probably should have won. The first real sign of vulnerability had come the previous month as Marcelo Bielsa's Athletic pressed and harried Barça into errors and were denied a 2-1 win only by an 89th-minute Messi equaliser. At the Bernabéu, an error from Valdés gifted Benzema an opener after 23 seconds. As Madrid pressed, Barça wobbled. This was the lesson Athletic had taught: Barça could be rattled; their possession game was not as invulnerable as it had once appeared. But then Messi came deep and with a typically penetrating run teed up Alexis Sánchez to equalise. Barça settled and goals from Xavi and Fàbregas decided the game in the first half of the second half. By the end, Barça kept the ball from Madrid with ease, but it had taken a moment of brilliance from Messi to turn the game their way. This was a truth that would become increasingly apparent as time went by: however good the theory, however sound the philosophy, however slick the interchanges and patterns of play, it always helps to have one of the greatest players of all time to drag a game his team's way.

Madrid still had a game in hand but with the sides level on points at the top, after such an emphatic second-half display, it seemed clear who had the upper hand. Guardiola, though, urged caution. 'Madrid will recover,' he said. 'There are no champions in December.'

The following month the sides met again in the quarter-final of the Copa del Rey. As Barça won the first leg 2-1 there was whistling round the Bernabéu. As the Barcelona press railed against Pepe for seeming to stamp on Messi's hand, the Madrid papers turned on Mourinho, unable to tolerate the idea their side could have had just 28 per cent possession and one shot on target in their own stadium. *Marca*'s cover spoke of the 'never-ending story' and inside observed that Mourinho 'still hasn't found the right key and he is left without excuses'. The cover of *AS* proclaimed that, 'Madrid offered dirtiness; Barcelona offered football.' *El País*, understandably, just seemed weary of the whole business: 'Madrid sully themselves for nothing,' it stated. Victory is often the great validator, redeeming almost any means applied to secure the right result, but Mourinho wasn't even getting the right result. 'If you're just going to keep losing,' *AS*'s editor Alfredo Relaño asked, 'what's the need to lose your decorum too?'

Worse followed as *Marca* reported, word for word, a disagreement between Mourinho and Sergio Ramos about marking at corners. What was significant was less the content of the discussion – Mourinho complaining that players had ended up marking different opponents to those he had stipulated before the game; Ramos explaining they had been forced to improvise because of Barça's screening – than the fact it was reported in such detail. There was a mole, and that knowledge fired Mourinho's paranoia.

That weekend, Madrid faced Athletic. Mourinho brought in six players who hadn't played against Barça, selecting a noticeably attacking line-up as though passive aggressively picking the team people seemed to want. Madrid won 4-1. It was a vital win, one that brought a measure of stability and offered a glimpse of a possible way of playing.

At the Camp Nou in the second leg of the Copa del Rey quarter-final, Madrid were again aggressive. Barça raced into a two-goal lead, but were probably a little fortunate to do so. The tie was won and although Madrid hit back with two late goals, it seemed an irrelevance, not even quite a face-saving rally. It was perhaps then, though, that the realisation dawned that Barça didn't have to be feared, that they could be taken on head to head and not merely by guerrilla tactics.

The league *Clásico*, anyway, hadn't derailed Madrid, who picked up where they had left off, winning 11 league games in a row to open up a ten-point gap as Barça drew at Espanyol and Villarreal and lost at Osasuna. When Madrid's run came to an end with a draw at home to Malaga, Mourinho immediately went back to the script of blaming referees. Of course when decisions went Madrid's way – as they had, for instance, at Sevilla, where they got away with two handballs in their own box and their winner could easily have been ruled out for offside – he said nothing.

Three days later, Madrid drew at Villarreal, undone by a late Marcos Senna free kick. In the circumstances, it was an astonishingly chaotic display. Having taken an early lead, Madrid left Özil, Ronaldo and Benzema upfield, sat the other seven outfielders behind the ball and sought to bypass midfield with a series of inelegant long balls. Lassana Diarra, whose attributes as a midfielder encouraged Mourinho to persist with him long after it had become clear that Diarra disliked his manager, had to be taken off 29 minutes after coming off the bench because he kept clattering into challenges despite having been booked.

Mourinho was sent from the touchline for his protests after the equaliser and Özil and Ramos were shown red cards after the final whistle. 'All they do is rob us,' moaned Ronaldo as he left the pitch. The referee, again, was used as the excuse. The corrosiveness of such behaviour, inflaming the belief in conspiracy, undermining officials and eroding the basic notion of truth, either didn't occur to Mourinho or he didn't care about the consequences. He was crying wolf to elicit sympathy in the most calculated and cynical way and doing significant damage to the integrity of Spanish football.

Yet his antics weren't really necessary. Madrid were, for the most part, playing superbly while Barça, at least by the standards of the previous few seasons, were faltering. The season reached its critical point in mid-April as Barcelona faced Chelsea in the Champions League semi-final, the two legs straddling the *Clásico* at the Camp Nou.

Barça were on top from the start at Stamford Bridge, playing most of the game in the Chelsea half. Alexis Sánchez and Adriano hit the post and Ashley Cole cleared off the line. Barça did more than enough to be comfortably ahead by half-time, and yet there was a sense that they were growing frustrated by Chelsea's resilience, too often looking for Messi, who was tightly marked. Messi himself ended up dropping deeper and deeper looking for space until, shortly before half-time, he lost the ball just inside the Chelsea half. Frank Lampard played the ball to Ramires, who got away from Xavi and advanced into the space left as Carles Puyol and Javier Mascherano both tracked Didier Drogba's run out to the right. Ramires crossed low from the left and Drogba, who had checked his run as his markers kept going, swept the ball in with his left foot. It was Chelsea's only shot on goal in the entire game. Barça had 24, but Chelsea won 1-0. That was a frustration, but Barça's away form in the Champions League had been disappointing for a while and they remained supreme at home. The expectation was still for Barça to go through.

Before that, though, came the league *Clásico* at the Camp Nou. Guardiola was clear about what his side needed to do: draw or lose, he said, and the title was gone. Khedira gave Madrid a first-half lead, bundling in after Valdés had misjudged a corner. Barça were generally poor, giving the ball away too often and looking short of energy but, midway through the second half, Sánchez levelled, poking in after Cristian Tello, who had wasted two earlier chances, saw his shot saved. But within two and a half minutes, Ronaldo had seized on Özil's brilliant pass to restore Madrid's lead and, with Mourinho's first win at the Camp Nou, the title was as good as theirs.

That, perhaps, added pressure to the second leg of the Champions League semi-final as Barça faced the prospect of their season collapsing in the space of a week. When Barça had lost the semi-final two years earlier, it had been the result not merely of Inter's resistance in the second leg but of the way they'd capitulated in the first leg. This time it was just a story of resistance. Chelsea defended pretty much as well as they possibly could have done, both individually and as a unit, showed admirable mental and physical resilience and rode their luck. The stats fundamentalists who see nothing in the game but numbers will say they were incredibly fortunate, which is true, but they also fought with the tenacity of an ageing side knowing this was its last – improbable – chance of European success. When Busquets turned in a Cuenca cutback after 35 minutes, both Gary Cahill and Piqué had already been forced off through injury. Two minutes later, Chelsea lost their other centre-back, John Terry, after he kneed Sánchez in the back and was sent off. When Iniesta converted Messi's set-up a minute before half-time to make it 2-0 on the night and 2-1 on aggregate, the tie seemed as good as over. Perhaps Barça thought so too, their defending bafflingly lax in first-half injury time as Lampard played a through ball into the path of Ramires, who finished with an uncharacteristically deft chip.

That put Chelsea ahead on the away goals rule but it hardly seemed to matter when Drogba tripped Fàbregas in the box four minutes into the second half. Messi, though, hit the bar from the spot. Still, such was Barça's domination that a third, decisive goal felt inevitable. But the longer the half went on, the more secure Chelsea, with Branislav Ivanović and José Bosingwa at centre-back, came to seem and the more predictable Barça looked. They completed 806 passes to Chelsea's 122, had 23 shots and hit the woodwork twice more and yet they seemed beaten long before Fernando Torres ran through an empty half, rounded Valdés and scored to seal an improbable 3-2 aggregate victory in added time. 'I look at the team and I try to think of what we have done wrong to explain why we are not in the final and I can't find anything,' Guardiola said. 'From the very first day I have said that we have to attack, attack, attack. There are times when we don't find the necessary *pausa*.* Maybe we have to learn that lesson in the future. We have to find the way of attacking better.'

There was a weariness about Barcelona towards the end of that season, but there was something more. Guardiola believes in the need for perpetual revolution. He is always fiddling, always adapting, always aware of the dangers of staleness or complacency. He converted Lionel Messi into a false nine. He signed Zlatan Ibrahimović to provide a different option in attack. And yet in his final season at Barcelona, he seemed to become like some figure from Greek tragedy, not merely unable to avert a destiny of which he was very aware, but finding that the measures he took to avert it were precisely those that ensured it came to pass.

Guardiola was troubled by teams sitting deep against Barça, worried that his side would end up following the same patterns and routines, and so he devised a way of getting more players, Dani Alves in particular, higher up the pitch to try to outflank blanket defences. All that did, though, was to make Barça more impotent: it is easier to mark a player who starts high than one coming from deep.

That wasn't the sole cause of that odd flatness Barça demonstrated in those final minutes against Chelsea, but it did explain why they never had players bursting at pace through the defensive lines: everybody was too near the box already – they couldn't build up enough pace to be travelling at speed when they ran on to the ball.

By then, you wonder also whether Guardiola, clearly contemplating the end, was in the grip of a fatalistic idealism. His approach seemed to become analogous to the concept of altruism envisaged by Ernest Becker in his reframing of Freud: Guardiola could not prevent

---

* The *pausa*, particularly celebrated in Argentina, is the moment of calm before a decisive pass; Guardiola, in other words, is suggesting his side had become too frantic.

the dissolution of the ego, but he could at least take control of the circumstances of its dissolution and thereby invest it with meaning. His principles might be leading him to destruction but rather than easing back he pressed on: he might fail, he would fail, but he would be failing in the most Barça-ish of ways.

Two days after the Chelsea defeat, Guardiola met with Rosell and told him he was leaving. He was replaced by his assistant Tito Vilanova. Mourinho had done what he'd been appointed to do. In the league, Madrid lost just twice and finished nine points above a weary Barça, accumulating a record 100 points and a record 121 goals. Their Champions League run was ended by Bayern on penalties in the semi-final but, still, this was Mourinho triumphant. Whatever disquiet may have been felt about his methods, the fact was that in the short term they worked. Guardiola finished with one final trophy, beating Bielsa's Athletic to win the Copa del Rey in an emotional final against one of his great coaching idols, but the way seemed clear for Madrid to create their own empire.

Empires, though, are not Mourinho's way. Before getting to Manchester he had always won the league in his second season at a club; he rarely lasted a third and when he did, he was never successful. With Barcelona managed by a novice in Tito Vilanova, their aura of invulnerability shattered, the – naïve – hope in Madrid was that Mourinho would emphasise the constructive side of his personality, that, the ends achieved, his means would become more palatable, something more in keeping with the club's self-image of *señorío*.

Mourinho, perhaps, recognised the reality better than anyone. He was never a fit for Madrid – hardly anybody is at a club that often seems to struggle to reconcile its status as a football club with its self-declared vision of being 'a content provider' like Disney – and that summer sounded out options in the Premier League before extending a contract to 2016.

For Barcelona, Vilanova represented continuity. 'They have different personalities,' Messi said of the new coach and his predecessor, 'but the work is the same.' Within a month it was clear there would be no peaceful era of Mourinho-led Madrid dominance. Although they overcame Barça on away goals to lift the Super Cup, Madrid began the league season with a draw at home against Valencia and defeat at Getafe. When they then lost away to Sevilla in their fourth league game, they were eight points behind Barcelona, even though Vilanova's side hadn't played particularly well. In Seville, Madrid had struggled to create chances after Piotr Trochowski had converted a first-minute Ivan Rakitić corner and lost 1-0. Players complained – as they had done in the previous two seasons – that too much time was spent practising the counter-attack and very little practising against massed defences. Mourinho, meanwhile, was keen to make clear the defeat was not his fault. 'We cannot train any more or any better on set pieces,' he said. 'Every player knows his position and his mission.'

A delegation of senior players, angered at their manager's denial of responsibility, confronted Mourinho, but the pattern continued. Madrid still had enough high-class players to win most games, but there was no fluidity to their play. Against Real Betis and Granada, there came 1-0 defeats caused primarily by a lack of invention and spark. In December, Mourinho became embroiled in a row with a journalist from Radio Marca in which he made the extraordinary claim that he was being undermined by 'three black sheep'. The tensions within the squad hadn't gone away and nor, it seemed, had Mourinho's paranoia. A week later, Casillas was left out of the side for a 3-2 defeat away to Malaga. Early in the new year, the goalkeeper was omitted again for a home match against Real Sociedad, only to be called into action after eight minutes after his replacement, Antonio Adán, had been sent off. Madrid ended up winning 4-3, but the crowd's frustration with Mourinho was clear.

Casillas soon suffered a broken bone in his hand, which took some of the heat out of that controversy as Diego López was signed from Sevilla to replace him. But there were too many fires for them all to be extinguished. The end was foreshadowed long before it came. 'Not many managers,' Mourinho noted long before the end of the season, 'stay here for three years.' That is true, but it's also true that Mourinho never stays at a club for four years.

Even when things went right they were wrong. Madrid drew at the Camp Nou and beat Barça at home in the league, and eliminated them from the Copa del Rey, but none of it brought silverware. In the Champions League, having scrambled through the group stage behind Borussia Dortmund, Madrid drew 1-1 at the Bernabéu and then fell behind at Old Trafford in the second leg. When Nani was controversially sent off for a high foot on Arbeloa, Mourinho seized the initiative, taking off the full-back and throwing on Luka Modrić. Within ten minutes Madrid had scored twice and the tie was as good as won. It could have been an occasion for celebration, for Mourinho to revel in his tactical mastery; as it was, when it was put to him that he had everything at Valdebebas, he sourly noted he had 'everything but team spirit'. Mourinho's apologists would note that that wasn't just an issue to do with him: in December that season, for instance, very few players turned up at a party for Michael Essien's 30th birthday. The whole atmosphere around the club was toxic.

The Champions League brought a humbling semi-final defeat to Jürgen Klopp's Borussia Dortmund, who seemed quicker, sharper, better at the counter-attack that was supposed to be Mourinho's strong point. Here, if Mourinho wanted it, was corroboration of his theory that having the ball was dangerous, but here too was a hint that the game had moved on. Counter-attacking takes on many forms, and Klopp's, based on a high press and winning the ball back high up the pitch, seemed more dynamic, more thrilling, more modern than Mourinho's.

Barcelona, having led from day one, won the league, matching Madrid's tally of 100 points for the previous season. In November 2012, there was even a glorious vindication for the policy of the *cantera*. When Barcelona won 4-0 away to Levante, the 11 players who finished the game had all come through their youth ranks. Van Gaal, Xavi pointed out, had 'always said that the club should strive to build a team with players only from its own schooling. Now we have achieved that goal… Van Gaal established the basis for this.'

Generally, though, 2012-13 was overshadowed by Vilanova's health. In the December it was announced that he had cancer for the second time. He had surgery and underwent chemotherapy, standing down for six weeks as Jordi Roura, his assistant, took temporary charge.

Entirely understandably, there was a lessening of intensity. When Barça lost to Madrid in the Copa del Rey, *El Periódico* spoke of 'a lack of ideas the like of which we had never seen before, miles from what this team was until very recently'. When they lost to Madrid in the league a week later, *El País* described them as a team with 'no soul, no football and [because of injury] no Messi'.

Messi returned to inspire Barça to overturn a 2-0 first-leg deficit against AC Milan in the last 16 of the Champions League and was then instrumental in an edgy away goals victory over Paris Saint-Germain in the quarter-final. 'Let's not debate *Messidependencia* any more,' Ramon Besa wrote in *El País*, 'his mere presence is enough. One day, a cardboard cutout of Messi will win a match.'

The league title had been all but assured by Christmas, but there was plenty of evidence of decline long before Barça faced Bayern in the semi-final. It was a crushing humiliation. Their 4-0 defeat in Germany echoed the 4-0 defeat Cruyff's side had suffered to Milan 19 years earlier; the 3-0 defeat in the second leg was limply pathetic. There were mitigating factors: Messi missed the second leg. Puyol, Mascherano, Busquets and Jordi Alba were injured. Abidal was returning from a liver transplant. Xavi and Dani Alves were exhausted. The signings of Alex Song and Cesc Fàbregas had not worked out. There were claims that the high Barcelona style was finished, that the more direct German counter-attacking approach had superseded a philosophy rooted in possession. But more than anything, there was a sense that this Barcelona were simply tired, that a cycle had come to an end.

And then, of course, there was their manager. Although it felt uncomfortable, insensitive even, to discuss, by the end of the season there was an acceptance that Vilanova's illness had led to a lack of direction from the top. He was able to return to the bench in late March, but Vilanova resigned in the summer. He suffered another relapse the following April and died a week later, aged just 45.

\* \* \*

On 7 May 2013, Mourinho arrived alone at the Sheraton Madrid Mirasierra to prepare for a league game against Malaga, having refused to travel with his players after accusing them of disloyalty. A contingent of the Ultras Sur, who saw themselves as Madrid's most devoted fans, were waiting for him with a banner that proclaimed their love for him. That Mourinho's fractious time at the club was coming to an end wasn't in any real doubt. And for Mourinho, things were about to get much worse.

The story broke that evening that Manchester United were going to appoint David Moyes as a successor to Alex Ferguson. According to Diego Torres in his biography of Mourinho, the Madrid manager was appalled. He'd been machinating for a return to the Premier League for most of the second half of the season; as the former *Sun* journalist Rob Beasley reveals in his book about his relationship with Mourinho, the manager told him where and when a photographer would be able to snap him in London to help fuel rumours he was returning to England. After Madrid had won at Old Trafford, Mourinho had been notably and unusually magnanimous, suggesting that the 'best team lost'; some sort of game, clearly, was afoot. Moreover, Mourinho had believed he had a special relationship with Ferguson, but the outgoing United manager hadn't even called him to let him know of the decision.

That night Mourinho was restless, fretful, constantly checking the news to see if there may have been some mistake. The following morning he called Jorge Mendes to see if it might be possible to derail the deal and reinsert himself into the picture. By the following day, Mourinho was insisting that his intention had always been to go back to Chelsea, that his wife wanted to live in London. Perhaps that was true, but perhaps he saw this as a second betrayal; he had been on noticeably good behaviour after the win at Old Trafford, fulsome in his praise for both Sir Alex Ferguson, in what turned out to be his last European match, and the institution of Manchester United. Worse was the sense that this was a decision that was only indirectly related to football. 'A United manager,' Bobby Charlton, at the time a United director, told the *Guardian* in December 2012, 'would not do what he did to Tito Vilanova... Mourinho is a really good coach, but that's as far as I'd go.' And his behaviour at Madrid had raised other doubts. 'The problem is,' one executive at Gestifute told Torres, 'when things do not go well for Mou, he does not follow the club's line. He follows José's line.'

By then, Mourinho's options were limited: other than PSG, Chelsea were the only club of sufficient stature who would still have him. Not only that, but he was, at least, going back to a club where he'd been revered, where he'd announced himself as 'a special one' and been loved for it, where the fans didn't seem to mind – perhaps even relished – his uncompromising approach (whether Abramovich was so keen on it was another matter).

As negotiations went on, there was a season to complete. With the league gone, the Copa del Rey final, played at the Bernabéu against Atlético, might have offered some kind of finale, a means of bidding farewell with, if not dignity, then at least silverware. There was none of that. Pepe was left out for siding with Casillas as Mourinho selected a 4-3-3 with Özil drifting in from the right. Madrid took the lead as Ronaldo headed in a Modrić corner after 14 minutes but, not for the first time that season, Madrid invited pressure by trying to sit on a lead. Diego Costa equalised and Miranda got the winner in extra time. Ronaldo was sent off for collecting two yellow cards, while Mourinho was, predictably, sent to the stands, ending his Madrid career the way he had spent most of it, fuming at the injustices of the world and making sure everybody was aware he felt hard done by. 'This,' Mourinho said in the post-match press conference, 'is the worst season of my career.'

Three days later, Pérez confirmed that Mourinho would be leaving the club. Two weeks after that, he was announced as the new manager of Chelsea.

# CHAPTER EIGHT

# COUNTER-REFORMATION

Just before the half-hour mark in the 2010 World Cup final, Xavi nodded the ball to his left towards Xabi Alonso as he broke through the centre circle. The Real Madrid midfielder got to the bouncing ball first and helped it on, and was then sent crashing to the ground as the studs of Nigel de Jong's outstretched boot thumped into his chest. It was a dreadful challenge, late and clumsy rather than malicious perhaps, but born of a profound cynicism, of the logic that if it didn't win the ball it would without question stop Alonso's progress and potentially do some damage to him as well. It was a mentality that ran contrary to the Cruyffian ideals but one that had characterised the Netherlands at that tournament, the third of nine yellow cards shown to Dutch players in the final, culminating in the dismissal of Johnny Heitinga 19 minutes into extra time.

The Netherlands had lost in World Cup finals before. They'd had great teams who had played great football and not quite come home with the trophy before. That was their identity, and victory in the Euros in West Germany in 1988 a glorious exception. Heroic failure with a sense of moral superiority was their culture. As the journalist Simon Kuper has observed,* that was true not only of football: from the sixties, Dutch political discourse had echoed the phrase 'Nether-

---

* In 'The Dutch Style and the Dutch Nation' in Issue Zero of *The Blizzard*.

lands, guide land' as the country became famous for its attitude of tolerance. As the political scientist Paul Scheffer, a former professor at the University of Amsterdam, noted, it's much easier for a small nation to be good than powerful. That's why what happened at the World Cup in South Africa was so painful. It was failure with no sense of moral superiority and that meant there were few plaudits for Bert van Marwijk's side for reaching the final. On the contrary, there was disgust. It was as though De Jong's boot had stamped not merely on Xabi Alonso's chest but on all the proudest Dutch traditions.

Johan Cruyff was distraught. 'They asked me from Holland, "Can we play like Inter?"' he told *El Periódico*. '"Can we stop Spain in the same way Mourinho eliminated Barça?" I said no, no way at all. I said no, not because I hate this style – I said no because I thought that my country wouldn't dare to and would never renounce their style. I said no because, without having great players like those of the past, the team has its own style. I was wrong... They didn't want the ball.' But the similarity between Van Marwijk's 4-2-3-1 – which had itself been the cause of a certain amount of hand-wringing from those who felt no truly Dutch side could ever playing anything other than 4-3-3 – and Mourinho's set-up at Inter was clear. Both involved employing six outfielders sitting deep to provide a platform for four more creative players, and Wesley Sneijder was central in each. It may not just be coincidence that Robben and Van Bommel, Van Marwijk's son-in-law and a hugely influential figure in the dressing room, had both lost in the Champions League final to that Inter weeks before the World Cup began; had that game, perhaps, reinforced in their minds the limits of idealism?

'Regrettably, sadly,' Cruyff went on, 'they played very dirty... It hurts me that I was wrong in my disagreement that instead Holland chose an ugly path to aim for the title. This ugly, vulgar, hard, hermetic, hardly eye-catching, hardly football style, yes, it served the Dutch to unsettle Spain. If they got satisfaction with this, fine, but they ended up losing. They were playing anti-football.'

It was Spain, not the Netherlands, who had become the truest exponents of post-Cruyffianism. 'I am Dutch but I will always defend the football Spain play,' Cruyff had said even before the final. 'If you play attacking football, like Spain do, you have more chances of winning. And if you try to play on the counter against a team that really wants the ball, you deserve to suffer.'

Two months later, Ajax, in their second season under Martin Jol, lost dismally in the Champions League to José Mourinho's Real Madrid. For Cruyff, that was the final straw and he was provoked into writing the column in *De Telegraaf* that would ignite his counter-reformation, the Velvet Revolution by which, in a typically oblique way, he took control of Ajax. This was not just about Van Marwijk, who had never played for or managed Ajax and had won only one international cap, nor was it just about Jol, who equally had never played for Ajax; it was about all of Dutch football. The only reason there was need for a counter-reformation was that there had been a reformation in the first place. A post-Cruyffian philosophy may have taken Barcelona to unprecedented heights but, back in the Netherlands, the classic Ajax style had been assailed by doubt. Realism had become the new mode and what was perhaps most disturbing was that it was a movement led by those who had previously identified themselves as being of the Ajax school, even if they had been regarded as part of its less idealistic wing.

For Kuper, that was a process that had started with the 1-0 defeat Van Gaal's Netherlands suffered away to Ireland that meant they failed to qualify for the 2002 World Cup. After '*het drama van Dublin*' it began to be accepted that the close passing approach that had previously characterised Dutch teams was no longer breaking opponents down and, thanks to the prompting of Guus Hiddink, they instead turned to an approach based more on transitions. At Euro 2008, Marco van Basten's Netherlands side, blessed with an extraordinary depth of talent and playing what was widely perceived as an updated version of the traditional Dutch approach, beat Italy 3-0 and France 4-1 before losing in the quarter-final to a team playing an even more modern version of the same style: Guus Hiddink's Russia. Another glorious failure.

Then something changed. Under Van Marwijk, the Dutch became a team that won, but cared little for the aesthetics. They won all eight of their qualifiers for the World Cup, but the attitude had changed. A Nike advert before the tournament gave notice of what was to follow. There were the Dutch, training hard, looking grim, sweating. This was emphatically not a bunch of players who would engage in something like the notorious pool party the revelation (or fabrication?) of which by the German media supposedly undermined morale before the 1974 final. 'Tears of joy are made of sweat,' read one caption. 'Destroy egos, starting with your own,' said another. This was not a team, the ad made clear, that would be satisfied with another glorious failure. 'Football is not total without victory,' another caption said. 'A beautiful defeat is still a defeat.'

What that meant in practice was made clear by the final. More than 600,000 turned out to welcome the Netherlands team home – and there were those who dismissed the disgusted as canal-belt intellectuals – but opposition slowly grew. The magazine *Hard Gras* ran a cover that featured a photograph of De Jong's assault on Alonso with the ironic caption, '*Hollandse School*'. Viewing figures for the national side dropped alarmingly.

Even Hiddink, who was widely seen as being responsible for beginning the shift to pragmatism, had no sympathy for Van Marwijk. 'I had no feeling with it at all,' he told Kuper. 'I watched, but I realised I wasn't watching eagerly. Around me in the house, I saw disappointed people. You hear it from people in international football: "Gosh, a shame that we didn't see much from Holland." That image of "that little Holland" hasn't been lost worldwide, but you don't want to do another one like that again.'

But the truth was that Van Marwijk's side was just an extreme example of a more general trend. Other approaches may not have been so violent but they were also a deviation from the Cruyffian tradition.

After his time as technical director of Ajax had come to an end, there had been a widespread suspicion that Van Gaal was finished, that he was another – like Arrigo Sacchi perhaps – who, inspired by a radical idea of how to play, had enjoyed remarkable early success in their managerial careers, only to discover that those theories did not fit so well in other environments. When Van Gaal returned to football, in January 2005, it was not with one of the continent's giants but with AZ. Based in Alkmaar, a town of just over 100,000 population noted for its cheese market and little else, they had won the league only once, and that as long ago as 1981, when they also reached the final of the UEFA Cup.

The step away from the limelight suited Van Gaal. Slowly, he began to build a side to his specifications. He was pragmatic enough to realise that the press-and-possess Ajax method was impractical at a club with such limited resources and so focused more on sitting deep, keeping an organised shape and striking rapidly on the break. 'Provoke the space then press,' Van Gaal explained. 'It depends on the quality of your team, the quality of your opponent… In the beginning I was always attacking and pressing with the defence always on the halfway line, but that was a big space [to leave behind]. Later, the evolution in my mind was that I had to adapt also to the qualities of my opponent.' That was an answer to those who had wondered whether the Cruyffian principles were relevant to smaller clubs, or whether that philosophy was a luxury in which only those blessed with the highest level of player could engage. Or at least it was a partial answer: it may be common sense that tweaks need to be made according to circumstance, but how many tweaks can be made before the philosophy has become something else?

Adaptation of style did not mean an adaptation of approach and Van Gaal remained as meticulous as ever. He divided games into 2,000 video fragments and would send each player an appropriately illustrated email outlining what they had done right and what they had done wrong. 'He always had a very special way of thinking; he could make virtually any formation in football work,' said the Georgian forward Shota Arveladze, who joined AZ from Rangers at the beginning of Van Gaal's first season in Alkmaar. 'He had two good strikers that could score a lot and wanted to play both of them with quick midfielders backing them up.'

By Van Gaal's second full season, AZ were, to widespread surprise, genuine title contenders. 'He always knows how to improve you,' Arveladze explained. 'Many people said that we wouldn't get along but everything he told you and did for you was to make you better; it was very easy to talk to him and discuss anything.' Although Arveladze left the club for Levante in the summer, he returned a year later to take on a role as assistant coach. AZ went into the final day of 2006-07, when they faced the bottom club Excelsior, leading the table on goal difference from PSV and Ajax. But after their goalkeeper was sent off, they lost 3-2 and, with PSV and Ajax both winning, AZ finished third.

AZ's top scorer Danny Koevermans left, disgruntled after Van Gaal had told him he was looking for an upgrade. That wasn't even the worst self-inflicted injury that summer, as Van Gaal suffered a double fracture of the leg while attempting to demonstrate the pole vault at a school reunion. The problem, he insisted, was that he had been wearing smooth-soled leather shoes rather than trainers. He was 56.

The break demanded the insertion of six pins into his leg and he was in a wheelchair for weeks. Van Gaal's focus remained undiminished and he took training from a golf buggy. The day after having surgery at the beginning of November, he went to the stadium to watch AZ play NEC, sitting in an executive box and communicating with his assistant Edward Metgod by walkie-talkie. AZ won 4-0 but that was a rare bright spot in a disappointing season. AZ finished 11th and Van Gaal announced he would resign, only to be persuaded by the players to change his mind. That August, on his 57th birthday, Van Gaal married Truus after a 14-year relationship.

AZ lost the first two games of 2008-09 but the return of Stijn Schaars after an injury that had kept him out for the entirety of the previous season proved crucial. Schaars was both tactically disciplined enough to screen the back four and a good enough long passer that when possession was won he could release the rapid front two of Mounir El Hamdaoui and Mousa Dembélé on the break. 'I had El Hamdaoui, a kind of Rivaldo, from a different football culture, egoistic,' Van Gaal said. 'He needed freedom but I felt he would score 25 goals.' On the left of the 4-4-2 he used another player who would not be regarded as a typical Van Gaal player, Maarten Martens. 'He wanted to play as a ten, but I put him on the left,' Van Gaal said. 'I convinced my players we had to do for him what we had to do. And he could run for 90 minutes.'

AZ went on a run of 17 wins and two draws in 19 league games. When Van Gaal had opened the Alkmaar cheese market in 2008, a fortune-teller had prophesied that AZ would win the league on 19 April. On 18 April, they could have won the title, but surprisingly lost to Vitesse. The following day, Ajax, their closest challengers, were beaten 6-2 and the title was theirs. It was, Van Gaal said, 'my greatest little masterpiece'.

Van Gaal might have stayed at AZ, a club small enough that he could dominate it as a dictator without needing to keep directors happy, but he lost an estimated €6m investing in Bernie Madoff's Ponzi scheme. Perhaps the offer Bayern made to him that summer would always have been too good to turn down, but his financial circumstances definitely made it more enticing.

Bayern were in transition. They had won the league under Jupp Heynckes in 2008 but had then appointed Jürgen Klinsmann as manager with a brief to rejuvenate and modernise. 'The Pre-Announced Revolution,' proclaimed the *Münchner Merkur*. 'Everything at Bayern will change under Klinsmann.' The former striker had overseen the transformation of the national team but Bayern never really took to him. It was never forgotten that he had demoted the Bayern favourite Oliver Kahn before the World Cup on home soil, or that there had been times during his playing stint at the club when it had been asked whether he had really bought into Bayern or if he were just there to tick the empty Bundesliga champion box on his CV. Although it was the work of a designer rather than Klinsmann, it seemed to encapsulate the prevailing spirit when four stone Buddhas were installed on the roof of the training centre before the season began. 'They give us a certain energy flow,' Klinsmann said, before revealing there were more golden Buddhas inside. They were taken down three weeks into the season when the Catholic Church complained.

As early as the opening day of the season, after Bayern had drawn 2-2 with Hamburg, Philipp Lahm was admitting, 'We lacked organisation and defensive stability.' In April, Bayern were hammered 4-0 in the away leg of their Champions League quarter-final against Guardiola's Barça. 'We've been given a masterclass in how to play the game,' said Franz Beckenbauer.

In the league, they lost 5-1 at Wolfsburg and slipped to third with a 1-0 defeat to Schalke. The threat of failing to qualify for the Champions League was too much and Klinsmann was sacked with five games of the season remaining. 'His concept convinced us,' said the club president Uli Hoeneß before adding the vital kicker, 'on paper.' Bayern had wanted modernisation, scientific method and a shift to a high-tempo pressing game. They got a sunny demeanour, banal motivational slogans, yoga classes, an ill-conceived dabble with 3-5-2, the even more ill-conceived signing of Landon Donovan and a general laxity when it came to detail. The more the world saw of Klinsmann's day-to-day methods, the more significant the role of Joachim Löw, his assistant with the national team, began to look.

Klinsmann was replaced, in a caretaker capacity, by Jupp Heynckes, who ensured Champions League qualification. As Wolfsburg won the title, Van Gaal represented a reliable older hand, somebody who could be trusted never to be lax and who favoured a style that, if not quite modern, at least had a background in pioneering the sort of pressing game that was becoming increasingly modish and that had proved so effective against Bayern in the Champions League quarter-final. Bayern, quite consciously, turned to a post-Cruyffian to lead them into modernity.

Van Gaal's start, though, was less than encouraging. In his first weeks at Bayern, as the doubts of others piled up, Van Gaal remained characteristically self-confident. 'I am like God!' he would announce.

'I never get ill and I am always right.' Once their form picked up, he backed off a little, confirming he was not God because if he were he would win all the time.

The pattern was typical. It takes time for players to absorb the Van Gaal method, to adapt to his schoolmasterly ways. Bayern failed to win any of their first three games under Van Gaal and by late October he was under pressure. There were rumours he would be sacked if they failed to beat Eintracht Frankfurt. After 86 minutes it was 1-1, at which Van Gaal, to general mystification and widespread booing, took off the centre-forward Luca Toni for the central defender Martin Demichelis. As Demichelis slotted into the back line, Daniel Van Buyten was moved up front. Shoving a big centre-back to centre-forward in the hope his height and strength might shake something loose is a tactic as old as football and can often seem like the last resort of a coach who has tried to create something by patience and method; certainly nobody could claim it was a classic ploy of Total Football. On this occasion, though, it worked, as Van Buyten converted a Thomas Müller cross for the winner.

That began to change the mood but a draw against Schalke the following month left Bayern eighth, having endured their worst start in 15 years. Toni, having been substituted at half-time, stormed out of the stadium. His relationship with Van Gaal hadn't recovered from the moment in pre-season when Van Gaal had seen him slouching at dinner and had pulled him up by the ears. But Philipp Lahm, significantly, struck a note of optimism in an interview in which he savaged the board for their lack of a coherent philosophy or transfer policy. This was not the same as it had been under Klinsmann, he said; he had 'hope, because I can recognise structure'.

At the beginning of December, Bayern were third in the league, having drawn six and lost two of their opening 15 games. Two defeats to Bordeaux left them needing to beat Juventus away to qualify for the knockout phase of the Champions League. It was in Turin that everything clicked: Bayern won 4-1. That was part of a run of 13 straight victories in all competitions. They went on to win the league and eliminated Manchester United and Lyon on their way to the Champions League final in which they were beaten by Mourinho's Inter. The former Bayern defender Paul Breitner spoke enthusiastically about how good Van Gaal's side were at 'controlling the ball', saying, 'I have not seen Bayern play this well in about five or ten years.'

This was not the old-style 3-4-3/4-3-3 but a 4-2-3-1 similar to the shape Van Gaal had used with the Netherlands national team. To an extent, the way he saw the system, the one was always implicit in the other. In his 4-3-3, the six was always more defensive than the eight with the ten as a playmaker in front of them. Here, all he had done was pull the shuttling midfielder a little deeper but even then there was no suggestion that he was fielding two out-and-out defensive players at the back of midfield. Mark van Bommel was the deeper-lying holding midfielder with Bastian Schweinsteiger, who had been a right-sided player, operating as a more progressive figure. The addition of an extra midfielder in the centre liberated the fullbacks, with Lahm in particular taking full advantage of the freedom he had to overlap as the wide forwards tucked in. A young Thomas Müller offered goals and inventive movement playing behind Ivica Olić, a prodigiously hard-working centre-forward, the ideal figure to lead the press.

Van Gaal's second season was rather less impressive. A defeat to Thomas Tuchel's Mainz in the sixth game of the season suggested they were susceptible to a hard-pressing game, an impression that was strengthened when they lost their next game 2-0 to Jürgen Klopp's Borussia Dortmund. After seven games, Bayern were 12th with just eight points and five goals. The timing of the launch of the German version of his book, *Biographie & Vision*,\* wasn't ideal, but Van Gaal's behaviour around it would have caused problems whatever the club's results. He invited Rummenigge and Hoeneß to the launch at a Munich hotel and, as he addressed the audience, Van Gaal picked up a copy and waved it at the two directors. 'It's important for you to read this,' he said. 'You can learn from this.' Perhaps it was meant as a joke, but then jokes weren't Van Gaal's forte. It ensured he had no allies in the boardroom.

There was a recovery of sorts, but when Bayern lost 3-1 to Dortmund at the end of February, they were, the sports editor of *Süddeutsche Zeitung*, Klaus Hoeltzenbein, said, 'like driftwood in a sea of yellow and black'.

Van Gaal blamed individual errors – a familiar excuse for those whose approach is rooted in the system – but Hoeltzenbein was unconvinced. 'A holistic system like the one presented by Klopp,' he wrote, 'takes errors into account and includes safety measures. Van Gaal's purely offensive model is courageous, attractive, but also risky and sometimes naïve because it doesn't pay enough attention to the opponents' abilities.'

That defeat was the first of a run of four in five games that saw Bayern eliminated from the German Cup and the Champions League and effectively ended their hopes of retaining the Bundesliga title. Breitner, by then, was bored. 'We swapped Bayern's traditional style for this high-possession game but there was still no flexibility in terms of players' positions and everyone had to stick rigidly to his own area,' he told Marti Perarnau in *Pep Confidential*. 'In some matches,

---

\* In Dutch, they came out as two separate volumes *Biografie van Louis van Gaal* and *De visie van Louis van Gaal*.

we ended up with 80 per cent possession but there was no real rhythm or pace. After half an hour, everyone in the Allianz Arena would be yawning at this display of constant passing. Our game was well executed but very, very predictable … the basic idea was sound. What we lacked was speed and regular changes of rhythm.'

World Cup fatigue and Arjen Robben's lengthy absence through injury offered some mitigation, but only some. 'Van Gaal is dogmatic without a plan B,' said the *Frankfurter Allgemeine Zeitung*. 'Now that explanations for the weakness of Bayern's season are no longer valid, he's at the centre of criticism. Why did he refuse to invest in defensive players? Why the constant positional changes? Why is he not interested in practising defensive dead-ball situations?'

'It's not easy to fire Van Gaal,' Van Gaal said at the beginning of March. 'The question who will follow is a very difficult one to answer.' But when a draw to Nürnberg saw them slide out of the Champions League qualification places in early April, he was dismissed. His assistant Andries Jonker took over and Bayern won five of their final six games to finish third. The answer to the question of who would succeed him turned out to be simple: it was the man who had preceded him, Jupp Heynckes.

* * *

On 15 September 2010, Ajax lost 2-0 in the Champions League to José Mourinho's Real Madrid. Few in Amsterdam were surprised. The glory Louis van Gaal had brought 15 years earlier was long in the past. There'd been the brief flicker under Ronald Koeman but the economic reality was clear enough. Ajax had become a minnow and in football's ruthless economic climate that meant they couldn't compete. Even if another great generation did emerge from De Toekomst, or if some astute sporting director put together a gifted squad on a shoestring, the brightest players would soon be sold off once Europe's biggest clubs caught the scent of something exciting emerging again. They hadn't won the Dutch league since that Koeman side of six years earlier. Failure in Europe had become commonplace: only once since 2003 had they got beyond the group stage of the Champions League.

Johan Cruyff was furious. 'This isn't Ajax any more,' he wrote in his column in *De Telegraaf.* 'Let me get to the point: this Ajax is even worse than the team from before Rinus Michels's arrival in 1965.' Few were surprised by that either. '*Gezanik*' – complaining just to have something to talk about – is common among Amsterdammers and Cruyff was a prime exponent. There was a growing sense that Cruyff had become bitter, angered by his marginalisation at Ajax, angered by modernity. As Elko Born, describing the general response, put it in Issue 14 of *The Blizzard*, 'Shit, Amsterdam wasn't really Amsterdam any more. The 1970s were gone and the yuppies had taken over. De Meer was gone, Ajax now played in the Amsterdam ArenA, the stadium that resembled a concrete spaceship and tried to impose a capital at the end of the name as well as the beginning. You couldn't take the tram there. Welcome to 2010, Mr Cruyff.'

But Cruyff wasn't just having a grumble; he was plotting a revolution. He had decided to reimpose his principles at their origin. The *Telegraaf* column, the final paragraphs of which demanded the board to be deposed, became a call to arms.

The former Ajax and Inter midfielder Wim Jonk was already employed at De Toekomst, as was Ruben Jongkind, an amateur footballer who had completed a Master's degree in business administration. Both were devout Cruyffians and although they were given a certain freedom to work as they saw fit, they had become frustrated by the constraints placed upon them. 'Because we were working from the under-eights up to the second team,' Jongkind said, 'we saw the whole picture, on a day-to-day basis. Both of us are conceptual thinkers as well. And I have an academic background in production systems and logistics. So, we were able to make a proper plan, which we presented to our former bosses, but they said, "Ah, you can't do this kind of thing here" – that it was dangerous politically, or whatever.'

Cruyff had persuaded Jonk to sign for Ajax from Volendam in 1988 but had moved to Barcelona before he arrived. As he plotted his takeover, Cruyff sounded him out. Jongkind put together a proposal for how youth development could be improved, how Ajax could be made Cruyffian again. 'So we had a secret meeting,' Jongkind said, 'with all these former greats, like Bergkamp and Van Basten and Rijkaard, Piet Keizer, they were all there at the table. And I just came in – I was brand new and green, with these books and the plan in my hand.

'Johan said after our explanation and presentation, "Ah, I'm not wearing my glasses, I can't read it, but it sounds good. You have to come to Barcelona and then we can talk further about it and then I can have it checked by my specialists." So that's what we did. And then we changed some things, added some stuff. Rijkaard had a lot of good additions and that became the Cruyff Plan.'

Working out a means of improving youth coaching, though, was only part of it. What Cruyff was calling for was a complete overhaul of the club from top to bottom. He wanted former players in key positions, he wanted a greater faith in home-grown talent rather than imported stars, he wanted, in his own terminology, to make Ajax Ajax again.

Ajax's general director Rik van den Boog and the chairman Uri Coronel didn't take Cruyff particularly seriously. What did he know about modern football? they asked. What did he know of economic realism and strategic planning? That was a big mistake. By taking that tone, Van den Boog and Coronel made clear they were part of the value system Cruyff was railing against. He was a populist and a romantic; that he cared little for strategic planning was part of his appeal.

Cruyff's closest advisor was the former Ajax defender Keje Molenaar, a practising lawyer. He advised Cruyff that the best vehicle for revolution was Ajax's Council of Members, so Cruyff targeted the eight seats on their 24-man board that came up for election in December 2010, filling them with former players who shared his outlook. Flanked by Jonk and Dennis Bergkamp, Cruyff delivered a speech outlining his vision, while making clear that he had no intention of 'wearing a jacket' himself. He didn't want a formal post in the new organisation; he wanted the position he had effectively occupied at Barcelona: that of moral compass and *éminence grise*.

Early in December 2010, after a 1-1 draw against NEC that left Ajax fourth in the league, Martin Jol resigned as manager and was replaced, initially on an interim basis, by Frank de Boer. It was his first senior managerial role, but his ideological credentials were impeccable. He'd played for Ajax and Barça, had managed the Ajax youth team and been an assistant with the Netherlands, albeit under Van Marwijk. But a change of manager wasn't enough for Cruyff; the structures and spirit of the club had to be changed as well.

The Velvet Revolution, as it became known, was a protracted process. There was no one moment when the barricades were manned or the statues pulled down. During the early months of 2011, in the 14th minute of every game at the Amsterdam ArenA, the chant would be raised by the supporters group VAK410 and the F-side, 'Stand up if you support Johan!' and dutifully the crowd would get to their feet.

Directors, recognising that Cruyff's popularity meant there was no chance of his challenge fading away, gave him a seat on the board in February 2011. Grumpily, he accepted, outlining his proposals for reform, making clear he felt there had to be changes of personnel and that the manager, Frank de Boer, had to be given more responsibility. 'At one point we gave a presentation of our plans,' Cruyff told the *VI* journalist Simon Zwartkruis. 'There was a chart on the table showing how power was distributed within the club. At the top was the supervisory board. Underneath that, the board of directors. Then you had marketing and finance. Some distance below were the first team and the youth team. So I asked the marketing guy, if the first team was ever to lose, how do you sell it? The answer was, then I sell nothing. Then I asked the finance guy, if the first team is losing, do you make profit or loss? The answer: we make a loss. Then I asked the board what they could accomplish if the first team loses. Same answer: nothing. That way, we tried to make it clear that when in football, everything stands or falls with the first team. And I told them I know how to make that good.'

At the end of March, Coronel and the rest of the board resigned on the understanding they would remain in their posts until replacements were found. On 6 June, Cruyff was appointed to the new board of advisors, although he insisted he had 'a weird feeling' about it from the start.

After months of sniping and backbiting, matters came to a head in November when Van Gaal was appointed to be general director. That was a move calculated to infuriate Cruyff, all the more so as the board waited until he was in Barcelona for his daughter's birthday to make the decision. 'You think you're on the right road,' Cruyff fumed, 'and suddenly this happens.'

With Cruyff only too aware that there was no way Van Gaal would be able to follow a plan drawn up by anybody else, he took legal action against Ajax NV (the public company that runs the club) and the club's other four commissioners – Steven ten Have, Marjan

Olfers, Paul Römer and Edgar Davids. In December, a court in Haarlem approved Van Gaal's appointment, only to suspend it to gauge the confidence of shareholders in the supervisory board. As Ajax NV appealed against that ruling, Van Gaal became increasingly convinced he couldn't take up the position. In February 2012, the court ruled that the appointment was not valid 'because of serious flaws in the notification process'.

Van Gaal departed, but not without a swipe at Cruyff. 'People say that Ajax are now following a Cruyff line,' he said in an interview with *De Telegraaf*. 'That's nonsense! There is no more a Cruyff line than there is a Van Gaal line. There is only an Ajax line and that has been in place for at least 25 years. I have contributed to that just as Cruyff has, with the difference that I was there longer.' He insisted that the vaunted 'Cruyff Plan' for individual development was essentially the same programme he'd implemented when he had been technical director back in 2004.

All five commissioners, Cruyff included, resigned which, if anything, strengthened his position. From Barcelona he pulled the strings while those loyal to him purged Ajax of his opponents. A new board was appointed. This time Cruyff was not a part of it, but it didn't matter: they were his men in charge; his spirit had conquered the club.

Jongkind was promoted to head of talent development at De Toekomst and, from 2012, implemented the Cruyff Plan. He describes the Cruyffian philosophy as having 'five pillars':

1. 'Attractive football' that is enjoyable both to watch and to play.
2. 'To produce home-grown players ... it's important to have a youth system which produces the core of your team.'

3. 'A system of smart transfers' which has two main component parts. The new signings should not 'block upcoming youth' and there should be 'a direct reinforcement for the team … from a technical, tactical point of view as well as a behavioural point of view'.

4. 'A high-performance culture … a flat organisation, with direct lines of communication, clear task responsibilities, and a lot of freedom but freedom with responsibilities.' Jongkind links this to Stephen R. Covey's business and self-help book *The Seven Habits of Highly Effective People*.

These four pillars, Jongkind believes, 'lead to quality and results' but must go hand-in-hand with a fifth pillar, an 'individual approach' to the home-grown players. There was also a recognition that it wasn't enough to develop young players from Amsterdam: Ajax had to look abroad and try to spread their philosophy to what were, in effect, feeder clubs.

As though the whiff of Cruyff was itself enough, Ajax won the title in 2011, ending the seven-year drought by beating the leaders Twente on the final day with a goal from the youth-team product Siem de Jong. De Boer managed to remain largely neutral through the wrangling. When pushed on the issue, he'd insist he was loyal to Cruyff, but he was also clear that, having played under him at both Ajax and Barcelona, he owed a lot to Van Gaal as well.

Edwin van der Sar became director of marketing, Marc Overmars was made sporting director and Dennis Bergkamp, having been assistant manager of the under-19s side, became De Boer's assistant. The training ground was dominated by former players, who would vote to settle disputes; Bergkamp had far more influence than most assistants. Spending on transfers was checked.

Ajax kept winning. De Boer's first championship was followed by three more as Ajax won four in a row for the first time in their history. But somehow that wasn't enough. 'While they might have been successful in the league,' Cruyff wrote in his autobiography, 'the quality of the football they were playing was variable, and it was clear that there was still a long way to go to reach our shared goal. Unfortunately, success tends to overshadow well-intentioned criticism.' The style wasn't quite right, it was too functional at times, too focused on holding the ball without necessarily looking to hurt the opponent, too much influenced by Van Gaal; there was rarely much sense of a Plan B beyond throwing a central defender forward and going long to him if the original idea hadn't worked. 'It was defensive possession,' Jongkind said, 'and that's something he [Cruyff] really disliked.'

There were other frustrations. Jongkind wanted Ajax to spend the money they were making on transfers on overseas investment, particularly in Ajax Cape Town, the South African club of which Ajax are the majority shareholder. 'The children were still training without food,' he said, 'and meanwhile the CEO was driving around in a Lamborghini. Really bad situation. Good talent over there, but no investment, "too difficult blah blah blah".'

Disillusionment perhaps necessarily follows any revolution: no reality can ever quite live up to the rhetoric of the campaign; no group of people – Dutch football people, perhaps, in particular – can ever agree for long; compromise and idealism rarely sit well together. Cruyff was sceptical about both Van der Sar and Overmars. 'They were educated in a country that doesn't actually count from a tactical point of view,' he said: England. 'And the English have never been that keen on tactics, so you couldn't expect them to take my tactical message on board.'

But then Cruyff never saw anything he didn't think he could do better. A journalist from *VI* tells the story of taking a walk with Cruyff through Amsterdam. As they passed two road workers on their knees, he told them they hadn't removed enough pebbles before beginning to lay the paving stones. Recognising their critic, neither said anything. A little later, a woman passed on a bike, holding a cigarette between her fingers. 'You shouldn't smoke on a bike,' Cruyff told her. 'It's not healthy.' She too didn't reply.

Cruyff moaning was Cruyff being Cruyff and, in a sense, relatively easy to dismiss. But he wasn't the only one beginning to doubt the revolution's progress. Jongkind was critical of 'all the wrong transfers'. When the central defender Toby Alderweireld left for Atlético, for instance, Ajax turned down the opportunity to sign Virgil van Dijk from Groningen for around €3m, and instead bought Mike van der Hoorn from Utrecht for €3.8m. Van der Hoorn never settled and Joël Veltman emerged from the youth ranks to be Alderweireld's replacement. Similarly, when Ajax took Yaya Sanogo on loan from Arsenal, it emerged they had barely scouted him and had simply gone on Arsène Wenger's recommendation. He started just three games for the club.

'We warned them beforehand,' Jongkind said. '"Don't buy this guy, don't buy that guy, we have a guy coming up." A lot of money was lost. Another pillar which was not followed. During many meetings, Cruyff tried in a very constructive way, and I was present, to change their minds to follow the plan.

'Of course, we did some things wrong on our part too. We went too fast, we didn't inform people well enough. If I look back, we should've done that differently. But still, the overall picture was that we followed the strategy.

'Another pillar that was not followed was "attractive football". People were really, really disappointed by the way we played, especially the fans.'

Jonk, meanwhile, became frustrated that meetings with the supervisory board tended to focus on, as Jongkind put it, 'how much holiday a trainer in the under-12s took, or that someone saw a physiotherapist training with the ball on Field 13' rather than transfer policy and playing style. Jonk stopped going to the meetings, at which the supervisory board, arguing that attendance was mandated by his contract, threatened to fire him. That created a split and in 2015, Jonk and Jongkind both left their posts while Cruyff asked to be dissociated from what was going on at the club. Twenty-four other staff also left. 'Overmars, Bergkamp and Van der Sar, who all got their positions thanks to the work Johan had done with us, decided to choose the side of the board and go against Johan and us,' Jongkind said. 'Even people like [Saïd] Ouaali, for whom Jonk had fought so hard to get him in, stabbed Jonk in the back and took Jonk's position as Head of Academy.'

\* \* \*

Even if the takeover had been entirely successful, it wouldn't have been enough. Ajax weren't the only club to have strayed from the one true path. After leaving Ajax in 2005, Ronald Koeman had gone to Benfica, but his time there was less than successful and he left after a year to take over from Guus Hiddink at PSV. 'The club,' noted *de Volkskrant*, 'was looking for a Dutch trainer who speaks Spanish.' Koeman certainly did that. Even at that stage, though, his tactical approach was seen as non-conformist. 'He is not a trainer that guarantees spectacular football,' the same article went on. 'At Ajax he deviated from the system preached in Amsterdam by playing strikers on the wings.'

By the following February, the same newspaper was reluctantly hailing Koeman as 'a results coach'. There had been a 1-0 victory over Ajax rooted in sitting deep and striking on the break and then, more impressively, victory over Arsenal in the first qualifying round of the Champions League. The home leg was won 1-0 thanks to Koeman's ploy of having his two central strikers split and take up wide positions to block in the Arsenal full-backs. 'Our tactical plan worked,' Koeman said. 'Arsenal are great when you lose the ball but if they have to build up from defence they hardly create any chances. It was obvious that their central defenders, who are used to marking someone, did not know what to do without a direct opponent.'

Although he still tended to play 4-3-3 that season, Koeman was more than willing to tweak the system for individual games. Arsène Wenger had complained even in 2002-03 about the 'negativity' of Koeman's Ajax against his side; on this occasion he was dismissive, saying PSV had 'played for a 0-0'. The seeds of Koeman's dissent, perhaps, had been sown at Ajax but had begun to flourish as he moved away from Amsterdam.

PSV began that season superbly but three key injuries meant they faltered in the second half of the season, taking just 19 of a possible 39 points and allowing Ajax and AZ back into the title race. A 5-1 victory over Vitesse on the final day, though, meant the title was won. Koeman, after much discussion, stayed on but by October he was gone, opting to move to Spain and take over at Valencia.

Koeman did win the Copa del Rey, but his time at Valencia was largely a disappointment and he was sacked in April 2008 with the team 15th in the table, just two points above the relegation zone. After Van Gaal had gone to Bayern, Koeman took over AZ in the summer of 2009 but he was fired by Christmas as the champions won just seven of their first 16 games of the season. It wasn't until

July 2011 that he was considered employable again, and then only by Feyenoord, who had just finished tenth in the league. They may be one of the traditional big three in the Netherlands, but they hadn't won the league since 1999. There were few expectations and the demand was simply for success, however it might be achieved. He got them to second in his first season. They fell to third the following season but then struggled at the beginning of 2013-14, losing their first four games in all competitions. There was a slow improvement but when they lost 2-1 to Ajax at the beginning of March, they were still only fourth. For the following game, away at Groningen, Koeman made a radical change, switching from his usual 4-2-3-1 to a system with three central defenders. This was emphatically not a Cruyffian 3-4-3; rather it was a very traditional 5-3-2 with Stefan de Vrij, Joris Mathijsen and Bruno Martins Indi presenting a solid central defensive block.

The game was won 2-0 and the back three experiment was quietly left to one side for a month before being employed gain for a 2-0 away win at PSV. Feyenoord ended up second again that season, thanks largely to a run of seven straight wins that began in Groningen. That victory in Eindhoven, though, would have far-reaching consequences.

# CHAPTER NINE

# THE ONGOING
# STORM

Cussed, awkward and dogmatic as Louis van Gaal was, he turned out to be far less fundamentalist than many post-Cruyffians. He had demonstrated that in Alkmaar with his counter-attacking approach, but AZ were AZ. They were far from a giant even in a Dutch context. The Netherlands national team was something else. If they didn't follow the Dutch school, then who would? Amid the soul-searching that followed the 2010 World Cup, Van Gaal, as somebody raised in the Ajax tradition, was seen as just the man to restore traditional values.

For a while he did. The Dutch qualified for the 2014 World Cup by taking 28 points from a possible 30. Nobody in the UEFA section had a goal difference as good as their +29. But Van Gaal wasn't convinced. Smashing Hungary 8-1 or Romania 4-0 is no great preparation for the final stages of a major tournament. A friendly against France in Paris the March before the World Cup brought matters to a head. The Netherlands lost 2-0, convincing Van Gaal that his defenders struggled in individual duels and so needed some additional form of protection. Even worse, four days later, playing for Roma against Napoli, Kevin Strootman, his playmaking deep-lying midfielder, suffered a serious knee injury, ruling him out of the finals.

The following month, Van Gaal took Robin van Persie to watch Ronald Koeman's Feyenoord win 2-0 away at PSV. He may have disliked and distrusted Koeman but in his side he had seen his solution. Feyenoord deployed a back three that was often a back five and didn't look to dominate possession but sat off and hit PSV on the break. It was not Total Football, nothing like it, but it was effective.

'With this system you defensively build some more certainty,' Koeman explained to *VI*, 'while attacking you can also take the initiative. *Oranje* have the players there too. Someone like Wesley Sneijder might work well in a tactical variant with some more certainty behind him. Everybody knows that *Oranje* is in a difficult situation and it will not be easy to survive.' In addition, three of the defenders Van Gaal intended to use in Brazil – Daryl Janmaat, Bruno Martins Indi and Stefan de Vrij – were in the Feyenoord side and so had some familiarity with the system.

Van Gaal used the new formation in two of the remaining three friendlies before the World Cup. Its impact was inconclusive – a 1-1 draw against Ecuador and a 1-0 win over Ghana – but after a switch back to 4-2-3-1 in a 2-0 win over Wales, the Dutch began their first game of the World Cup, against Spain in Salvador, with a three-man central defence. That in part, Van Gaal explained, was 'because of the quality and the profile of my defenders' and in part 'to provoke the space behind the defenders of our opponents'.

There was criticism from those who thought the Dutch should only play a 4-3-3 but for Van Gaal stylistic principles overrode concerns about the formation. 'I believe in this system also because the covering over the pitch is fantastic…' he said. 'You have always triangles … always occupation of the width. I wanted Van Persie, Robben and Sneijder as my creators. Then I changed because I found at the training sessions that they were not strong enough, not connecting well with each other.' His solution was to shift Nigel de Jong – 'normally not my favourite player at the six position, a more defensive type' – to a position in front of the back three and to pull Sneijder deeper rather than using him as a number ten. 'I thought I needed him to put Van Persie and Robben free on the goalkeeper,' Van Gaal said, 'but they were good enough to do it because they liked the freedom I gave them. Sneijder didn't like his structural task but he did it for me so it was good.'

Spain were not just any opponent. They were the world and double European champions and, more than that, had reached their position of supremacy by adopting a more cautious version of the approach that had taken Barcelona to their two Champions League successes under Guardiola. There were five Barça players in Spain's starting XI; two of them, Xavi and Iniesta, had played under Van Gaal, while Piqué had been dismissed by him as not tough enough. Only one side in that game played the classic Dutch way and it wasn't the Netherlands. Xabi Alonso put Spain ahead from the penalty spot but Robin van Persie equalised just before half-time with a remarkable diving header from the edge of the box.

What happened in the second half was wholly unexpected, a resounding vindication for Van Gaal. Arjen Robben's pace, in an unexpected second striker role behind Van Persie, devastated Spain. He scored twice as the Dutch won 5-1. They wouldn't quite reach those heights again in the tournament but a third-place finish was far better than anybody had anticipated – and came to look even better as the Netherlands failed even to qualify for Euro 2016 or the 2018 World Cup. But the style was a concern. It wasn't the brute physicality of Bert van Marwijk's side four years earlier but there were those, Cruyff among them, who saw the 5-3-2 as a betrayal of the Dutch tradition. Van Gaal's response was characteristically blunt. 'I have been appointed,' he said, 'to win.' Maybe so, but that was a significant step away from the idealism of ten or 15 years earlier, and a significant step away from the ideals Cruyff was trying to reinstil at Ajax. The classic Dutch principles may have carried Guardiola's Barcelona to great heights, but they increasingly seemed to have little place in the Netherlands, despite Cruyff's efforts.

* * *

Mourinho, perhaps, had changed. As he rejoined Chelsea in 2013, he spoke of being 'the happy one'. He seemed mellower, and that seemed reasonable. What, after all, did he have left to prove? In the 11 years since taking over at Porto, he'd won two Champions Leagues, a UEFA Cup, seven league titles and six domestic cups. He'd toppled Guardiola. He'd left Madrid in strained circumstances, but who didn't? He'd been their longest-serving manager in a decade. And he was back at a club where he had been adored, by players and fans – and by the media. There were a handful who had been captivated by him on a personal or tactical level but, beyond that, the return of a man whose every press conference could turn into a week of back-page leads was welcomed to the extent that the Football Writers' Association chose to honour Mourinho at their annual tribute dinner in January 2014. Yet even then, six months after his reappointment, the old narratives were beginning to play out again.

The happy Mourinho had begun the season seemingly trying to play expansive football, as though even he had begun to wonder whether his thinking had become overly negative. He regularly used Óscar, Eden Hazard and one other (Kevin De Bruyne, Juan Mata, André Schürrle or Willian) behind a striker. There were some promising runs – a block of three wins against Norwich, Cardiff and Manchester City in which Chelsea scored nine, and another streak of three wins, against Southampton, West Ham and Sunderland in which they scored ten – but no real consistency. By mid-December, 16 games into the season, Chelsea were second behind Arsenal but there was a clear sense that this wasn't quite a Mourinho side. In the win over Sunderland, in which Hazard had been sensational, they'd let in three. They'd also lost 2-0 at Newcastle and 3-2 at Stoke and been very fortunate to get away with a 2-2 draw at home to West Bromwich Albion with a disputed late penalty. This certainly wasn't the ruthless Chelsea of his first spell in charge.

An extra-time defeat in a League Cup quarter-final at Sunderland forced a change. Afterwards, Mourinho looked tired and dishevelled. Others might have dismissed the significance of elimination from the secondary cup competition but it had been good to him in the past – he'd never lost a League Cup tie in 90 minutes until the quarter-final defeat to Bristol City in December 2017 – and he was clearly both angry and concerned. He spoke of the need to return to basics. By a quirk of the fixture list, he had nine days before Chelsea played again and when they did, they stifled Arsenal at the Emirates in a tedious 0-0 draw. Afterwards, Mourinho seemed almost gleeful; there was a sense that the old style had returned and with it some of the old swagger.

But that meant the self-consciously relaxed Mourinho of the early part of the season had gone as well. That January, at the FWA tribute dinner – attended by most of the Chelsea hierarchy but not Abramovich – he spoke of wanting to stay in the job for life. For a moment it was possible to believe that he thought he had returned home and dreamt of founding an empire, but then came a classic Mourinho inversion. Perhaps he was seeking merely, out of gratitude to his hosts, to express his love for England, but given subsequent events it looks like a warning: if he were to be sacked, Mourinho said, he wouldn't leave, he wouldn't seek a job in Italy or Spain again, he wouldn't even return to Portugal; he would stay and manage another Premier League club.

Not that anybody was thinking of that then. Their solidity bolstered by the re-signing of Nemanja Matić in January, Chelsea went unbeaten through the following 13 league games, during which they conceded just four goals. Hazard, in particular, played excellently, although his relationship with his manager was never straightforward. From the start, Mourinho would provoke Hazard in front of the squad, telling the team, 'Today we're playing with ten', to try to goad him into great defensive effort. Initially, Hazard, used to more overtly supportive managers, was troubled. 'If he looks you in the eye, it's terrifying,' he said. But Hazard is not a natural rebel. He accepted his manager's ways, even if he preferred to go home and spend time with his family after training rather than staying at Cobham for extra gym work.

However well Chelsea were playing, though, Mourinho was adamant his side was not ready to win the Premier League. 'The title race is between two horses and a little horse that needs milk and needs to learn how to jump,' he said that February. 'Maybe next season we can race.'

On 8 March, Chelsea went seven points clear at the top by beating Tim Sherwood's Tottenham 4-0. They had played a game more than Arsenal and Liverpool, and three more than City who were two points further back, but they seemed to have the remorselessness of champions, that same implacable quality they had had in their first two seasons under Mourinho.

But Chelsea then went to Aston Villa and had Willian, Ramires and their manager sent off as they lost 1-0. They responded by beating Arsenal 6-0 in Arsène Wenger's 1,000th game in management, but then lost 1-0 at Crystal Palace.

Four days later, Chelsea lost 3-1 away to Paris Saint-Germain in the Champions League quarter-final, only to rouse themselves to win

2-0 in the second leg with a typical Mourinho performance. Every stage of the game, John Terry revealed afterwards, had been planned in advance: the players knew exactly what substitutions were going to be made when, depending on whether they were still chasing the game or not, even down to the remarkable system with three centre-forwards plus Schürrle plus Willian they used for the final ten minutes when in need of a vital second goal. This was the Mourinho of Porto, predicting and shaping the future. When Demba Ba scored the winner with three minutes remaining, Mourinho even celebrated as he had in his Porto days, charging down the touchline to join his players as they piled in a gleeful heap by the corner flag.

A 0-0 draw away to Atlético in the first leg of the semi-final seemed promising, particularly when Fernando Torres gave them the lead eight minutes before half-time in the second leg, but they ended up losing 3-1 at Stamford Bridge. Unwisely, Hazard suggested on Belgian television that Chelsea were rather better at counter-attacking than they were at taking the game to the opposition, a perceived criticism that prompted Mourinho into a public response. 'Eden is the kind of player who is not so mentally ready to look back at his left-back and give his life for him,' he said.

In the league, there were wins over Stoke and Swansea but Chelsea went down 2-1 at home to a Sunderland side rousing themselves for another great escape. It was Mourinho's first ever league defeat at Stamford Bridge and it handed the advantage in the title race to Liverpool and Manchester City. Their next game, the fourth-last of the season, was at Anfield.

A draw would have kept Liverpool ahead of Manchester City. Their manager Brendan Rodgers had espoused a philosophy perhaps best described as Barcelona-lite before that season adopting a more direct approach to make best use of the pace of Luis Suárez, Raheem

Sterling and Daniel Sturridge. Mourinho turned to his Madrid manual for big games. Chelsea spoiled and wasted time from the off, set their back four deep and almost never played out through it, showed little interest in the ball, had 23 per cent possession and won because of a Steven Gerrard slip just before half-time and a late goal on the break from Willian. Wait long enough and the opponent will eventually make a mistake: 'Whoever has the ball has fear.' Mourinho made his point and City won the title.

* * *

Confirmation that Vilanova was too ill to carry on forced Barcelona into a decision. The success of Guardiola had led to a general commitment to appoint always from within, to preserve the ideological line, but events can overwhelm the best-laid and best-intentioned of plans. The Athletic coach Ernesto Valverde was considered, but they ended up appointing the Argentinian Gerardo 'Tata' Martino.

The reasoning wasn't hard to fathom. Martino, like Messi, was from Rosario and seemingly had the support of his compatriot. He had played for Bielsa's great Newell's Old Boys' side of the early nineties and, although he was far more pragmatic than Bielsa, he had a clear grounding in his principles suggesting he should be able to adapt to the environment Guardiola and Vilanova had left at the Camp Nou.

Martino moved into coaching in 1998 and pursued a peripatetic career. When he returned to Newell's in 2012, it was his ninth club in 14 years, five of which had been spent with the Paraguay national team, taking them to the quarter-finals of the 2010 World Cup and the final of the Copa América in 2011. He had won three Paraguayan titles across two spells at Libertad.

He returned home holding his nose, calling Argentinian football 'hysterical' and 'dirty' and lamenting the physicality of a game in which the result overshadows everything else. 'Aesthetics are despised,' he said in an interview in *La Nación*. 'Some would say that a game was bad and finished 2-1 but others make you think it was a great match.'

The focus on process rather than results was a classic trope of the *bielsistas* and Cruyffians but it sat a little uneasily with how his Paraguay had played. Back at Newell's, though, he readopted something closer to the classic *bielsista* model, taking a side that had finished 18th and sixth in the previous season's Apertura and Clausura and shaping them into a purposeful, attractive team. Perhaps they didn't score as many goals as some would have liked but they pressed hard, defended well and passed neatly. And then, like so many *bielsista* teams, they ran out of steam on the run-in, surrendering the Torneo Inicial* to Vélez Sarsfield. But they regrouped and came back refreshed for the Torneo Final, winning it by three points and answering criticism of their lack of goals return by racking up 40 in 19 games, 12 more than anybody else. Their Copa Libertadores run was ended only by a penalty shoot-out defeat to Atlético Mineiro in the semi-final.

Past record, though, was only a small part of it. Vilanova's only experience as a club coach, after all, had been to relegate Palafrugell out of the Tercera and neither Guardiola nor Rijkaard would have got the job had their managerial CVs been the most important consid-

---

* From 1990, the Argentinian season was split into two halves: the Apertura and Clausura. In 1990-91 the winners of each played off for the championship; thereafter two championships were awarded each season. The format was changed again in 2012-13, with the two halves of the season renamed Inicial and Final; each of which was accorded the status of a championship but the winners played off for a third championship, the 'Campeonato' (which Vélez won 1-0 in a game played in Mendoza). Even in Argentina, a country that revels in bewildering formats, that was considered absurd and the play-off was abandoned for 2013-14, after which, following a transitional half-season championship, one league title was awarded per season. By then the top flight consisted of 30 teams, each playing everybody else once, apart from a designated rival whom they played twice.

eration. Far more significant were his beliefs about how the game should be played and specifically that he had been influenced by Bielsa, whom Guardiola had visited in Rosario to discuss his theories before taking the Barcelona job.

Martino, though, was far from the biggest arrival at Barcelona in the summer of 2013. Neymar signed from Santos for a reported fee of €57.1m. That would later turn out to have actually been €86.2m, a discrepancy that had far-reaching ramifications. The season began for Barcelona with two major questions: would Messi and Neymar be able to function in the same side, and would Martino be able to impose himself and restore the intensity that had been lost the previous season, particularly given how little time he was given before the start of the campaign? The answers soon became apparent, the latter proving far more troublesome than the former.

For somebody who supposedly prioritised the process over the results, Martino had a very strange start to the season. Barcelona went 20 games undefeated. They took the Spanish Super Cup on away goals against Atlético. They beat Carlo Ancelotti's Real Madrid in the first *Clásico* of the season and established a comfortable lead at the top of the table. Their style, Fàbregas said, had become more 'anarchic': they were more direct, less controlled. They got the ball forward quicker, but they lost it more often as well. In a 4-0 win away to Rayo Vallecano on the fifth weekend of the season, they had less than 50 per cent possession in a game for the first time in five years. Even then, doubts began to be expressed: was this really the style Barça wanted to be playing? Was this remaining true to Cruyffianism?

They lost away to De Boer's Ajax in the fifth group game in the Champions League. In practical terms, it didn't matter. They were already through. But it did matter a little, perhaps, both because it brought to the surface a lot of anxieties that had been festering for a year or more, and because it was against Ajax, in whose name there would always be an echo of the standards to which Barça aspired. Martino, seemingly contradicting the view he'd expressed in *La Nación*, said he'd happily take another run of 21 games with only one defeat.

But the next defeat came in the very next game. When they went down 1-0 in Bilbao against Athletic the following weekend, those anxieties burst forth. That game may have marked Barça's 53rd successive week at the top of La Liga, equalling the record set by the Real Madrid of Emilio Butragueño and his Quinta del Buitre 25 years earlier, but *Sport*'s front page screamed, 'That is not our Barça!'

Martino, mystifyingly given what he'd said after the Ajax defeat, and given that Barça were at that point still top of the table, attacked journalists for focusing only on results, then suggested he wouldn't have been given such a hard time had he been 'Dutch or from within'. He, like Bobby Robson, seemed bewildered by the *entorno* and the politicking around the club. He did, though, have a point: the defeat in Bilbao had been given added edge by the fact that Athletic's coach was Valverde, somebody who had seemed a possible appointment at the Camp Nou since the dog days of Rijkaard's reign.

Barça won their next seven games. They didn't lose for 13 games. At the end of January they were top of the league with 54 points from 20 games, level on points with Atlético and a point clear of Real Madrid. But none of it felt right. Only at Barcelona in the age of the superclubs could six points dropped in 20 games have been seen as a crisis, but it was, compounded as Sandro Rosell was forced to resign as president over irregularities in the signing of Neymar.

A 1-0 defeat at lowly Valladolid at the beginning of March was their third in six league games. 'The players threw away the league … and we were ashamed of them,' *Sport* raged, as Xavi made excuses about the state of the pitch. Again there came a rally and again Messi was at the heart of it. He scored a hat-trick in a barely credible 4-3 victory in the *Clásico* at the Bernabéu and when Madrid then lost to Sevilla, Barça had the title back in their grasp. They beat Manchester City to reach a Champions League quarter-final against Atlético, but then came the reckoning.

They drew the first leg 1-1 at the Camp Nou. When Koke put Atleti ahead five minutes into the second leg, there still seemed plenty of time to get back into the game. They didn't use it. Barça were desperately uninspired and could easily have lost more heavily. In the space of a week, their season collapsed. Three days after defeat at the Vicente Calderón, Barça lost away to Granada in the league, surrendering the initiative to Atlético. Four days after that, Real Madrid beat them in the final of the Copa del Rey. 'Tataclysm,' as *El Mundo Deportivo* had it. Martino had never had time to properly assess the job, had been plunged into a difficult situation at an extremely difficult time, and then, their editor Santi Nolla, a committed Guardiola sceptic, later wrote, 'the fundamentalists destroyed him for not respecting the model'.

The problems, though, went far beyond the manager and the style of play he had encouraged. Pre-season had been a shambles, an extended tour from Germany to Norway to Poland to Malaysia to Thailand that allowed little time for either tactical or fitness work. The result was a crippling lack of sharpness in the final third of the season. The failure to sign a central defender left Barça exposed as Mascherano lost form. Their pressing game lacked any of the intensity of the Guardiola years.

But the biggest fear of all was age. Puyol had announced he would retire at 35. Víctor Valdés had decided to move on. Xavi was 33. All the talk had been of the *cantera* and the production line of talent that could slot into the first team, but players such as Bojan Krkić, Cristian

Tello and Ángel Cuéllar had not developed in the way that had been hoped. Perhaps it was unreasonable to expect them to. As Piqué acknowledged, it might be that the generation that had emerged from La Masia over a handful of seasons – Iniesta, Messi, Xavi, Víctor Valdes, Busquets, Pedro, himself – was 'unique'; Barça had to face up to the possibility that 'it might not happen again'.

\* \* \*

Exhausted by his final season at Barcelona, Guardiola spent 2012-13 on a sabbatical in New York. There were rumours that he might move to Manchester City but, in January 2013, it was announced that he would replace Jupp Heynckes as coach of Bayern Munich at the end of the season. Heynckes would be 68 by then and, it was said at the time, had told the club before Christmas that he wished to retire. Subsequent reports suggested the situation was perhaps not quite as comfortable as that. There was, though, no public complaint from Heynckes. He just got on with the business of winning the first treble in Bayern's history. They finished 25 points clear of Borussia Dortmund in the league, losing just once. They beat Stuttgart in the final of the Cup and they won the Champions League at Wembley, beating Dortmund in the final.

The semi-finals, of course, had been almost more significant than the final as Bayern and Dortmund had beaten Barça and Madrid, looking quicker, stronger and sharper, their systematic pressing and counter-attacking overwhelming the possession-focused approach of the Spanish sides. There had been predictable snide comments about Bayern's folly in appointing as their new manager the high priest of a style their outgoing manager had just exposed, but that was to miss the point. The new German style was less an antidote to the Spanish game than a variant of it. What clouded the issue was the focus on possession. Barcelona at their best, like Ajax before them, had excelled not merely at keeping the ball but at winning it back and it was that aspect of the game, followed by rapid transitions, that characterised the German approach.

Besides, as Louis van Gaal put it in characteristic style, the appointment made sense on an ideological level. 'Guardiola follows the Van Gaal philosophy, so I'm not surprised Bayern have hired Guardiola,' he said. 'Bayern always hire the best managers.' Van Gaal had done what Klinsmann had been brought in to do and instilled a sense of modernity, moved the club on from its obsession with grit, effort and *Führungsspieler*.* 'Van Gaal represents the crucial turning point,' said Lahm. 'He introduced a specific idea of the game – a striker, two wingers, two defensive midfielders – and shaped the club with this philosophy.' Heynckes had been adaptable enough to build on Van Gaal's work, to carry on pressing.

Van Gaal was never shy of claiming credit for what his successors later achieved but here he seemed to have a case: appointing Guardiola was another stage in the process of changing the culture of the club. Not that Hoeneß saw it that way. 'His problem,' he told *De Telegraaf,* 'is that Louis doesn't think he's God – but God the Father. Before the world came into existence, Louis was already there. But the world doesn't work as he sees it.'

Whatever groundwork had been done, this was a major test of Guardiola's interpretation of post-Cruyffianism, whether it could be applied outside the unique environment of Barcelona and whether it was still at the cutting edge of the game. After Mourinho's title success and Chelsea's Champions League semi-final victory in Guardiola's last

---

* Literally 'leader player'; as Raphael Honigstein outlines in *Das Reboot*, until the late nineties German football tended to focus on the psychological aspect of sides rather than their tactical make-up.

season in Spain, and then the strides made by German clubs, there were reasons for doubt and Guardiola did not find adaptation an easy process.

'When I first arrived in Munich,' he said, 'I thought I could more or less transfer Barça's game to Bayern, but what I actually did was marry the two. I brought the Barça philosophy and adapted it to Bayern and the players there.' That willingness to adapt has led some, most notably Martí Perarnau, to assert that there is no 'guardiolisme'. At best, though, that's a semantic point. Just because Guardiola can be flexible doesn't mean that he doesn't have core tenets that guide his decision-making, just as Van Gaal increasingly adapted his philosophy according to circumstance as his career progressed. Again and again Guardiola has come into press conferences and has dealt with scepticism, real or perceived, about his side's emphasis on attack by saying, 'Sorry, guys, this is how I play...' while Perarnau himself lists 'ten main pillars' of Guardiola's philosophy, which can be summarised as playing high up the pitch, maintaining structural discipline, spreading the play as wide as possible and using possession as both an attacking and defensive tool – but not, crucially, as an end in itself.

That final point is perhaps the one that requires the greatest emphasis because it explains why Guardiola loathes the term 'tiki-taka', which was habitually applied to his style at Barcelona. It is, he says, 'total shit. It's a meaningless concept which basically describes passing the ball for the sake of passing. Aimlessly, with no aggression or particular plan.' That apparent rejection of a theory with which for a time he was commonly credited (in the English-speaking world at least) has caused some confusion, but the issue, surely, is that the use of the term differs from country to country. In Spain, the term was coined by the former Athletic coach Javier Clemente to deride what he saw as the pretty-pretty approach of Barça; it was initially a term of abuse. It was subsequently applied by English speakers to the Cruyf-fian doctrine that Guardiola would term '*juego de posición*' to describe the possession-focused approach that has characterised Barcelona since Rijkaard took over.

There's no reason to doubt Guardiola when he insists that the possession is a by-product of the positional strategy rather than an end in itself, but Cruyff always stressed that when you have the ball, the opposition cannot score. As time has gone by, Guardiola, perhaps, came to prioritise the positional aspects more than his great mentor. Overhead shots of Bayern's Säbener Straße training ground from Guardiola's time there show a couple of pitches divided into zones. The lines marking the penalty areas are extended for the full length and width of the pitch, while the vertical lines marking the sides of the six-yard box are picked up again at the edge of the 18-yard box and extended to the edge of the other 18-yard box. The zones nearest the touchlines are then split again, halfway between the 18-yard and halfway lines. The pitch is thus divided into 20 zones: five vertical bands by four horizontal ones. The basic idea of *juego de posición* is that players adjust their position according to which zone the ball is in. But that's just the foundation: ideally players should be flexible enough to fill a zone that would, in the initial template, be filled by somebody else, creating a level of rotation to overman in key areas while maintaining a structure that should both offer passing options and maintain a defensive shape that can react effectively to the loss of possession and a counter-attack by being immediately prepared to counter-press.

At its simplest level, the zone principle should mean that no more than three players are in a line horizontally and no more than two vertically: if a player moves into a zone that means four in the same horizontal line are occupied, one of the other three should automatically move. That should ensure that the man on the ball always has two or three passing options. That allows possession to be retained – the endless *rondos* that Guardiola favours in training making his players supremely adept at giving and receiving the ball in tight spaces – which is why, he would claim, his sides regularly have so much possession.

Possession is a metric that must always be taken in context, a gauge less of *how well* a side plays than *how* it plays, but the change in style from Heynckes to Guardiola is undeniably striking. Completed passes per game rose from 567 per game to 726, average possession from 61.35 per cent to 70.47 per cent. According to Perarnau, the defensive line under Heynckes was at an average 36.1m from goal; by the third season under Guardiola it was at 48.5m, so that eight of the team had an average position in the opposition half.

When it is not aimed directly at the opposition goal, passing is designed to allow the team to generate the right structure, whether to mount an attack or to be prepared to counter-press. Guardiola has said it takes 15 passes for that structure to be created. There is, in other words, a direct link between offensive and defensive strategies, and no demand for the instant transition to attack that characterises Bielsa or Klopp. This is pure Cruyff. 'To be able to attack,' he wrote in his autobiography, 'you have to defend by pushing forward, and in order to do that you have to put pressure on the ball. To make this as easy as possible … you have to create as many lines as you can. The man with the ball will always then have someone in front of him and someone behind him. The space between the man with the ball and these two teammates should never be more than ten metres.'

That is linked to the way in which the team attacks. 'Do you know how Barcelona win the ball back so quickly?' Cruyff asked during Guardiola's spell as coach at the Camp Nou. 'It's because they don't have to run back more than ten metres as they never pass the ball more than ten metres.' Instilling those positional ideas is difficult. While basic elements such as a holding midfielder dropping between the two centre-backs to overman when playing out from the back against two centre-forwards, or even the full-back coming inside when the winger goes wide and vice versa, can be readily grasped, the principle of responding constantly to a mental pitch map is rather harder. At Barcelona, Guardiola was dealing with players who had been prepared for his extreme interpretation of the theory from their upbringing at La Masia; at Bayern, he was dealing with players who had been instructed in a (more cautious) variant of the philosophy by Van Gaal. At Manchester City, he was virtually starting from scratch, which is perhaps why implementation there proved so much trickier.

But whatever foundations had been left by Van Gaal, Guardiola found himself having to compromise. His Bayern played at a higher tempo, more verticality, than his Barça had. They also played in a far greater variety of formation as Guardiola began to adapt his own thinking. Whereas at Barça he'd essentially played either a 4-3-3 or a 3-4-3, at Bayern, according to Perarnau, he used 23 different formations (Bielsa has said there are 29 viable shapes in the modern game).

'Football obeys the players, not the managers,' Guardiola said as he was unveiled in June 2013. 'The fans come to see the players, not me. I will adapt 100 per cent to the high quality of players who are here.' Maybe so, but it didn't take long for Bayern's players to realise that, whatever the talk of continuity of philosophy, things would be very different under Guardiola.

'I've never had a manager who changed so many things,' the 34-year-old forward Claudio Pizarro said, while there was scepticism about such positional experiments as fielding the full-back Philipp Lahm in midfield and the striker Mario Mandžukić on the flanks.

'Pep Guardiola turns the most successful team in the history of Bayern Munich on its head,' *Der Spiegel* wrote from Bayern's training camp in Italy. 'The club's bosses are impressed by his enthusiasm – but also worried whether everything will turn out all right.'

Those worries soon faded. A 3-1 win away to Manchester City in the Champions League at the beginning of October was mesmerisingly brilliant. There was one period of three minutes and 27 seconds in which Bayern held the ball through a sequence of 94 passes. 'For 80 minutes this was a football that I have rarely seen in my life, against a team of the same standard,' said Uli Hoeneß. 'It was amazing how we passed the ball around.' Any doubt Bayern would win the league disappeared as they won 3-0 away to Dortmund the following month. That game showcased Guardiola's new versatility as he initially fielded Javi Martínez high up the pitch alongside Mandžukić, having his defence play long to bypass the Dortmund press, and then reverted to a false nine in the second half to exploit the spaces left by a panicking Dortmund.

The title was sealed with a 3-1 victory over Hertha Berlin at the end of March. In that game, they enjoyed a record 82.3 per cent possession and completed 1,078 passes, the first time any side in the Bundesliga had racked up four figures. Lahm, whose role in midfield no longer seemed outlandish, completed all 134 passes he attempted. It was Bayern's 20th win in a row, their 52nd game unbeaten. When Guardiola had arrived it had been asked where, after their Treble, he could take the club but downwards. That spring it seemed he might win another Treble – but win it better. The Cup did follow, but the Champions League did not.

Bayern beat Arsenal and then Manchester United to set up a semi-final against Real Madrid, who by then were managed by Carlo Ancelotti. They set out in the first leg in the Bernabéu, Guardiola said, 'to show they are real footballers, to take the ball and play, then play again'. After 18 minutes they had had 82 per cent of the ball. But then Madrid countered and Fabio Coentrão squared for Karim Benzema to score. Bayern continued to dominate the ball; Madrid continued to look the more dangerous. It finished 1-0. 'Possession,' Franz Beckenbauer said on Sky Italia, 'is meaningless if you give away chances. We should be grateful Madrid didn't score more.' That has always been the main criticism of the post-Cruyffian style: it may look pretty, but does it always hurt opponents?

During the post-match dinner in Madrid, Guardiola decided for the return leg he would play a 3-4-3. He also knew that the issue in Madrid hadn't just been tactical; Bayern's form had dipped after wrapping up the title, their intensity diminished. But on the flight home, he changed his mind. They hadn't used a back three since December: he would play a 4-2-3-1 that would liberate Arjen Robben and Franck Ribéry.

That Friday, Tito Vilanova died.

On the Saturday, Bayern beat Werder Bremen 5-2. Ribéry played well and Robben scored after coming off the bench, but there were defensive concerns.

Monday's training was light. Guardiola asked his players how they felt. They were excited. They spoke of great comebacks of the past. The desire that had disappeared after the Hertha game seemed to be back. Guardiola decided to yield to passion. He would attack, not with a 4-2-3-1 but with a 4-2-4. It was, he later said, 'the biggest fuck-up' of his career.

Madrid sat deep, counter-attacked at pace through Ángel Di María, and won 4-0 thanks to three goals from set plays.

\* \* \*

This was the great crisis of post-Cruyffianism. With Barcelona fading and Bayern thrashed in that semi-final, Spain's embarrassment at the World Cup seemed the continuation of a trend. Just as their rise had seemed an adjunct of Barcelona's success, so their fall reflected Barça's struggles. The 5-1 defeat to the Netherlands was met with a sense of shock. Only two World Cup matches, after all, had been played between their 1-0 victory in the previous final and the capitulation in Salvador. How could the Dutch suddenly seem so dynamic and modern? And especially when they were managed by a ghost of Barcelona's past in Van Gaal? It was only the third time Spain had conceded five in their history and the first time for 64 years. In the second half, like Bayern against Madrid – players conforming to style rather than nationality – they seemed lost, dazed, helpless against the counter-attacking thrusts.

Spain were only marginally better in their second game, beaten 2-0 by a dynamic and well-organised Chile side coached by Jorge Sampaoli, a devout *bielsista* whose approach, based on hard pressing and direct play, would lead to him being linked with the Barcelona job three years later. Spain were the fifth champions to be eliminated in the group stage of the following tournament and the third in the previous four tournaments, but they were the first to go out losing their opening two games.

To watch that defeat was to be reminded of Hemingway's observation on bankruptcy: the end came gradually, and then suddenly. There had been slight signs of vulnerability over the previous couple of years, in the 3-0 reverse against Brazil in the Confederations Cup final and in surprising defeats in friendlies that perhaps shouldn't have been blamed as readily as they were on weariness brought on by the Spanish federation's determination to capitalise on its champions by flogging them around the world in search of cash.

'We've made lots of mistakes,' said Xabi Alonso. 'We've lost a bit of our know-how, and we've paid for it with our solidity that had helped us win so many games. We've not been able to keep the same levels of ambition and hunger, perhaps the real conviction to go for the championship.'

But there were also tactical issues, most notably the fact that Spain's ball-playing defenders, although an integral part of that plan of maintaining possession – and the Spain national side was always more risk-averse, more prone to sterility than Guardiola's teams – looked vulnerable when they actually had to defend, an issue numerous sides who have prioritised ability on the ball have come up against.

'The death of *tiki-taka*,' screamed the more excitable pundits, but it was not that, nor was it the end of *juego de posición*. Rather it was the end of a cycle, the end of a generation of players. 'Barcelona's end of an era has passed on to the national team, as is natural,' said *Sport*. 'The players are exhausted, mentally and physically.'

Nobody doubted that a chapter had closed. 'Eras end with defeats …' said Xabi Alonso, 'and this was a painful defeat.'

# CHAPTER TEN
# EVOLUTION

Johan Cruyff's last act as manager of Barcelona had been to persuade Luis Enrique to leave Real Madrid for the Camp Nou. He had come through the ranks at Sporting Gijón, his home town club, before joining Madrid in 1991 at the age of 21. He won the league there in 1995 and then, after Barça signed him in 1996, he added a Cup Winners' Cup under Bobby Robson and two league titles under Louis van Gaal. Technically gifted, versatile and with extraordinary stamina, he was the perfect fit for Barcelona and remained at the club until he retired, with a degree of truculence, in 2004. He remained incredibly fit, running marathons in New York, Amsterdam and Florence (in which he dipped under three hours), riding in the *Quebrantahuesos* 'bone crusher' cycle race 205km through the Pyrenees and finishing an Ironman event in Frankfurt before, in 2008, completing the Marathon des Sables, 255km through the desert with a 10kg pack on his back.

After four years away from the game, Luis Enrique returned, taking over the Barcelona B-team when Guardiola was elevated to the first team. He left in 2011 to take the Roma job but, after initial promise, resigned at the end of the year having failed to qualify for any European competition. A year at Celta Vigo offered attractive football and moderate achievement, but his only tangible managerial success by 2014 was to have led Barça B to promotion.

That might not have made him an obvious choice to replace Gerardo Martino, but Barcelona rarely appoint managers with much concern for prior achievement. What matters is style and identity and Luis Enrique had that in abundance. 'I have come home,' he had said on returning to the club in 2008.

After Martino's comments about how he had been treated as an outsider, the arrival of Luis Enrique was seen as a return to trusted, traditional values. He had, after all, played alongside Guardiola in Van Gaal's first side, that crucible in which modern football was formed, while the fact he had stayed at the club through the difficult days between Van Gaal's first departure and the arrival of Rijkaard, that he was the only bridge between those two periods of success, meant he was popular with fans who chanted his name in his first match in charge, something they had never done for Martino.

But it also meant his relationship with his squad was different. 'Tata idolised some of the Barça players because he never imagined he would be coaching them,' Lluís Mascaró wrote in *Sport*. 'Now the players at Barça revere Luis Enrique (as they did with Pep Guardiola) because he is an idol at the club who won titles as a player at Camp Nou. Xavi's case is the most clear, and shows that Enrique can conduct the club in a way Martino could not.'

With hindsight, his introduction gave warning of what was to come. Although his tone was light, he insisted he would be 'a leader' and hinted that he knew there would be some dressing-room disputes. Given the sense of aimlessness and the lack of urgency of the previous two seasons, that was probably a necessary assertion of authority.

But Barça didn't just rely on philosophy. That summer, they signed Luis Suárez from Liverpool for €82.3m to form the MSN forward line with Messi and Neymar – although not until 25 October as the Uruguayan was banned for four months after biting Giorgio Chiellini at the World Cup. Reaction was mixed: although the prospect of that front three was undeniably exciting, signing superstars like Neymar and Suárez in successive seasons did seem to go against the *cantera* model, a bit like something Madrid might do. Cruyff himself was sceptical. 'I do not understand how the club will play a joined-up game with Messi, Neymar and Luis Suárez all in the team,' he wrote in *De Telegraaf*. 'All three are individuals. Clearly then this is a club that prefers individuals rather than a team that plays good football. '

Before the season began, Luis Enrique briefed journalists on his tactical plans, which essentially were ways to vary the classic model, none of them especially radical. The basic shape would remain 4-3-3, but with the capacity to switch to a back three, either in a 3-4-3 or a 3-2-3-2, something the players worked on during pre-season at England's training base at St George's Park. To combat teams pressing high against Barça, he wanted his goalkeepers to become more involved in the play with their feet. Recognising the strain on Busquets, operating both as a holding midfielder and an auxiliary defender, the plan was for Mascherano to take on some of the burden.

Luis Enrique vowed to remain true to the Cruyffian philosophy, saying that to win with *patadóns* – aimless punts – was worthless, but at the same time he acknowledged the need for adaptation, for the introduction of 'nuances that enrich our approach'. 'We have to evolve that idea,' he said, 'perfect it, improve it, so that we can surprise opponents and so that they don't know what type of play we will use.'

Ivan Rakitić, the Croatian signed from Sevilla that summer as Xavi's long-term replacement, added pace and aggression to the midfield, offering the possibility of a more direct style, something Martino had already tried to instil.

Barça won 12 of the 16 league games before the winter break, but when they lost the 17th, 1-0 away at Real Sociedad, Luis Enrique was on the brink. Again, it felt a very Barcelona crisis. They were still in the Copa del Rey, had qualified with some ease for the last 16 of the Champions League and were only a point off the top of the table, albeit having played a game more than the leaders Madrid. But even in a league in which the standards of consistency required from the two giants were preposterously high, it wasn't really about results or positions, it was about the sense that with each day, Barça moved further from the highs of the Guardiola years, that drift had become decline had become decay.

That wasn't just about performances on the pitch. The day after the defeat in San Sebastián, Andoni Zubizarreta, the former Barça goalkeeper and captain, was dismissed from his post as director of football. His assistant Carles Puyol announced his departure soon after. The previous week, the Court of Arbitration for Sport had upheld the decision by FIFA to ban Barcelona from signing players for two transfer windows for a breach of regulations relating to the registration of players under the age of 18 between 2009 and 2013. Although Barcelona insisted the issues were largely administrative and the result of a discrepancy between Spanish and FIFA rules, Zubizarreta had suggested in a television interview on the Sunday evening that the Barça president Josep Maria Bartomeu bore some responsibility for decisions taken during his time as vice president. None of that was easy to square with the *més que un club* moralising of the high Guardiola years.

The interview wasn't the only reason Zubizarreta had gone. The priority over the summer had been to strengthen the defence, but the Belgian centre-back Thomas Vermaelen, brought in from Arsenal, hadn't started following surgery on his knee, while the Brazilian full-back Douglas, signed from São Paulo, had begun only one game and looked hopelessly out of his depth. The French central defender Jérémy

Mathieu had been more of a success after his move from Valencia, but the arrival of one solid but unspectacular 30-year-old wasn't enough.

There were, anyway, more immediate practical concerns. Zubizarreta had been the main driving force behind Luis Enrique's appointment. His departure left the manager exposed, which was of particular concern given the circumstances around the defeat to Real Sociedad. Messi, Neymar, Dani Alves, Rakitić and Gerard Piqué were all left on the bench. The three South Americans had only just returned to training after extended Christmas breaks and it was the sixth year in a row Messi had been rested from the first game back but their omissions felt significant because the Argentinian, blaming a gastric complaint, missed training the following day, Epiphany, traditionally a special open session for children. Unhelpfully, Xavi had revealed the previous week that if players wanted to duck out of training or a game, stomach problems were a useful excuse. Inevitably, the question was raised of whether Messi, angered at being left on the bench and sceptical of his coach, was making a point.

The uninspired performance against la Real without Neymar and Messi had demonstrated just how reliant Barça had been on the pair, which in turn raised again the doubts about how true Luis Enrique's side was to the post-Cruyffian ideal. It's hard to reconcile a dependency on two star forwards with the team ethic on which the philosophy is based. Cruyff, Eusebio Sacristán said, 'wouldn't let the individual qualities of one player be more important than the collective but he did enhance that individualism'. Left on his own, Suárez disappointed, highlighting his difficulties in settling, which in turn exposed the underwhelming start made by the MSN as a unit.

Piqué's form had been erratic, but in his absence, Barça lacked any aerial presence, making clear how inadequate the defensive reconstruction had been. Superclubs play by different rules to the rest, different rules to previous generations. However good results may have appeared, there were plenty of reasons to ask whether Barça were drifting into difficulties. Messi and Luis Enrique had squared up on the training pitch and there were suggestions that the coach had wanted to take disciplinary action against his biggest star. In public, Luis Enrique did nothing to play down talk of a crisis, admitting he had been 'weakened' by the removal of Zubizarreta and Puyol.

The *entorno* had struck again. Luis Enrique had even anticipated it, observing at the beginning of November, when defeat to Real Madrid had been followed by a first-ever defeat at the Camp Nou against Celta Vigo, that the 'hunting season is open'. Mix a couple of disappointing results with stylistic doubts and the result was that fans sided with Messi. One poll suggested 68 per cent wanted Luis Enrique sacked. 'I live among extremists,' he noted.

The following Wednesday, Bartomeu called an election for the summer to 'reduce the tension'. The immediate impact was limited. That night, Barça beat Elche 5-0 in the Copa del Rey. It was the first time all three of Messi, Suárez and Neymar had scored in the same game but that detail was rather lost in the prevailing atmosphere. There were only 27,000 at the Camp Nou. Some chanted Luis Enrique's name but when they did they were drowned out by boos and whistles. Bartomeu went to the dressing room after the game where, reports claimed, Messi urged him to get rid of Luis Enrique, threatening to leave at the end of the season if the situation didn't change. Those rumours were never confirmed, but what is clear is that Messi was upset and that the intervention of senior players, Xavi foremost among them, in the days that followed was vital in placating the Argentinian.

That Sunday, Barça played Atlético. The previous season, they'd met them six times, failing to win and scoring a total of only three goals. More than any other manager, Diego Simeone seemed to have worked Barcelona out; Atlético were the worst possible opponents for Luis Enrique, just the team to deliver the final blow.

But they did not. Rather Barça were elevated, as though the presence of an external threat allowed them to forget internal issues. There was a sharpness to them, a snap to their tackling that had been missing for months. Again, each member of the MSN scored as they won 3-1. Messi, reconciled and re-energised, warned the press to 'stop throwing shit'.

Luis Enrique was more phlegmatic. 'Victories are the only thing that can calm this wave,' he said. 'As soon as we make mistakes, the crisis will be back.' But, by and large, they stopped making mistakes. The win over Atlético was the second in a sequence of 11 straight victories in which Barça scored 42 goals. When Real Madrid lost at Athletic on the first weekend of March, Barça went top of the table.

They consolidated that position a fortnight later in the *Clásico*. Barça went ahead when Mathieu headed in a set play after 16 minutes and then endured a pummelling. Cristiano Ronaldo levelled on the half hour and for the rest of the half Barça struggled. But eight minutes after the break, a long ball from Dani Alves released Suárez. His first touch cushioned the ball to his right away from Sergio Ramos, his second fired it low past Iker Casillas and inside the far post. 'He's not just an old-style striker,' said Luis Enrique. 'He can also combine with his teammates, he reads the game well and he doesn't need many touches to score. He also has the physique which is good for us and the character which is useful for a team like us … which is colder.' As Sid Lowe pointed out, his words recalled what Cruyff had said when he'd signed Hristo Stoichkov: the Bulgarian brought '*mala leche*' – literally, bad milk – a fire and a hunger and a ruthlessness that added edge to the cerebral passing behind him.

Barça won with a goal from a set play and a long ball over the top. They won with just 52 per cent possession, their lowest figure in a *Clásico* since before Pep Guardiola had taken over. Just as Luis Enrique had promised when he took over, the style had evolved.

By the beginning of May, the outlook could hardly have been more different to that of four months earlier. The front three dove-tailed after Messi moved to the right, allowing Suárez to take up a central position. Suárez, who had perhaps simply needed time to find his rhythm after his ban, suggested the players had happened upon the combination during a game and, seeing how well it worked, had not switched back. If that were the case, then the only credit due Luis Enrique was for letting it happen. But whoever was responsible, Barça had a highly gifted forward line who, at least for a while, seemed to relish playing together and were able to function as a devastating unit without egos getting in the way. They saw off PSG in the Champions League quarter-final and warmed up for the semi-final by putting six past Getafe and eight past Cordoba.

Two years after being hammered by Bayern at the same stage, they met Bayern again. But this time, of course, there were ramifications beyond the immediate context of being a Champions League semi-final because Bayern were managed by Pep Guardiola. This was the modern interpretation of Cruyffianism being tested against its greatest exponent.

\* \* \*

The defeat to Madrid in the previous season's semi-final had shocked Guardiola. He became aware of the issue of over-pressing, of Bayern lacking the wherewithal to drop off, to yield space and then counter, much the same problem Barça had had in his final season there. He began to encourage his side, after they had conceded a chance or a goal, to seek 'stability', by which he meant putting together a run of 20 passes. As Juanma Lillo likes to say, 'The faster the ball goes, the faster it comes back.' Teams can become locked in an infinite regress, counter-pressing and then counter-counter-pressing and then counter-counter-counter-pressing, leading to a fury that works against the more gifted side.

The desire to right a wrong through the immediate expenditure of physical effort, Guardiola found, was more of an issue in Germany (and later England) than it had been in Spain – an indication of how tactical developments can be shaped by temperament, culture and emotion. This, perhaps, represents the clearest distinction between the Guardiola model and the philosophy of the hard-pressing German school as represented by Jürgen Klopp.

While both believe in the importance of pressing, Klopp's version of the game is based on rapid transitions, on catching the opposition before it is set. It's a frenetic, occasionally harum-scarum vision of the game; Guardiola also sees the value of quick counters, but prefers to slow the game down to reset, relying on the technique and movement of his side to prise apart an opposing defence, even after it has had a chance to reorganise. 'It's just not the same,' Guardiola said, 'if the winger gets the ball from the centre-half rather than from an inside-forward. If he gets possession from the centre-back it gives the other team time to organise their defence. But if the play's been worked forwards until it's the attacking midfielder who delivers the ball, it's far harder to defend – especially if the midfielders have drawn the defenders to them.'

Charles Reep, the father of British match analysis and the first theoretical proponent of direct football, found that roughly 80 per cent of all goals stemmed from moves of three passes or fewer.* It might be expected that for a Guardiola side that figure would be lower, but how much lower is remarkable. In his third season at Bayern, 72 per cent of goals scored came from moves of five passes or more. At the same time, the number of goals scored from counter-attacks dropped by more than half.

Whether that is a positive or not is highly subjective. Bayern's total goals scored fell from 98 in the Bundesliga in 2012-13, Heynckes's last season, to 94 in Guardiola's first season to 80 in each of his last two. Goals conceded went from 18 in the last season under Heynckes to 23 to 18 to 17. That suggests a slight downturn, but such numbers are largely academic. Heynckes's treble-winning season was freakishly good and unlikely ever to be repeated and besides, when a team is scoring that many goals, slight fluctuations are largely irrelevant. Bayern blazed though the Bundesliga in each of those four seasons, as they did in the one that followed under Carlo Ancelotti when they scored 89 goals to 22. If a few 6-0s became 4-0s, who really cared?

That's the biggest issue in terms of assessing Guardiola's time in Germany. Winning the league was a given. It's irrelevant to point out that such domination is unprecedented in German history; the economics of football have never previously been so starkly stratified. That has had an enormous impact on how the game is played and how it is consumed. The superclubs are so dominant that league titles in many countries become almost box-ticking exercises, Champions League revenues meaning their success is self-perpetuating. The result is that whole seasons can rest on one or two games at a key stage of the Champions League.

---

* Reep was dogmatic and misguided, the central flaw in his reasoning laid out in *Inverting the Pyramid*, but there's no reason to doubt his raw figures.

And perhaps the fact that the superclubs have become global brands means they lose their identities and become almost inter-changeable to top players. It's a minor example and one that it would perhaps be a little unfair to see as definitive, but it seemed telling that when Paul Pogba rejoined Manchester United he spoke of his dream as being to win the Ballon d'Or; in a previous age, winning the league or the Champions League with his new club would surely have outweighed an individual bauble. Such a focus on stars may be inhibitive to creating a fluent and effective style, but it makes sense for clubs: a great player can always turn a one-off game and, in terms of marketing, what is easier to sell? A glamorous player or a philosophy? It is against that mentality that Guardiola had set himself.

Just as Paris Saint-Germain dominate in France and Juventus in Italy, so Bayern dominate in Germany. Their revenues are roughly two-thirds greater than those of their nearest rival, Borussia Dortmund. Of course they win the league; as Mourinho hinted, not to do so would require a season of monstrous underperformance.

The feeling among Bayern directors was that Guardiola had developed the club, that he had moved them into the tactical avant-garde. But in terms of winning trophies, rather than engaging in intellectual and aesthetic exhibitions, that meant Guardiola needed success in the Champions League and that he never achieved.

Guardiola's second season followed a similar pattern to his first. Bayern were again unbeaten at the winter break, and again cruised through their Champions League group. But his side were evolving. Guardiola increasingly deployed his full-backs as auxiliary holding midfielders. The idea that full-backs should be de facto midfielders is a familiar one in the modern game and Guardiola had success-fully used Lahm in central midfield the previous season, describing him as 'the most intelligent player' he had ever worked with. Essentially fusing those two ideas, Guardiola had his full-backs, rather than advancing down the line to support the wide midfielders, tuck in front of his defensive line, with the holding player dropped back to operate almost as a third central defender. The five-man platform that provided, Guardiola said, was 'a security system' that allowed him still to attack with five players without suffering the sort of breakdown suffered against Madrid. The shape out of possession might have been a fairly orthodox 4-3-3 (which its modern form is usually a 4-1-2-3), but with the ball it morphed into a 3-2-2-3, resembling the W-M that had been the default formation for most sides between 1930 and 1960.

A first domestic defeat of the season came in the 18th game, a 4-1 reverse against Wolfsburg. Guardiola blamed himself and wrote what he came to refer to as 'the bible' on the whiteboard in his office. It was a very short bible, containing just three key strictures. He would deploy:

- Two against four in attack
- An extra man in midfield
- An extra man in defence

Those, of course, are very Cruyffian values, the second and third commandments echoing the line Guardiola had written, when explaining the Cruyffian philosophy in his 2001 memoir, about the need 'to fill the centre of the pitch in order to play having numerical superiority'.

But vulnerabilities remained. Bayern were held 0-0 away by Shakhtar in the last 16 of the Champions League, but won 7-0 at home. They lost 3-1 away to Porto in the quarter-final, but won 6-1 at home. Both ties were ultimately won easily enough, but there was

THE BARCELONA INHERITANCE

a clear pattern of Guardiola sides failing to dominate the away leg in knockout ties.

The league again was sealed against Hertha, this time with four rather than seven matches of the season remaining. But again, once the title was wrapped up, standards dipped. Bayern drew in the Cup semi-final against Dortmund and lost on penalties. They lost at Leverkusen in the league. And then came the Champions League semi-final against Barça.

The principles Guardiola had written on his whiteboard after the Wolfsburg defeat suggested that when facing a 4-3-3 such as Barça still played, he should field a 4-4-2, which would provide an extra man at the back and in midfield and two against four in attack. But this was no ordinary opponent. For one thing it was debatable whether Barça's full-backs, Dani Alves in particular, could be categorised as defenders. And for another this was a team with Lionel Messi. 'There is no defensive system that can stop him, and no coach either,' Guardiola acknowledged and then, boldly, decided that meant there was little point trying, deploying a man-marking back three against Messi, Neymar and Luis Suárez. Barça, he reasoned, are used to playing against teams that pack men deep, the result of which is that most of their players have time on the ball. By leaving only three men back, Guardiola had seven to pressure Barça, to enforce the highest and most intense of high presses. It didn't work, but the shock might have done.

Barça repeatedly sliced through Bayern in the opening stages and had missed two clear chances when, after 16 minutes, Guardiola called a halt to his experiment, pushing Juan Bernat from a left-sided midfield role to right-back and adopting a 4-3-3. The flow of chances was staunched and it wasn't until the 77th minute that Barça went ahead, Messi taking advantage after Bernat had been dispossessed. The problem was that they then scored twice more, Messi toppling Jérôme Boateng with a rapid change of direction then dinking the ball over Neuer, before Neymar added a third on the break in injury time.

It was a win born of the rapid transitions that come from winning the ball back high up the pitch, something on which Luis Enrique had focused. 'He understands the club's philosophy: he has really driven home the idea of pressing high,' Javier Mascherano said.

Barça, Guardiola observed, were the best counter-attacking side in the world. He meant it as a compliment and it was taken as such, but there were times in the previous couple of seasons when it would not have been. For only the second time in 442 matches, Barcelona had less possession than their opponents. The other had been the 4-0 win at Rayo Vallecano that was widely seen as being the moment at which Martino had begun to lose the faith of the club.

Bayern's 3-2 win in the home leg, in which they did play a version of 4-4-2, merely confirmed another semi-final exit. The former Bayern president Franz Beckenbauer blamed the defeat on the way Bayern had 'laid down [their] arms' after the first goal in the first leg and in the obvious sense of when the goals were scored, it was that final quarter of an hour in the Camp Nou that undid Bayern; a rapid burst of goals conceded that would become such a bane for Guardiola. But it seems probable that the seeds of their collapse had been planted in the first 16 minutes. Would Bernat have been dispossessed so easily had he not been exhausted? Even the corner from which he was leading a counter when he lost the ball came about because Bayern had – wearily? – squandered possession. Would Boateng have been quite so leaden-footed had he not been given such a runaround early on? Certainly, a less tired Bayern might have closed down Rakitić more effectively before he released Messi in the build-up to that second goal. And had they not been two down, would Bayern have been quite so reckless in chasing an away goal late on, leaving the space behind their defensive line that Messi and Neymar exploited?

Perhaps it would have been different had Arjen Robben, David Alaba, Javi Martínez and Franck Ribéry been available, or had Robert Lewandowski and Bastian Schweinsteiger been fully fit, but then even Bayern's injury list was arguably in part a result of the intensity of Guardiola's demands.

It's impossible to be definitive, but it seems reasonable to conclude that Guardiola's initial tactical approach cost Bayern the tie. Just because a gamble does not come off does not mean it was not worth taking but, once again, Guardiola had refused to countenance compromise and had failed by pursuing his attacking ideals to the utmost.

* * *

Five days after completing their 5-3 aggregate victory over Bayern, Barcelona sealed the league title with a 1-0 win away to Atlético, 364 days after Atlético had won the league against them. 'We believed at difficult moments,' said Javier Mascherano. 'We overcame adversity. We laughed when we had to laugh and suffered when we had to suffer.'

They beat Athletic to lift the Copa del Rey and, five months after they had seemed on the brink of collapse, they completed another Treble by beating Juventus 3-1 in the Champions League final in Berlin.

Their opening goal wasn't just of awesome quality but seemed to embody a style. Luis Enrique's Barça may have been more varied than the Guardiola model, but this was a goal born of the classic Cruyff philosophy. In a perfect narrative, perhaps, it would have come last: would have been the final flourish to round off the masterpiece. Instead it came after four minutes and was of such class that it almost seemed to overshadow the first quarter of the game.

It began, unpromisingly enough, with a throw-in on the Barça left, about ten yards inside the Juve half. The ball was worked across the pitch and back again, until Dani Alves presented it to Lionel Messi just outside the centre circle. Suddenly there was an injection of urgency, a change of direction. The ball was slipped out to the left flank, where Jordi Alba was surging forwards from left-back, into the space inevitably – and probably necessarily – left by the narrowness of Juve's midfield diamond. He knocked it inside to Neymar, who waited until Andrés Iniesta had made a burst away from Arturo Vidal. From there it was all extremely straightforward: a ball inside, a square pass across goal and a simple finish for Rakitić.

With greater ruthlessness, Barça would have had the game sewn up by half-time. As it was, Álvaro Morata equalised before Rakitić's perfectly weighted ball – a typically direct pass – laid Messi in. His shot was saved but Suárez knocked in the rebound. Neymar added a third on the counter with the final kick of the game. At the final whistle, Xavi, who had come on for Iniesta after 77 minutes, taking the armband in the 767th and last game of his Barça career, was chaired around the pitch. He had been an unused substitute in the 2006 final and had played in the victories of 2009 and 2011. In a decade at the top, he had made the sideways pass a key part in the midfielder's armoury and had demonstrated over and over that the best route to goal wasn't necessarily the most direct.

For Julen Lopetegui, Xavi was both the embodiment of the philosophy and the player who made it possible. 'Xavi changed football,' he said. 'He helped us to build, or to see, a new player profile that ended up running through all levels of the national team. He killed off the myth of physicality being above all else and opened people's eyes to the qualities of small, technical players, proving that you can attack and also defend with the ball... The intensity with which he played was vital and it showed that intensity is not what people often think it is. It's the rhythm of the game, the speed and intensity of the play itself: quick, simple, constant. He made every other player better. He gave the right pass, he gave continuity and he was always well positioned.'

It was no coincidence that it was as he aged and his influence diminished that Barça moved away from Guardiola's interpretation of their style. This version was more direct than Guardiola's side had been. There was still a sense of the (positive) 'anarchy' Fàbregas had spoken of early in Martino's reign. 'Our games don't look like handball any more,' said Piqué. They got the ball forward more quickly, which meant they lost it more often, but also meant they were more prone to catch opponents on the counter, before they were set. The front three, meanwhile, were all dribblers. Each of them – not just Messi – had the capacity to break a marking structure by beating two or three men in a tight space. They weren't as pure as the Guardiola model but they were less predictable. Luis Enrique, Eusebio said with evident scepticism, was 'a coach who has been able to express what he was as a player: competitiveness, desire to improve, every detail, work … in that spirit he has been close, on the inside, of a club that has things that he has learnt and he has impregnated himself with those things, assimilated them, and used them.'

Yet for all the differences of style, these were largely the same players: when Pedro came on as an injury-time substitute in Berlin, it meant six of their side had also played in the final in Rome six years earlier. Eight had played at Wembley in 2011. That represents a remarkable level of consistency: Real Madrid won the first five European Cups but only four of those who played in the 1960 final had also played in 1956.*

---

\* Marquitos, José María Zárraga, Francisco 'Paco' Gento and Alfredo Di Stéfano

Were they better? That's more an aesthetic judgement than anything else, but what was true was perhaps that their variety made them less vulnerable, less susceptible to opponents who set up merely to stop them, and yet at the same time limited the heights they could scale when everything went right. Barcelona's 2015 Champions League winners were a very good side; their 2011 winners were arguably the greatest ever.

\* \* \*

Guardiola's third and final season in Germany began with a penalty shoot-out defeat to Wolfsburg in the Super Cup, but there followed a run of 12 straight wins in all competitions, a familiar remorselessness about their excellence. By Christmas, though, as it became apparent Guardiola would not carry on, doubts began to be raised. Was he too intense? An ongoing dispute had led to the departure of the long-serving club doctor Hans-Wilhelm Müller-Wohlfahrt, but that was just the most public manifestation of a wider issue. Guardiola, said the *Süddeutsche Zeitung* in a slightly overwrought profile, had proved himself 'a very good-looking, very erotic but also, at times, totally prissy lover that you look at, next to you in bed, with pride each morning, even if you never know what kind of mood she's about to wake up in'.

The league was again won at a canter, and the Cup was won with a penalty shoot-out victory over Dortmund, but the Champions League again evaded Guardiola. Bayern, in truth, were never as impressive in Europe that season as they had been in the previous two. It took a last-minute equaliser from Thomas Müller to force extra time in a thrilling last-16 victory over Juventus, and the 3-2 aggregate quarter-final win over Benfica was unexpectedly shaky. Then came Atlético in the semi-final.

To some consternation, Guardiola left out Müller for the first leg in Madrid, preferring a 4-1-4-1 with Kingsley Coman and Douglas Costa wide and Arturo Vidal and Thiago Alcântara breaking forward from midfield to support Robert Lewandowski. Müller was hugely popular among Bayern fans, a native Bavarian who had come up through the youth ranks and had a knack of scoring vital goals, but he perhaps lacked the supreme level of technical ability Guardiola's rat-a-tat possession football demands.

Saúl Ñíguez put Atlético ahead after 11 minutes, a brilliant jinking run that took him past three Bayern players before he squared up Alaba and, using the defender's body to block Neuer's view, curled a low shot just inside the post. Bayern settled after that, though, and had the better of the game before, with 20 minutes remaining, Guardiola took off Thiago for Müller. His initial selection was almost immediately vindicated as Bayern, suddenly unbalanced, lost momentum and ceded the midfield, Fernando Torres hit the post and, although Bayern had arguably had the better of the game, by the end it felt as though they'd done well to get away with a 1-0 defeat.

This, Guardiola knew, was it. This was his Bayern legacy. The Bundesliga was regarded as a given. Insiders might have admired the style of his hat-trick of titles but others saw the Champions League as the truest test. A third straight defeat in the semi-final would, inevitably, leave a taint of failure.

He fretted over his approach for the return leg, his constant tinkering meaning that, for Guardiola more than most coaches, this was seen as a direct examination of him and his ideals. He thought he had seen a vulnerability between Filipe Luis, the left-back, and Stefan Savić, the left-sided centre-back. Koke usually protected it, but Guardiola believed Lahm could draw him away, creating an opportunity for Müller. He suspected Atlético would press hard early on and so planned to go long to Lewandowski, switching to Bayern's more orthodox possession-based game when Atlético dropped off.

His plan nearly worked. It should have worked. Bayern went ahead through a Xabi Alonso free kick before half-time and Müller missed a penalty soon after. But nine minutes into the second half, Atlético caught them on the break, Fernando Torres laying in Griezmann to equalise. Bayern needed two. Lewandowski got one of them, heading in a Vidal cross with 16 minutes to go, but as Bayern grew increasingly frantic, they became increasingly ragged. Torres missed a late penalty but it didn't matter: Atlético went through on away goals.

Over three seasons, Guardiola averaged 2.52 points per game in the league, an unprecedented figure. 'German football owes him a lot; he's taken the game to the highest level, tactically and strategically,' Bayern's executive chairman Karl-Heinz Rummenigge wrote in the programme for Guardiola's final league game. He later described him as 'a coach like no other at Bayern in terms of intensity and quality'.

But he did not win the Champions League.

# CHAPTER ELEVEN

# A BRIDGE TOO FAR

José Mourinho always won the league in his second season at a club. In the summer of 2014, Chelsea added Cesc Fàbregas and Diego Costa and so dealt with the two most obvious deficiencies of the previous season: a lack of midfield guile and the absence of a tough, awkward, goalscoring leader of the line.

The relationship between Eden Hazard and José Mourinho entered a productive phase: when Hazard had been named Players' Player of the Year the previous season, he had joked that the other nominees would have to work harder, a dig Mourinho appreciated. That was the height of their connection. The manager recognised Hazard as a humble, diligent player lacking a little ambition. Hazard's father announced that he saw Mourinho as the manager to give his son 'a little more ego', to make him 'a wonderful player' as well as the 'fantastic dad and wonderful husband' he already was. Mourinho began to acknowledge his respect for Hazard, highlighting an opponent in team meetings and saying he was 'no Maradona, no Messi, no Hazard'.

From their opening game, a 3-1 win at Burnley, Chelsea looked like champions. The little horse had grown up. They lost only three times all season, and one of those was after the championship had been wrapped up. Hazard was named Football Writers' and PFA Player of the Year. To those who had known him the longest, this was the same old Mourinho. 'I didn't feel any difference when it came to communication with the players,' said Maniche. 'I did some work with Chelsea and some of the processes were the same when it came to training. The warm-up, for example, was practically the same I had at Porto.' However damaging Real Madrid had been to him, the anti-Cruyff was still relevant, was still a winner.

Liverpool, having lost Luis Suárez to Barcelona and Daniel Sturridge to injury, were never the same in 2014-15. Arsenal were still beset by their familiar problems. United were struggling to get used to Louis van Gaal. As City collapsed in the January, Chelsea's progress was relatively unhindered and they ended up confirming their title with a 1-0 home win over Crystal Palace in the fourth-last game of the season.

It was neither a great game nor a great performance, but Chelsea had been looking weary for a couple of months. It was a day of relief as well as exultation, as fatigued limbs were dragged over the line to give Mourinho his third title with the club and only the fifth they had ever won. Nobody then, perhaps, realised quite what a struggle those final yards had been, had any notion just how difficult things had become.

Yet Mourinho in his post-match press conference was neither tired nor celebratory. Usually in such circumstances, reporters just want a quote or an anecdote to drop in their features on how the title was won: what the key game was, when he'd felt the momentum swing his way, a promise, perhaps, that Chelsea would be even better the following season. But instead he took another barely disguised swing at Guardiola. 'For me,' he said, 'I'm not the smartest guy to choose countries and clubs. I could choose another club in another country where to be champion is easier.'

He didn't name Guardiola, but the reference was clear. Guardiola had gone to Germany where the question was less whether Bayern would win the league than how many points they'd win it by. To some extent he was right, of course, and if he'd been making a general critique of the iniquities of global football finance, he might even have come across as statesmanlike, but his point was limited to Guardiola and his personal feud. 'I chose a club where I was happier before and a country where I was happy before,' he went on. 'I took a risk. I am so, so happy because I won another Premier League title ten years after [my first] in my second spell at the club. I was champion at every club I coached. I came to Inter, Real Madrid and Chelsea. Every title is important, to win the title in Spain with 100 points against the best Barcelona ever was a big achievement that I enjoyed so much. Maybe in the future I have to be smarter and choose another club in another country where everybody is champion. Maybe I will go to a country where a kitman can be coach and win the title. Maybe I need to be smarter but I still enjoy these difficulties. I think I'm at the right place. I'm here until [the Chelsea owner Roman] Abramovich tells me to go.'

Even for Mourinho, this was very strange. Why would anybody, having just lifted the title, choose to belittle their rival, particularly when he operated in another country? And not just a passing jibe, an under-the-breath aside, but a full-on assault. Mourinho could have criticised Guardiola by implication, by pointing out he had come back to Chelsea for love, by outlining the difficulties he had faced, by paying tribute to the competitiveness of the Premier League, but instead he chose to sneer about how easy the league was to win in certain countries – the reference to the kitman was perhaps a nod to the way his enemies in Spain referred to him as 'the translator'. In the moment of his triumph, Mourinho chose to make the conversation about Guardiola.

In hindsight, that final sentence seems strange too: there until Abramovich told him to go? Mourinho had said on his return to

Chelsea that he wanted to found a dynasty, that in a career laden with silverware that was something he still hadn't done. Yet that line, seemingly so throwaway, hinted at an insecurity. Perhaps it was merely part of his contract negotiations – he did, after all, sign a new four-year deal a few weeks later – but it echoed the remarks he had made at that FWA tribute dinner the previous season, the uneasy sense that his stay at the club might not be as long as most people expected it to be.

But still, nobody anticipated what happened next.

Chelsea had shown signs of fatigue in winning the title – oddly scratchy performances against Burnley and Southampton, away at Hull and QPR – but the context was such that nobody paid them much heed until the following season. At the time, with the title race reduced to a slightly laboured procession, the issue of who would win was replaced by the question of how a champion should win. Were Chelsea, those masters of closing the game down with their manager who had apparently said that whoever had the ball had fear, boring? 'That question doesn't even make sense to me,' said Jorge Costa. 'It's obvious the most important aspect of coaching is winning. I hated to lose when I was a player, and I still hate it as a coach. I really don't think there was a team playing better than Chelsea last season.'

For Maniche, similarly, the question is simply naïve. 'The ideal was to do what we did in Porto, which was win and play very well and attractively in practically every match,' he said. 'But football has changed completely and it will be completely different again in ten years. Those critics have no idea of what football is, apparently. Arsenal seem to enjoy having a coach who does not win titles, but ask their fans if they wouldn't like Mourinho better, ask any team in the world if they would not have Mourinho as their coach. What would you prefer? Winning is not only part of the game, but it's also a part of your life. You need to win, and to win, you need Mourinho.'

Mourinho himself is unapologetic about prioritising winning. 'I don't think it's changed from one century ago … there is no kid, even playing with his cousin or his father,* even in the garden, there is no kid that plays to lose,' he said shortly after the end of that season. 'The nature, the sense of it – doesn't change. They play to win. I used to play a lot in my neighbourhood. And I don't remember it ever being any other than a big fight to win. I don't think that's changed. And football at the highest level, that's even more so. Because the objective is to win.'

Was there not a new generation of coaches who had developed the ideas of Cruyff and Bielsa, the likes of Guardiola and Klopp, who tried to win in a more exciting, more dynamic way? 'What I think,' Mourinho said, 'is people will try to disguise that [the importance of winning]. People try to create what is not true. When people talk about a new generation of coaches … what is that new generation? The generation will always be the ones that win. And the ones that win occasionally or never win will always be something else.'

That's certainly not how everybody sees it. 'He has more belief in defence than attack,' Van Gaal told Patrick Barclay for his biography of Mourinho. 'My philosophy is always – because I believe we must entertain the public – to have attacking play. His philosophy is to win! That is the difference.' Yet did Van Gaal's AZ Alkmaar side, with its compact 4-4-2, really set out always to attack? Did his Netherlands team at the 2014 World Cup with its counter-attacking 5-3-2? How attacking, really, were his United with all their sideways passing and risk-free possession?

---

* Or, presumably, his servant.

'There is no new generation,' Mourinho went on. 'What there is, is people who've got some idea, some philosophy, and want to create something like, "We build very well from the back, we have a very good ball possession, we don't play counter-attack…" If you don't play counter-attack then it's because you are stupid. Because counter-attack is a fantastic item of football. It's an ammunition that you have and when you find your opponent unbalanced – because a counter-attack always has a connection with some losing of position because of attacking movements – and when you recover the ball, you have a fantastic moment to score a goal. So if you're not playing counter-attack it's because you're stupid. Because you have to. So I think people are creating – and it has influenced some people in the public opinion. But football will never change in that aspect. Football is to win.'

The perfect example of that had come in the April as Chelsea had faced Van Gaal's United at home. They'd been sluggish in winning at QPR the previous week and had to go to the Emirates the following weekend. There was a feeling that if they were going to slip up it would be then, particularly as Diego Costa was out with a thigh problem. Chelsea played the centre-back Kurt Zouma alongside Matić at the back of midfield, defended deep, allowed United the ball and won 1-0 despite having only 30 per cent possession. Van Gaal claimed his side had 'dominated' but the truth was that Chelsea had looked comfortable for the vast majority of the game. 'It's simple,' said Mourinho. 'We didn't have important players in our attacking structure. We didn't have Diego Costa. We didn't have the natural replacement for Diego which is [Loïc] Remy. We didn't have depth in our attacking game. We don't have Óscar [he came off the bench], we didn't have a lot of our attacking potential. We needed a point – and our opponent needed three points. It's as simple as that.

'If I don't concede a goal my objective is there. And if my opponent needs to score a goal and their defensive structure, when they lose possession of the ball is very unbalanced – because of the positions they adopt in ball possession, with defenders very exposed, because they project the full-backs a lot and they leave one holding midfield player in front of two central defenders with a big distance in between them … then when you analyse them and you know they do that all the time, if you don't prepare your team for that then you are not coaching.

'Coaching is about recognising the good qualities of the opponents and recognising the fragilities of the opponent. And, more than that, it's to recognise the good qualities of my team – and the bad qualities of my team. Because my team also has bad qualities, and it's very important that me and my players, we recognise our bad qualities. One of the secrets of good coaching is, "Can you hide from your opponents and even from the pundits your bad qualities?"'

Yet the oddity of Mourinho was that the older he got, the more defined his tactical approach, the more apparent his bad qualities, his insecurities, were.

For the fifth time in a row, Mourinho had won the league in his second season with a club. Almost immediately, though, those powers of disguise began to desert him. From the very first game of the following season, Mourinho's bad qualities were on display. Chelsea were drawing 2-2 with Swansea City. They'd been poor and were slightly fortunate to be level. Jefferson Montero, Swansea's speedy right winger, had eviscerated Branislav Ivanović. Thibaut Courtois had been sent off. As the game went into injury time, Hazard received the ball from Radamel Falcao and was challenged by Ashley Williams. He went down and rolled onto his right side, clutching his groin, then slid onto his back. The referee Michael Oliver gave a free kick and, after checking with the Belgian whether he needed treatment, signalled to Chelsea's medical staff. When they didn't immediately respond, he nodded at them. On ran the physio Jon Fearn, closely followed by the team doctor, Eva Carneiro. A photograph taken from beside the goal shows Mourinho's reaction as she ran past him, his right arm flying up, his face crumpling into anger.

As the pair left the pitch having attended to Hazard, Mourinho exchanged furious words with Carneiro and berated Fearn. He subsequently described them as 'naïve' because Hazard, having received treatment, had to leave the field reducing Chelsea temporarily to nine men. FA regulations and medical ethics, though, had given them little choice. Carneiro and Fearn were subsequently demoted from working with the first team. Carneiro sued for constructive dismissal and eventually reached an out-of-court settlement for a reported £5m. Symbolically, it was the moment at which the countdown began on the end of Mourinho's Chelsea career.

The seeds of Mourinho's decline had been planted much earlier and lay perhaps in his character. It certainly wasn't the first time everything had begun to go wrong in the third season. There were practical reasons but many of them seemed to come back to Mourinho's methods, the strategies that had made him great coming to undermine him. Particularly when he was at Inter, he was compared to Helenio Herrera, another charismatic figure who was regarded as dangerously pragmatic. Herrera, the high priest of *catenaccio*, had led Inter to the European Cup in 1964 and 1965. They were favourites to beat Celtic in the 1967 final, but as the team was corralled in isolation in a hotel in Estoril, the constant focus on stopping their opponents, the accumulation of negativity, became too much. The full-back Tarcisio Burgnich remembers being kept awake at nights by the sound of teammates vomiting with anxiety. They lost the final, precipitating a collapse in Serie A that cost them a title they had seemed sure to win and led in the end to Herrera's departure. He only ever won one other trophy and that was the Copa del Rey 14 years later with Barcelona. The process of playing on fear, of seeking always to counter an opponent and expose their weakness rather than accentuating your own abilities, led eventually to a psychological disintegration. The process of reactivity proved ultimately degenerative.

Historical parallels are rarely exact, but there were echoes. The first evidence that all was not quite right at Chelsea probably came in those final games of 2014-15. Would Chelsea have been so weary had Mourinho not been so determined to stick to a small core of key players, his 'untouchables'? In a world in which the increasing physical demands on players had made other managers regard rotation as essential, was his reliance on a small band of acolytes still viable? Mourinho was aware of the fatigue and delayed pre-season, the intention presumably being twofold: to give them time to recover and to try to have them peak later in the year. But that in itself was a major departure from past policy: his three league titles in England had come from starting quickly, building up a lead and holding on.

The effect was that Chelsea began 2015-16 looking undercooked. Ivanović, Fàbregas and Diego Costa all looked off the pace. Hazard, struggling with a hip injury, found Mourinho ramping up the pressure on him, describing him as 'my new Messi' while urging him to take more defensive responsibility. At one point a frustrated Mourinho allegedly told him, 'You're not good enough for the top. I'll have to sell you.' He began to criticise him in press conferences again.

Swansea, Manchester City and West Brom all scored from simple balls in behind the Chelsea back four, with Courtois, perhaps mindful of the goal he had conceded from the centre circle to Stoke's

Charlie Adam the previous season, seemingly reluctant to leave his line. As the sweeper-keeper ideal became the orthodoxy across other top clubs, Courtois was notably conservative.

But a lack of physical preparedness and individual losses of form could only explain so much. The pre-season tour of the USA had been characterised by uneasiness. Mourinho, perhaps, had sensed then that there was something amiss, had felt the lack of hunger, had recognised that certain players had begun to doubt him. By the end of September, it was being widely rumoured that players had been disturbed by Mourinho's attack on certain Sky Sports pundits after they had highlighted misbehaviour by Diego Costa, echoing the unease felt by many at Real Madrid over his constant attacks on referees, schedulers and Barça.

So utterly had English football bought into the cult of Mourinho, seeing him as some great Machiavellian puppet-master, that his every gesture was analysed for deeper purpose. Why had he arrived unshaven for the Community Shield in a sloppy tracksuit, his hair long and uncombed? He had built his image in part on his good looks and sharp sense of dress, but here he was at Wembley looking like he'd just popped out from doing up the bathroom to buy some more paint at the local DIY store. Was he making it clear he didn't care? Arsenal won 1-0 thanks to a goal from Alex Oxlade-Chamberlain, and Mourinho lost his 13-game unbeaten run against Arsène Wenger. Had he anticipated such a defeat and taken pre-emptive measures to downplay its significance? He went through the whole repertoire of diversionary tactics. He provoked a handshake spat with Wenger by making a point of congratulating every Arsenal player as they came down the steps after collecting their medals then turning away before their manager reached him. He then accused Wenger of having abandoned his principles and adopted a defensive approach.

But the problem was that the world had got wise to Mourinho's tactics. His provocations were reported less for their substance than for the fact that he was playing his games again. In his first spell at Chelsea, he had been a master of deflection, drawing pressure away from his team and onto himself. By his second spell he was a magician who had lost his sleight of hand.

At first, the outburst at Fearn and Carneiro had been seen as one of Mourinho's manipulations. He was deflecting again, picking a ridiculous fight to draw the headlines away from a disappointing performance. But then the full video emerged. That wasn't an actor putting on his face before his performance in front of the media: that was genuine rage. This was the great paradox of those opening weeks of the third season of his second spell: just as his act lost its power, just as his deflections began to be reported for what they were, it became apparent that there were times when this was no longer an act, that Mourinho was a brooder whose emotions occasionally boiled over.

The Carneiro affair had profound consequences. She was popular in the dressing room. She, like many team doctors, was somebody players trusted and liked, a confidante bound by medical ethics with whom they could discuss issues they would be reluctant to talk about with a coach or a teammate. If certain players had begun to have doubts about Mourinho, his treatment of Carneiro magnified them.

Chelsea went to Manchester City and were hammered, 3-0. Mourinho took off John Terry at half-time, the first time he had substituted his captain in a league game. Mourinho spoke afterwards of how 'fragile' Chelsea had looked in the first half, of how he needed to move the defensive line closer to the midfield. Perhaps the move was purely tactical. Terry, after all, has never been quick and City, with Sergio Agüero, Raheem Sterling and Jesús Navas up front most certainly were. But the problem with Mourinho and his endless machinating is that you never quite know what's real and what is a gesture towards something else. Was this a tactical decision or was it the sacrifice of a major figure *pour encourager les autres*? Or was it even designed to persuade Abramovich that the signing of John Stones from Everton was a matter of some urgency?

The wide forward Pedro did join from Barcelona, apparently rejecting Manchester United after talking to players about what it was like playing under Louis van Gaal. He scored on his debut away at West Brom as Chelsea survived the dismissal of Terry nine minutes into the second half to win 3-2. But he was the highest-profile figure to arrive. Falcao, after a miserable season at Manchester United where he seemed to be struggling with the after-effects of a knee operation, came in on loan from Monaco. Asmir Begović was signed from Stoke as back-up to Courtois. The promising but unproven Ghanaian left-back Baba Rahman joined from Augsburg and the Senegalese centre-back Papy Djilobodji was, to general mystification that time never dispelled, bought from Nantes. The usual handful of young prospects – Kenedy, Michael Hector, Matt Miazga – were brought in to be spun off on the loan circuit, but not the big names Mourinho demanded.

His criticism of Chelsea's recruitment policy became gradually more overt. 'You say if you stand still you get worse,' he said after the opening draw against Swansea. 'It's right.' Chelsea then lost 2-1 at home to Crystal Palace in the final game before the transfer window closed. 'I gave my club the report of the season projection on 21 April,' Mourinho said, the clear implication being that he had done his job in highlighting targets – John Stones and Paul Pogba most notably – and he could hardly be blamed if others hadn't done theirs. It was very reminiscent of what Mourinho had said in that small room off the tunnel at Adams Park in 2006 and, to his critics, a classic case of Mourinho promoting his own rather than the club's interests.

And why, it seemed legitimate to ask, had Mourinho been so keen to sign Radamel Falcao? Perhaps it was just a misjudgement. Perhaps he really did think that, despite the evidence of the previous season at Manchester United and the 2015 Copa América, the Colombian, another client of Mendes, could become again the striker he was before his knee injury – and, in fairness, he did show glimmers of his old form the following season after rejoining Monaco. But again a theme of the Torres book seemed relevant, namely the perception among certain Madrid players that Jorge Mendes clients enjoyed a privileged position at the club. That is not to imply any wrongdoing, but the closeness of a relationship can lead to misjudgement.

It is one that had had major consequences, largely because of Costa's dismal form. He went from being a poacher to a wrestler, the moments of gamesmanship that could once be accepted as a corollary to his edge now the dominant feature about him. He admitted he had returned for pre-season overweight.

Chelsea's preparations for the season in general came under scrutiny. A number of key players – Costa, Branislav Ivanović, Cesc Fàbregas, Eden Hazard, Nemanja Matić – all looked off-form simultaneously. The only player who started the season well was Willian, who had perhaps maintained his levels by playing for Brazil at the Copa América.

Results got worse. Chelsea lost 3-1 at Everton to a Steven Naismith hat-trick, the only league goals he scored for Everton that season. They beat Arsenal – some of the old certainties, at least, remained – but then drew 2-2 at struggling Newcastle and lost in the Champions League at Porto. Then, at the beginning of October, they lost 3-1 at home to Southampton.

It was then that it became clear this was more than a blip. Chelsea were slow, sluggish, weirdly disinterested. Chelsea fans booed the decision to replace Willian with Pedro after 64 minutes, the first major show of dissent against a manager they idolised. When he took off Matić 28 minutes after bringing him on at half-time, the crowd seemed dumbfounded.

On the touchline, Mourinho had looked impotent; after the game, he was apparently determined to show that he was standing obdurate amid the rubble. Jaw set, he delivered a seven-minute monologue in which he took aim at a host of foes, foremost among them the Chelsea board. 'No way I resign,' he said. 'No way. Why? Because Chelsea cannot have a better manager than me. There are many managers in the world that belong to my level but not better, not better. So no chance I run away. Why? For two reasons: because I have my professional pride and I know that I am very good at my job and secondly because I like this club very much. If that's not the case that could be different, but I want the best for my club and the best for my club is for me to stay, so I stay. When we were champions last season I said I'm going to stay until the owner and the board want me to leave. No club can persuade me to leave, no financial offer.'

What followed that seemed aimed at an audience beyond the press conference. 'If the club wants to sack me, they have to sack me because I am not running away from my responsibility, my team,' he went on. 'I think this is a crucial moment in the history of this club. You know why? If the club sacks me, they sack the best manager this club had. And secondly, the message is again the message of bad results. The manager is guilty. This is the message, not just these players, the other ones before, they got [the message] during a decade.

'I assume my responsibilities. It's time for everyone to assume their responsibilities. When you go down, to so many individual mistakes and fear to play, they have their responsibilities. Players that are performing really, really bad individually. I cannot come here and say, "You and you and you", it's not my job, but I think it's clear that we are being punished by too many individual mistakes. Sadness brings sadness. Bad results, they attract bad results. The first mistake is just the first because after comes another one. They still need to finish the first half winning two-three nil, the fear disappears, we come into the second half and play with a free brain, a free spirit. This is what this team needs. Unfortunately for them this is not happening.'

There followed a more predictable and wholly ludicrous attack on the referee Bobby Madley and his decision not to give a penalty following a collision between Falcao and the Southampton goalkeeper Maarten Stekelenburg (he also turned down two far better penalty shouts for Southampton): 'When we are in the top, I understand there is quite a big pleasure in putting us down. But when you are so down, I think it's time to be a little bit honest and to say clearly, the referees are afraid to give decisions for Chelsea.'

But it was those earlier words about Chelsea and the endless throughput of managers that seemed most significant. Mourinho was right, of course: the constant turmoil, the sacking of any manager who failed to win the league, was counter-productive, not least because it created a core of senior players who were resistant to change and who knew, essentially, that they were likely to outlast any coach who tried to take them on – and that, in turn, made the job less attractive to the world's great coaches. There were many factors behind André Villas-Boas's failure at Chelsea but the breakdown in his relationship with that core was probably the major reason it went wrong so quickly. Mourinho throughout his career has been seen as an impact coach, not somebody who could create a dynasty, yet his influence lingered at Chelsea, with mixed results, for several years after his initial departure. One of the many ironies of his return was it came just as Rafa

Benítez had taken a significant step towards breaking his hold by marginalising John Terry.

Beyond the narrative, of course, there was the metanarrative and what it said about his outlook. Had Mourinho's attack been more focused, had it dealt exclusively with Chelsea's previous managerial instability, it might have been possible to regard his words as a clever counter-offensive, a warning to the board that could also serve as a pre-emptive excuse were he to be sacked. But what he said about Madley was evidently ridiculous – as, given the way he toned down that part of his criticism in the written press conference that followed his monologue on television, he seemed belatedly to realise. He was lashing out indiscriminately against foes real and imagined, a wounded animal backed into a corner.

Bad got worse. Chelsea beat Aston Villa 2-0 at home, but everybody was beating Villa: it was their seventh defeat in eight games. They went to West Ham and, trailing 1-0, Matić was sent off for a second yellow just before half-time. It was perhaps too easy to suggest his judgement had been affected by his early substitution a fortnight earlier, but equally the possibility couldn't be ruled out. Mourinho approached the referee Jon Moss at half-time, called him 'fucking weak' and twice refused to leave his dressing room. Moss sent him from the touchline and Chelsea lost 2-1. Was that a genuine loss of control or was this another example of the trait outlined by Torres of him helping create the appearance of conspiracy to absolve himself of responsibility?

As reports surfaced that Hazard and Mourinho had fallen out, they met to discuss the situation. Hazard asked to play centrally and Mourinho agreed for the home game against Liverpool at the end of October. With the score at 1-1, though, Mourinho took him off, shattering what remained of Hazard's confidence as Chelsea went on to lose 3-1. They then lost 1-0 at Stoke. There was a brief rally with victories over Norwich and a 0-0 draw away to Tottenham, although that game emphasised that Hazard wasn't the only one frustrated with his manager. Mourinho had left Diego Costa out, preferring to use Hazard as a false nine. The Spain forward seemingly refused to take part in the pre-match warm-up and then, after Mourinho had brought on his three substitutes without turning to him, Costa threw his bib at his manager as he returned to take his place behind the bench, an extraordinarily blatant act of insubordination.

When Glenn Murray's late header consigned them to a 1-0 defeat at home to Bournemouth, it meant Chelsea went to Leicester at the beginning of December with Mourinho's future in very obvious doubt. And, given football's love of coincidence and narrative, who should be waiting to inflict the fatal blow but Claudio Ranieri, the affable Italian who had been ousted by Chelsea to make way for Mourinho in 2004?

Half an hour in, Eden Hazard went down after a heavy challenge from Jamie Vardy. He received treatment on his troublesome hip, trotted back on and almost immediately walked off the pitch again. Mourinho clearly wanted him to carry on but the Belgian dismissed his manager with a curt waft of the hand. Perhaps it would have been written off as the frustration of an injured player had it not been that Hazard had pointedly shaken off a hug from his manager as he was substituted late in the Champions League win over Porto the previous Wednesday. Four minutes later, Leicester took the lead, Vardy stealing between Terry and Zouma to volley in a cross from Riyad Mahrez. Three minutes into the second half, Mahrez jinked exhilaratingly in the box before drilling in a second. Loïc Remy did pull one back as Chelsea dominated the final half hour having switched to a back three, but it finished 2-1.

Mourinho seethed. He blamed the ballboys for supposed time-wasting late on, but then turned on his own players. 'I feel my work is betrayed,' he said. 'I worked four days in training for this match. I identified four movements where Leicester score a lot of their goals and in two of the four situations I identified they scored their goals. I went through it all with the players, you can ask them.'

Betrayal had become a familiar theme; Mourinho had spoken of 'rats' in the camp and had also accused one of his players of leaking his team line-up before the game against Porto. The conspirators – perceived and blamed if not necessarily real – were circling.

Defeat at Leicester left Chelsea 16th in the table, a point above the relegation zone. It proved the final straw. The following Thursday, Mourinho returned from a staff Christmas lunch to find Eugene Tenenbaum, a Chelsea director and one of Abramovich's closest allies, waiting in his office. Ten minutes later, Mourinho had left the club 'by mutual consent'.

Third-season syndrome had struck again.

# CHAPTER TWELVE

# THE MANCUNIAN REUNION

As Louis van Gaal celebrated Manchester United's victory over Crystal Palace in the 2016 FA Cup final, he received a text from his wife Truus telling him he was to be replaced by his former protégé José Mourinho. He maintains that was the first time he knew he was to be dismissed, although Truus had realised much earlier. 'My wife had said from December because she noticed that the board was reacting differently to her to before. Women...' he said, touching his nose to indicate his wife's capacity to sense a change in the atmosphere. 'But I never accepted that because all the normal things, all the meetings, the scouting meetings, with Ed Woodward were going on and they were supporting me. It was a big surprise.'

Mourinho and Van Gaal had maintained warm relations until that point; they haven't spoken since. 'That was not the right way to handle it, I think,' Van Gaal said. 'But I can imagine because Manchester United is the biggest club of England or the world that he wants it very much. That I can understand. But I think he had to call me.'

What should have been a moment of great satisfaction, ensuring he had won a trophy at every club he had managed, was soured. By the time he came into the press conference, brandishing the cup as evidence of his achievements, Van Gaal was furious. 'At the press conference,' he said, 'I put the trophy on the table for the media because they had been writing for six months already that I didn't play good and didn't win anything. That was my present for the media. At that moment I did not *know* that I was sacked. It was afterwards. We had also a celebration but the rumour was filling more and more the room. Officially I didn't know. We had to celebrate and the board was not there. You win the FA Cup – and it was a long time since they won it* – so then I knew and the players knew so it was a very sad evening for the players and for me. Then the next morning without knowing officially, I performed a farewell speech for the players at breakfast time.'

Van Gaal's departure from football management was not as ignominious as Cruyff's, but neither was it the farewell his career deserved. However unsatisfactory the way it was announced, though, there was no disguising the fact that Van Gaal's time at United was not a success. His reign had been very different to that of his predecessor David Moyes, but it was just as unfulfilling to those who believed United belonged, almost as of right, at the top of the table. Moyes had been a rabbit in the headlights, seemingly intimidated by the magnitude of replacing Sir Alex Ferguson as United finished seventh in their one season under him. If Moyes had seemed overawed by United, Van Gaal gave the impression United should be overawed by him.

His introductory press conference was remarkable. Usually they're relatively tame events, full of hope and corporate mutual congratulation, of note only when a manager goes off script and either offers a pithy tag that will be used to define them ('a special one') or fails to offer the requisite homage to the club's history, thereby turning fans against him from the off (Roy Hodgson at Liverpool). Van Gaal, though, took clear aim at United's hierarchy. Asked a fairly routine question about fulfilling expectations, he replied, 'I think I can, but it

---

* Their previous success in the competition had come in 2004.

is difficult because the greatness of this club is more than other clubs. And this club is guided in a commercial way and it is not always possible to meet commercial and football expectations.'

It was a message popular with fans long sceptical about the Glazers and their motives, but also a telling insight into a power struggle within United that would have significant consequences for Van Gaal and what came next. More immediately and more practically, Van Gaal's dissatisfaction with how the club was run came to the surface during the pre-season tour of the US during which he insisted on moving the players to a hotel nearer the training ground than had initially been arranged. He was adamant things would be done his way.

Pre-season went well and the 2014-15 season began with a mood of optimism – a sense, perhaps, that Moyes had been a necessary fall guy, a buffer between the Ferguson years and a new future. United lost the opening game of the season at home to Swansea. Van Gaal preached patience. 'You have to believe in the philosophy that we make again a big club but it needs time and it's not an overnight job,' he said. References to his 'philosophy' or 'process' would become a familiar part of his dealings with the media.

United went to Sunderland and drew 1-1. There was a lack of drive from midfield, a sense of players playing without spontaneity, shackled by the system. Van Gaal warned it would take three months for his philosophy to be assimilated. United went to Milton Keynes Dons in the League Cup and lost 4-0. 'For the fans,' Van Gaal said, 'it's very difficult to still believe in the philosophy of Louis van Gaal but you have to do that because I am here and I am here to build a new team and a new team is not built in one month. It takes time.'

But how much time? There was a goalless draw at home to Burnley, a 5-3 defeat away to Leicester and a 1-0 defeat at Manchester

City. After ten games, United had 13 points, half the total of the league leaders Chelsea and their worst start since 1986-87 when Ron Atkinson was sacked. Even Moyes had picked up four more points than that. Van Gaal pointed out his contract was for three years; his three-month timetable shelved as October slipped into November.

'I was talking always about the process,' Van Gaal said in 2018. 'Then everybody became crazy because I was saying that. When before it was not like that then it takes longer. Then you need also quality in your selection.' That quality, he insists, was lacking which was why, as he had with the Netherlands national team, he dabbled with a back three to try to offer additional defensive security.

The squad he inherited was ageing, including six players over the age of 30: Rio Ferdinand, Patrice Evra, Nemanja Vidić, Darren Fletcher, Michael Carrick and Robin van Persie. The first four of those were offloaded immediately. 'First of all I had at United to minimise the players above 30,' Van Gaal said. 'Then you have to buy players because they don't have players in youth education. At Barcelona I could use Xavi, Puyol, Valdés, Motta and Iniesta out of the youth. At Bayern I could use Müller, Badstuber, Alaba. At United, no. OK, [James] Wilson was there and [Tyler] Blackett, [Paddy] McNair … that was the level of my players. When you are honest and you see the players I had and where they play now … I had to buy other players. Then your scouting commission has to be good. In Manchester that was also a problem. The quality of the group … the year before they had been seventh with Moyes, so then you know: when you are seventh you are not seventh because of nothing.'

Even the infrastructure Van Gaal felt inadequate. 'The culture in England is not a training culture,' he said. 'When I came to Manchester United there was no light. No floodlights. I came to the biggest club in the world and there were no floodlights. So they were not used to training two times in one day.'

So Van Gaal was forced to adapt. It's hard to imagine that using Marouane Fellaini as a battering ram from midfield was ever part of his 'philosophy' but it worked. United's form improved without there ever being a moment of everything clicking as it had for Bayern in that 4-1 win away to Juventus.

And then it came, or at least it seemed to. United were superb in beating Tottenham 3-0 at home in mid-March and they followed that up with impressive victories over Liverpool, Aston Villa and Manchester City: four successive wins, three against top sides, all achieved with a measure of élan. This, it seemed, was the true beginning of the post-Ferguson era. But towards the end of the derby, Carrick had limped off and without him, United's renaissance faltered. They lost at Chelsea and then against Everton and West Brom. They finished fourth, and so qualified for the Champions League, but more important was that there had been a glimpse of a greater future.

It never crystallised into anything more meaningful. Ángel Di María, apparently unsettled by a burglary at his home, left, and an option on Radamel Falcao, still far from his best after knee surgery, wasn't taken up. In came Bastian Schweinsteiger, who had been such a key part of Van Gaal's Bayern side, Morgan Schneiderlin, Matteo Darmian, Sergio Romero, Memphis Depay and Anthony Martial. But for all the expenditure the football didn't improve, either in terms of results or style.

There was control, but little penetration. It was the manifestation of every criticism Sjaak Swart and Paul Breitner had made of the risk-averse nature of Van Gaal's approach. Van Gaal hinted that the major problem was players taking him too literally, regarding his theory as an absolute framework rather than a guide for them to extemporise upon. 'In the Netherlands,' he said, 'the players always say, "Yes, but..." and then comes their own opinion. In England, Germany and Spain, they are never saying, "But..." They are doing. They are performing. But then I have the problem that they are not thinking. I want my players thinking, reading the game, so they know they have to change the shape because of something. I want to train my players so that they can make decisions themselves as a team.'

By the turn of the year, United had drawn 0-0 seven times in all competitions and scored just nine goals before half-time in 19 league games. December was grim. United went out of the Champions League in the group stages with defeat at Wolfsburg, the beginning of a run of four successive defeats that, with Mourinho hovering after his dismissal from Chelsea, looked as though it might bring the end.

Van Gaal struggled on, but United never won three league games in a row after that. They'd gone out of the League Cup on penalties to Middlesbrough and went out of the Europa League to Liverpool. A subsequent flurry of victories – United won nine of their final 12 games of the season – brought the FA Cup, but it could not redeem the league campaign and United finished fifth, out of the Champions League qualifying slots.

The style of those four successive wins the previous season proved unrepeatable, an elusive dream that remained forever out of reach. Even on the morning of the FA Cup final, *The Times* was citing a source within the dressing room describing the 'bafflement' players regularly felt at Van Gaal's approach: 'Sometimes the players turn up and think, what the fuck are we doing this for?' Van Gaal, meanwhile, had been booed during United's final league game of the season, a 3-1 win over Bournemouth as fans displayed banners calling for his exit.*

The tendency Van Gaal had identified and railed against in his introductory press conference ultimately did for him. Mourinho had not been the right man when Ferguson had retired, so why did he become the right man three years later? If his behaviour, his existence in a perpetual fug of controversy, had ruled him out in 2013, what had changed in 2016? Certainly there'd been nothing about his time at Chelsea to suggest he had in any way amended his approach. Two trends, though, came together to open the door.

The influence of old-school board members such as Bobby Charlton, who had opposed Mourinho on moral grounds, had been diminished as a brasher, more commercially minded attitude took hold. The eight-game winless run over Christmas had coincided with a series of discordant announcements about new commercial deals – an official lubricant oil or mattress here, a coffee or formal footwear partner there – as United became the richest club by revenue in the world according to the Deloitte report of 2017. At a time when every penny was being wrung out of the brand, United couldn't afford not to be in the Champions League – not only for the revenues it brings directly but also for what it means in terms of exposure.

City's appointment of Pep Guardiola to replace Manuel Pellegrini forced United's hand. They had to react. They couldn't risk another season of drift, of waiting for the process to be internalised. Mourinho

---

* The game was played on the Tuesday, two days after everybody else had completed their league seasons, because of a bomb scare that had forced the evacuation of Old Trafford. It turned out a dummy device, used for the security team to practise sweeping the stadium, had been left strapped to a pipe in a bathroom. Somewhere amid the chaos and farce lurked a metaphor about the dangers of letting training get in the way of playing the game.

was available. At that point, he was the only manager ever to have prevented Guardiola winning a league title. Just as Real Madrid had swallowed their principles and accepted him as the only solution to the Guardiola problem, so United found themselves reaching in desperation for an unpalatable antidote.

* * *

The world settled back in expectation. The very best players on the planet may still have favoured Spain, but at the start of 2016-17, the Premier League boasted an astonishing collection of managers. At Liverpool, there was Jürgen Klopp, with his intensity, enthusiasm and manic pressing. At Tottenham there was Mauricio Pochettino, strict and likeable and also preaching a pressing game. At Chelsea there was Antonio Conte, another advocate of pressing, a demonic touchline presence and somebody with a ruthless focus on shape. At Arsenal there was Arsène Wenger, ageing and fading but still respected. At Everton there was Ronald Koeman, ready to take his version of post-Cruyffianism to a higher level than had been possible at Southampton where he had exceeded expectations by finishing seventh, then sixth. And in Manchester, there was Pep v José, a revisitation of the most apocalyptic rivalry in managerial history, the Cruyffian Messiah against the fallen angel. And that was without even mentioning the defending champions, Claudio Ranieri's Leicester City.

Guardiola and Mourinho should have met in a pre-season friendly in Beijing, but torrential rain forced the game to be called off. Their first encounter, though, could not long be delayed: United met City in their fourth league game of the season.

City beat Sunderland, Stoke and West Ham. United beat Bournemouth, Southampton and Hull. Both went into the first derby with 100 per cent records, but neither had proved anything. City, perhaps, had looked the slicker, but they had conceded a goal in every game. This was the most eagerly awaited derby in years and it became a humiliation for United. It may not have been as bad as Barça's 5-0 win over Madrid in the first Pep v José *Clásico* but City were quicker, sharper, smarter. For 40 minutes they passed the ball around at pace as United chugged in pursuit. This was what Guardiola's Barça had done to United in the 2009 and 2011 Champions League finals; it was what his Bayern had done to City in the Champions League group stage in 2013. It brought two goals: first Kelechi Iheanacho, in for the suspended Sergio Agüero, flicked on Aleksandar Kolarov's long ball for Kevin De Bruyne to score. Then a rat-a-tat of passes found Iheanacho in the box. His heavy touch let him down but De Bruyne seized on the loose ball, worked space and bent a shot that bounced back off the post for Iheanacho to poke in.

At that stage, City were rampant. With Raheem Sterling and Nolito staying wide and dragging out the United full-backs, Luke Shaw and Antonio Valencia, David Silva and, especially, Kevin De Bruyne, were able to exploit the channels outside the full-backs, something that exposed the positional limitations of Paul Pogba and Marouane Fellaini.

Guardiola appeared to have imposed his method at City remarkably quickly. Seven of City's players had played in the previous Manchester derby when they'd lost 1-0 – and two of those missing were Agüero and Vincent Kompany who might both have played if available. Van Gaal had told United it would take three years for his methods to be absorbed; Guardiola seemed to have instilled his in three weeks.

Perhaps Mourinho underestimated how slick City would be; perhaps that's why he stuck with his 4-2-3-1 rather than switching to a 4-3-3 with the *trivote* he had tended to favour in *Clásicos*. But what was striking was the lack of reaction. He took off Henrikh

Mkhitaryan and Jesse Lingard at half-time, but what had kept him? Why had there not been a change earlier? 'I didn't want to destroy the players,' Mourinho said afterwards, but when had that become a concern? This was the coach who had taken off Joe Cole and Shaun Wright-Phillips after 26 minutes of a 1-0 Chelsea defeat at Fulham in March 2006. He had taken off Nemanja Matić 28 minutes after he'd gone on as a substitute in Chelsea's 3-1 defeat to Southampton in October 2015. He'd even taken off Juan Mata after he'd come off the bench in United's 2-1 Community Shield victory over Leicester in August 2016. So why the delay here? It's true that two of those early moments of ruthlessness had still brought defeat, but was this mellowing or paralysis?

But then United were invited back into the game as Claudio Bravo came for a deep cross, collided with John Stones – the goalkeeper was widely blamed, but replays seem to show him shouting so it may be the fault was the defender's – and presented the ball to Zlatan Ibrahimović, who scored with a beautifully controlled shot at the top of the bounce. Had Ibrahimović not scuffed his shot, allowing Stones to clear off the line, Bravo would have gifted United an equaliser before half-time after a mix-up with Bacary Sagna.

United changed shape. Rooney went out to the right and Ander Herrera formed a three-man central midfield with Pogba and Fellaini. City changed approach and the game became far more even. Bravo, dallying in his own box, let the ball run towards Rooney and lunged in wildly. He took the ball first and then the man and Mark Clattenburg, the referee, decided against awarding a penalty; with the benefit of replays it was clear it was a foul and a red card. De Bruyne also hit the post and, despite the wobble, the impression that was left was of the first 40 minutes that City had controlled rather than the end-to-end football of the second half.

Mourinho railed against Clattenburg but also against his players. 'I made a couple of decisions because I thought the individual qualities of certain players would give me what I wanted,' he said. 'But I didn't get it.' That seemed a criticism of Mkhitaryan and Lingard who had presumably been included for their pace but were never involved.

'But it is not just about them,' Mourinho went on. 'We lost the ball very easily. Even our central defenders [Eric Bailly and Daley Blind], who were top-class until today, lost easy balls. What I told them at half-time was: "For some of you, it looks like you are trying to do what I told you not to do." I had told the players 20 times never to play a first-station ball [that is, a short pass to a central midfielder] – "never, because they [City] want to press, so never do that" – and they did it 20 times.' It wasn't his fault: he had given the players instruction and they had ignored him. It all sounded worryingly like his comments the previous December after Chelsea's defeat to Leicester in his final game at the club.

Alex Ferguson, following one of his great mentors, the former Rangers manager Scot Symon, made it a point of principle never to criticise players in public, whatever rollickings he may have given them in private. For Mourinho to do so after just four games in charge seemed a needlessly provocative stance and, worse, one that could be perceived as an attempt to safeguard his own reputation.

Then there was the deeper question: why had the players ignored his instructions? Why had Bailly and Blind played those short balls to Pogba and Fellaini, inviting pressure? It spoke of tactical confusion, as did the build-up to City's first goal. Kolarov had the ball under no pressure to the left of his own box. Mkhitaryan held his position but the crowd and Rooney urged him to close the full-back down. He didn't. Kolarov played the ball inside to Bravo who, hounded by Ibrahimović, returned it to the Serbian. This time Mkhitaryan did advance, but so slowly that Kolarov had time to measure his pass. What had the instructions been? To keep the shape or to press? Mkhitaryan in the end did neither, leaving his post but with so little intensity that all he did was take himself out of the game. Mkhitaryan was taken off at half-time and didn't play for another two months.

And perhaps there was an issue even deeper than that: Mourinho's aversion to passes played into the middle of midfield. Guardiola occasionally went long to avoid the press, most notably against Dortmund, but for Mourinho this was a wider point of principle. Cruyffian theory demanded passes through midfield, thrived on exploiting the qualities of passers and creators in that area, the likes of Guardiola, Clarence Seedorf and Xavi. Mourinho's rejection of the theory was so absolute that in big games he didn't want the ball in that area at all: he who has the ball has fear.

That game was the start of a pattern: United played badly and Mourinho blamed his players. United lost away to Feyenoord in the Europa League then away at Watford. Mourinho criticised Luke Shaw, accusing him of the same laxity Mkhitaryan had been guilty of. '[Nordin] Amrabat on the right side, our left-back is 25 metres distance from him, instead of five metres,' he said. 'But even at 25 metres, then you have to jump and go press. But no, we wait. This is a tactical but also a mental attitude.'

There followed the first rumblings of discontent, suggestions that some players were unhappy with a teammate being publicly criticised like that, particularly one battling to return to fitness following serious injury. Quite how serious they were was unclear but the parallel with what had happened at Real Madrid, when Mourinho had turned on Pedro Léon and provoked a squad rebellion, was clear. The criticism of Shaw went on unabated.

An edgy United beat Northampton 3-1 in the EFL Cup. Mourinho turned on the 'Einsteins' in the press who had doubted him. It seemed a strange platform from which to launch a counter-offensive but United then beat the champions Leicester 4-1, all the goals coming in a 20-minute spell, three of them from corners. For all those desperate to see the victory as evidence that momentum was building, there were at least as many who saw a slightly freakish game against a team that was prioritising the Champions League. United drew against Stoke City, then drew 0-0 away to Liverpool, successfully killing the game and becoming just the second team to stop Liverpool scoring. Mourinho, perhaps, still had the old capacity to thwart opponents – even if United were the first team to fail to score against Liverpool in the league.

The question then was whether he could repeat the trick six days later on his return to Stamford Bridge. He could not. Chris Smalling, Daley Blind and David de Gea combined to present Pedro with an opening goal after 30 seconds and United never recovered, losing 4-0. Mourinho, deflecting desperately, accused Antonio Conte of having disrespected him by whipping up the crowd with the score at 4-0. Aside from being ludicrous hypocrisy, it was such an obvious ploy it was widely derided.

The following weekend Mourinho was sent to the stands after abusing the referee Mark Clattenburg as the players returned to the pitch after half-time in a 0-0 draw against Burnley. United did then beat Swansea 3-1, with Mourinho banished from the touchline, but he seemed addicted to controversy, asserting both on television and in his press conference that he thought certain players were insufficiently 'brave' and were too willing to withdraw from games with injury. On MUTV he named them: Shaw and Smalling. Given Shaw had only just returned from a horrendously broken leg and that Smalling subsequently was ruled out for a month with a broken toe, it seemed an astonishing lapse of judgement. Perhaps he was right that United were in the grips of a collective hypochondria but singling out players who had very good reason to declare themselves unavailable just made him look unreasonable.

Whatever Mourinho did at Old Trafford in that season he lived perpetually in the shadow of what Conte was doing at Chelsea. There was no season of transition for the Italian: he took the squad that had rejected Mourinho, added to it N'Golo Kanté, David Luiz and Marcos Alonso and, aided by a lack of European football, not merely won the league but finished 24 points clear of United. They also beat United in the FA Cup quarter-final, a grim game in which Mourinho essentially set out with a narrow back four flanked by two wing-backs. Ander Herrera was sent off in the first half amid a flurry of fouls on Eden Hazard and Chelsea won 1-0.

Before the game, Hazard had been asked what the main difference between the two managers was. 'Tactical training,' he replied. 'We do more with Conte. We know exactly what to do on the pitch, where I have to go, the defenders [know] where they have to go. With Mourinho it was just he put the system [in place], but we didn't work a lot [on it]. We know what to do because we play football, but maybe the automatism was a little bit different.' Conte, in other words, had his players practise pre-planned moves, ready to adapt and apply in game situations; he organised not only the defence but also the attack.

For those who would claim that Mourinho is no longer quite at the cutting edge of the game, this, perhaps, was evidence: his systematisation went only so far. That echoed complaints made by various Real Madrid players who felt insufficient time had been spent planning how to break down massed defences. But of course that's inherent in Mourinho's whole process, his belief that football is too complex, too random, for automisations truly to be effective and that the best a manager can do is to instil the right mindset in his players to react appropriately to any given situation.

In 2016-17, that mindset seemed grindingly negative. United struggled to break teams down and although they went 26 games unbeaten in the league, and beat Southampton to win the League Cup, they were never really in the title race. As the joke had it following the drab 0-0 draw in the Manchester derby in April 2017, where Matt Busby had told his United team to go out and enjoy themselves, Mourinho told his to go out and ensure nobody enjoyed themselves.

\* \* \*

The mood around that second derby of the season was almost unimaginably different from that around the first. While the first time round had seemed like the most important game in the world, by the end of April it had become a scrap between fourth and fifth. Even a late red card for Fellaini couldn't rescue a drab 0-0 from being almost instantly forgotten. City, after an excellent start, had collapsed; United, having never really got going, were by then focused on the Europa League.

Claudio Bravo, having been left out for two and a half months before returning for straightforward wins over Hull and Southampton, was forced off by injury with 11 minutes remaining. It would be more than a year before he started another league game for City. The Chilean came to embody the problems of City's first season. Cruyff's philosophy demanded a goalkeeper who could play the ball out from the back and operate as an auxiliary outfielder if required, and it soon became clear to Guardiola that Joe Hart would be unable to fulfil that function. The decision to offload him provoked consternation in certain quarters – Hart was, after all, still the England goalkeeper – but it would be vindicated with time. What was not was Guardiola's choice of a replacement.

Claudio Bravo's stats looked excellent – he had completed 84.2 per cent of his passes the previous season, playing for Barcelona, while Hart had completed just 52.6 per cent – but the figures were misleading. Pass completion for goalkeepers was in general much higher in Spain than England, presumably because of a slower pace and greater focus on passing out from the back. Hart actually had the seventh-best figures of any keeper in the previous season's Premier League. That's not to say Bravo wasn't a good passer of the ball. He was; it was the other aspects of goalkeeping with which he struggled. His record with Barcelona and Chile suggests he is a very talented keeper, but he never looked comfortable in the Premier League. His struggles under crosses hammered his confidence to the extent that he seemed eventually almost to dematerialise when facing a shot.

Not that his shakiness provoked too much anxiety as City won ten straight games in all competitions from the start of the season. It had seemed then that Guardiola was set to dominate the Premier League as he had dominated La Liga and the Bundesliga. City often played with the two full-backs tucking in and Fernandinho dropping deep between the two central defenders to create the W-M shape Guardiola had employed at times at Bayern, with Kevin De Bruyne and David Silva as 'free eights', almost like old-fashioned inside-forwards.

But a Champions League group game away at Celtic demonstrated that City were not invincible. Brendan Rodgers's side pressed hard against City and, put under pressure, they crumbled, drawing 3-3. Tottenham then inflicted a first defeat, winning 2-0, and suddenly City couldn't win. They drew against Everton and then came the first of two Champions League group games against Barcelona.

A Fernandinho slip gifted Messi the opener after 17 minutes but City, pressing Barça and unsettling them, remained the better side until a dreadful misjudgement led to Claudio Bravo being sent off for handling outside his box nine minutes into the second half. Barça went on to win 4-0, confirming the impression of City as immensely gifted, capable of beautiful passages of play but essentially soft-centred. The clichéd criticism of the press-and-possess style turned out to be so true in this case that even Guardiola took to noting that they were fine apart from in the two boxes.

The run without a win stretched to six games, the last of them a 1-0 defeat, with a much-weakened side, to United in the League Cup. City's season never really recovered. They did beat Barcelona 3-1 at home, pressing them to distraction, but they were dogged by inconsistency. Perhaps it would have been different had De Bruyne not hit the bar from four yards with City 1-0 up against Chelsea, but that chance was squandered and Conte's side were ruthless on the break, winning 3-1 as City lost their discipline and had Sergio Agüero and Fernandinho sent off.

There were other, baffling defeats. They went down 4-2 at Leicester in December when City pushed high, leaving space for Jamie Vardy to exploit. Guardiola, afterwards, insisted he didn't 'coach tackling' and seemed vaguely outraged by criticism of his approach. When they lost 4-0 at Everton a month later, City slipped to fifth in the table. Guardiola moaned about the number of second balls in English football, his tone suggesting he was furious at English football for taking such a primitive form, angered at opponents who – understandably – sought to eschew a passing contest against De Bruyne and Silva. At that point, it seemed possible he might fail, that his version of post-Cruyffianism might not work in the Premier League.

City promptly went on a run of 11 games unbeaten that included a spectacularly open 5-3 win in the first leg of the Champions League last-16 against Monaco. A two-goal lead, though, was not enough. City were fine so long as they could control the ball, but against opponents who were able to mount attacks against them, basic defensive failings dragged them down. A 3-1 defeat meant an away-goals exit. Another wobble followed, a run of two wins in nine games that culminated with defeat to Arsenal in the FA Cup semi-final. City did win their final four games of the season to finish third, nine points clear of United, but there was no doubt that Guardiola's first year in England had been a disappointment.

\* \* \*

The first English battle between Guardiola and Mourinho may have been anti-climactic and Barcelona seemed to be moving away from classic Cruyffian principles, but in the Netherlands, at the home of Cruyffian football, Ajax's fortunes had begun to change after the failure of the Velvet Revolution. For all the gripes of the fundamentalist Cruyffians, who would perhaps argue that the consequences of their point of dispute will only become apparent in the long term, perhaps five to seven years after their split with the club, Ajax reached the Europa League final in 2017.

Frank de Boer had left for Inter in 2016 after two years without winning the title and had been replaced by Peter Bosz. Bosz had never played for Ajax but he 'had only one idol', as he put it; he had a season ticket at Ajax between 1981 and 1983 so he could watch Cruyff's farewell, even though he was a player for Vitesse at the time. Looking back, it seems as though a playing career that took him from RKC Waalwijk and Feyenoord to France, Germany and Japan was merely preparation for management. 'I knew from the age of 16 that one day I would become a coach,' he said. 'So I was preparing by writing down what my coaches were doing right but also reading a lot from Johan. With some friends, we more or less wrote our own book. Every article, all his interviews were in there. We collected them and tried to organise them – this is for attacking, this is how you defend, this is tactical.'

So fascinated was he by the Ajax method that as a player at Feyenoord in the early nineties he would regularly drive to Amsterdam to watch training sessions. The problem, as the fundamentalist Cruyffians saw it, was that those sessions were taken by Louis van Gaal. Guardiola was also an influence, with Bosz listing *Pep Confidential*, Marti Perarnau's explanation of Guardiola's first season at Bayern, as his favourite book. But where Guardiola gave his players three seconds to regain possession through a hard press before dropping off into a more defensive structure, Bosz concluded, 'We're not Barcelona, so I put two seconds on.'

Bosz also worked briefly at Maccabi Tel Aviv where Jordi Cruyff was sporting director, and where Cruyff senior would occasionally oversee his training sessions, but for some he still wasn't pure enough. Of the eight key playing principles Wim Jonk had tried to instil at De Toekomst, Ruben Jongkind claimed Bosz was applying only three. 'If you only use three principles,' Jongkind said, 'you already can see what happens, like the transition five-second rule – completely different game.'

Not that anybody could accuse Bosz's football of being boring. There was certainly no De Boer-style resting with the ball and many argued that they could have been a little more pragmatic during the Europa League run as they beat FC Copenhagen, Schalke 04 and Lyon in a series of thrilling but fraught games. They finished second behind an inspired Feyenoord in the league and then, in the final of the Europa League, they ran into Mourinho's United, pitting Cruyff acolyte against Cruyff apostate.

Ajax were never allowed to get going, were never allowed to play with the sort of fluency that had characterised them for most of the season. 'I didn't see that Ajax here,' Bosz said. United pressed early on, effectively forcing the central defender Davinson Sánchez to be a playmaker from the back by allowing him possession while shutting down every other option. A deflected shot from Paul Pogba put United ahead after 18 minutes and a 2-0 win was sealed as Henrikh Mkhitaryan hooked in a Chris Smalling knockdown from a corner three minutes into the second half. 'High pressing was difficult because Manchester United only played long balls, didn't take any risks and played only on second balls,' said Bosz. 'I think it was a boring game.'

Perhaps it was, but that was of no concern to Mourinho. 'There are lots of poets in football,' he said, 'but poets don't win titles.' He had got his strategy just right, cutting off the supply to the Ajax centre-forward Kasper Dolberg so effectively that the first time he touched the ball was to kick off after Pogba's goal. The victory, Mourinho claimed, was 'a victory of the pragmatism, a victory of the humble people, a victory of the people who respect the opponents, a victory of the people who try to stop the opponents and exploit their weaknesses'.

Even by Mourinho's standards, that was a moment of astonishing chutzpah. The suggestion that there is something hubristic about looking to impose your style on opponents rather than stopping them from playing represented a remarkable attempt to invoke the anti-establishment, underdog shtick he employed so successfully at Porto, Chelsea and Internazionale. That's a much less convincing posture to take, though, when you manage one of the two richest clubs in the world by revenue. It's hard to reconcile having an official noodle partner in every territory with claiming your reactive football is a necessary gambit in the face of an overwhelming inferiority of resources.

Mourinho had mocked the Europa League when Rafa Benítez had won it, saying it was embarrassing for a club of any stature to be involved in it. Yet his delight in victory was obvious. As his players celebrated with the Europa League trophy, José Mourinho brandished a red flag. He walked in front of his squad and tried to plant it into the pitch. The plastic pole, though, was too flimsy and bent, leaving Mourinho to prop the flag awkwardly against a hoarding reading 'Stockholm Final 2017'. As a metaphor for his first season at United it could hardly have been bettered: grand gestures thwarted but the job eventually, just about, done.

Two other details stood out, both of which offer insights into Mourinho's mentality. As he received his medal from Aleksandar Čeferin, the UEFA president, he leaned in close and spoke into his ear, telling the Slovenian that he had just become the first manager to be presented with medals by three different UEFA presidents (Lennart Johansson had been in charge in 2003 and 2004 when he won the UEFA Cup and Champions League with Porto; by the time he won the Champions League again with Inter in 2010, it was Michel Platini). He texted the detail to various friends and associates in the days that followed. To others it might have been a curiosity, but it delighted Mourinho: if he has set a record, he is going to know about it and make sure others know about it.

Perhaps it's trite to suggest that hints at a fragile ego constantly in need of bolstering, but it certainly illuminates Mourinho's mindset. As does the other notable feature of the celebrations. Mourinho, and a number of players apparently acting under instruction, kept holding up three fingers to signify the number of trophies won that season:

the Europa League, the League Cup and the Community Shield. It might have been the least impressive treble in history, but it suited Mourinho's purposes to remind everybody just how much silverware he had brought to the club in his first season.

And it was, after all, three trophies more than Guardiola had taken to City.

# CHAPTER THIRTEEN

# IDEALISM AND THE MODERN GAME

Pep Guardiola's hand went to his face. Slowly, he swept it up from his chin over his mouth and nose, over his left eye and across the sparse bristle of his scalp. As his hand reached his neck, his head fell forward, lips pursed in resignation, and he looked down at his feet. He rocked back and slumped. It had happened again – only this time he wasn't even on the bench to try to change it but exiled to the stand at the Etihad, able to communicate with his players only by shouting up the steps to a sheepish-looking coach in a magenta tracksuit who would then run down to the bench to convey his instructions. For Guardiola, who micromanages every game from the edge of his technical area, this was agony.

Guardiola's Manchester City had played football of extraordinary beauty all season. They were 13 points clear at the top of the Premier League table. If they'd beaten Manchester United the previous Saturday – and they'd led 2-0 at half-time – they would have won the league earlier than anybody else in English football history. As it was, they equalled the record by clinching the title five days later as United lost at home to West Bromwich Albion. But, once again, a Guardiola side, dominant in every other aspect, had faltered in the knockout stage of the Champions League.

His interpretation of the philosophy he'd learned as a player from Johan Cruyff and had refined under Louis van Gaal seemed to have a fatal flaw: it could produce historically low numbers in the goals against column over the course of a season, but if opponents could get through the midfield press, his defence had a tendency to crumble. Three goals conceded in rapid succession had sunk his Bayern in successive Champions League semi-finals against Real Madrid and Barcelona, had sunk his City against Leicester in the Premier League the previous season, away at Liverpool in the league three months earlier, and then again in the first leg of the Champions League quarter-final against Liverpool the previous Wednesday. Just in case the message hadn't got through, United had then scored three in 16 minutes in the second half of the derby the previous Saturday. It kept on happening.

Three goals down from the first leg, Guardiola had picked a remarkably attacking team for the second leg against Liverpool, a sort of 3-1-4-2 with the full-back Kyle Walker deployed on the right side of the three-man defence. And for 45 minutes it had seemed to be working. Gabriel Jesus had put City ahead in the second minute and most of the rest of the half was played at Liverpool's end as Jürgen Klopp's side struggled to break the siege. Bernardo Silva had hit the post with a deflected shot and then, just before the break, Leroy Sané had a goal wrongly ruled out for offside, none of the officials seeming to realise that the ball had bounced to him not off a City player but off James Milner.

As City's players forcefully made that point to the Spanish referee Antonio Mateu Lahoz as they left the pitch at half-time, Guardiola had intervened, seemingly to remove his players from confrontation. But as he dragged Fernandinho away, something in him snapped. Lahoz, after all, had awarded three penalties against City in the Champions League the previous season. More significantly, he had decided Sergio Agüero had dived against Monaco as City went out in the last 16 when replays suggested the correct decision should have been a penalty and a red card for the goalkeeper Danijel Subašić. Guardiola had turned back. He didn't, he later claimed, 'say a bad word'. Perhaps not, but the sustained nature of his aggressive pointing made his expulsion from the bench inevitable. What should have been 2-0 was still 1-0 and, worse, he was removed from the fray, left to sit impotent as Liverpool confirmed their progress with two goals in the second half and a 5-1 aggregate win.

Guardiola's City had not merely won the league but had done so by breaking records for the most points won and the most goals scored and yet there was a palpable sense of disappointment about the end of the season. In part that was a result of how straightforward the league success had been. From around November, City's triumph had felt inevitable. There was no crescendo and the one opportunity to offer that, by beating United and Guardiola's arch-rival José Mourinho, had been squandered. The result was a feeling of anti-climax. That might not have been fair – and for City to win the league so emphatically was a rather greater achievement than winning the Bundesliga by similar margins with Bayern had been – but it did mean that the enduring sensation was one of disappointment.

Yet it had been an astonishing season both statistically and by less quantifiable measures. City's football had at times been extraordinary. Aesthetic judgements are necessarily subjective but there had been at times, particularly in the late autumn when there had been an almost transcendental beauty to their play, a sense that Guardiola was redefining what was possible in football, that he had taken the style first developed in the Netherlands almost half a century earlier and refined it to dominate the modern age. But then that flaw recurred, Guardiola undone again by a quicker, more physical team. This was not the domination he had achieved with the great Barcelona side that won the Champions League in 2009 and 2011; rather his style, or rather his interpretation of the philosophy Johan Cruyff had developed at Barcelona in the late eighties, was merely one approach among many at the top of the game.

\* \* \*

For Barcelona, Paris came as a dreadful shock. They may have achieved a remarkable comeback in the second leg, exposing the fragility of the Parisian project as they did so, but their 4-0 defeat to PSG in the first leg of their Champions League last-16 tie was damning. All those fine words about Luis Enrique in his first season, all the praise they had garnered after their success in Berlin, all of it was left looking a little hollow. What if the fundamentals weren't right? What if their treble in 2014-15 was down less to a reinterpretation of the post-Cruyffian philosophy than to the simple fact that their forward line comprised three of the best forwards on the planet?

There had been suspicions all season that something wasn't quite right. The same intensity wasn't there. Sergio Busquets, in particular, had looked out of sorts while both he and Andrés Iniesta had struggled with injuries. Johan Cruyff had always said that Barça wouldn't realise how important Busquets was until he was gone, and this was the proof of it: he may still have been there in body, but he was not the same player, not even close. The benefits of that stellar front three, the individual brilliance that could unpick packed defences, began to be outweighed by their lack of defensive work, the disconnection to the midfield.

Barcelona's league season featured the usual thrashings of sides still petrified by their aura, but there were plenty of warning signs, not only in the autumn defeats to Alaves and Celta Vigo but in strangely lifeless draws against Malaga, Villarreal and Real Betis.

The Champions League group stage games against Guardiola's Manchester City also offered hints of what was to come. Barça may have won 4-0 at the Camp Nou, but it was a scoreline that said little about the balance of the game.

The message was clear: Barça had once terrified teams with their pressing, but this iteration was susceptible to just such a tactic. They could be outpressed. At the Parc des Princes, Paris Saint-Germain took full advantage. What was remarkable was that Barcelona were never in the game: it was a total annihilation. The PSG coach Unai Emery had previously won only one of 23 matches against Barça, but in his three seasons at Sevilla he had regularly shaken them. He knew that they could be got at. He knew they were vulnerable, that the spirit and the energy and the hunger that had once underpinned the passing and the technique was waning. But still, even he can't have expected Barça to wilt quite as they did. PSG's press was ferocious. At one point the goalkeeper Marc-Andre ter Stegen was pressured into slicing the ball out of play while inside his six-yard box. Midway through the first half, Barça ended up being forced to play back to Ter Stegen from an attacking corner.

Ángel Di María scored the first with a free kick. Julian Draxler got the second before half-time, following a neat interchange with Marco Verratti after Messi had been dispossessed by Adrien Rabiot. Di María, given a ludicrous amount of space, bent in the third after a move that had swept the length of the pitch. Edinson Cavani lashed in the fourth following an unchecked 40-yard surge by the right-back Thomas Meunier. Again and again in the final quarter of the game, as Barça's discipline disintegrated, PSG players were allowed to carry the ball without opposition for 40, 50 yards.

Sergi Roberto, at right-back, was repeatedly left isolated by the right-sided midfielder André Gomes, a glaring indication of Barça's problems with renewing the squad. Dani Alves had been able to dominate the right flank almost single-handedly. Perhaps Aleix Vidal, his start at the club ravaged by injury, would have fared better than Sergi Roberto, a converted midfielder, but that didn't excuse the lack of coherence, the lack of recognition, the sheer lack of battle elsewhere. 'This is not Barça,' roared the headline in *Sport*, going on to describe the club as being 'shipwrecked without a manager'.

The following weekend, Barça hosted Leganés, who were fourth bottom of the league having won just four games all season. They won 2-1, but only thanks to a last-minute penalty from Messi. When he scored, he didn't celebrate. He didn't point at the sky as he usually does, to dedicate the goal to his grandmother, Celia. There was no outburst of anger as there had been when he'd scored a late penalty winner at Valencia earlier in the season. He just stood there and in so doing seemed to express the sense of numbness at the heart of Barça, the feeling that something fundamental had misfired.

In that game against Leganés, Barça for the first time fielded only one Catalan player. In modern football the initial reaction, perhaps, is surprise that it has taken so long for the figure to fall that low, but it is not a detail to be glibly dismissed. Barça's strength, at their best, was the congruence of their political and tactical identities. They had a Catalan core and that core had been brought up at La Masia to play the Barça way; that had been one of Cruyff's first lessons. It was an ecosystem that often found it difficult to accommodate outsiders but it also meant basic familiarity with the system from those who had grown up within it. There was always another youth player who could slot in. He might not reach the heights of Xavi, Iniesta, Busquets or Piqué, but he knew what he was doing. There was a moment in that Leganés game when Lucas Digne played a ball down the line to Neymar, who controlled it, waited for a run and then, when it hadn't come from the static left-back, made a series of chopping gestures with his arm. This wasn't the Barça way: Digne, who cost £14m when he joined from PSG in the summer of 2016, was not attuned to the movements Neymar, in his three and a half seasons at the club, had come to expect.

But Digne was far from the only one. Neymar and Suárez, of course, changed the dynamic, as did Rakitić. They made Barça more direct, brought them perhaps more in line with the general tactical evolution of the game, certainly made them more varied. But it was within recognisable parameters. The signings of Arda Turan and André Gomes in midfield seemed utterly contrary to the post-Cruyffian philosophy. They are shuttlers, hard workers, gifted in their way, but not players to spin those beguiling long skeins of passes. And that, in turn, caused problems elsewhere, most notably on the right but also in terms of the role of Busquets. With Iniesta and Xavi (then Rakitić) in front of him, he could sit deep, operating at times almost as a third central defender; with a slowing Iniesta and Gomes or Turan there, he was forced to play higher up the pitch, exposing his lack of pace and mobility, which is one of the reasons PSG found themselves running so frequently at an exposed back line. As Sid Lowe pointed out in the *Guardian* after the Leganés game, it was indicative of how far Barça had shifted from their roots that there wasn't a Barcelona player in the top ten passers in the league at that point in 2016-17 and not a Barcelona midfielder in the top 25. Busquets, having by far the worst season of his Barça career, wasn't even in the top 80.

Luis Enrique, inevitably, bore the brunt of the criticism, but it was notable that the hard core of Barça fans chanted his name during the Leganés match. To an extent, of course, Barça's decline was the inevitable result of a great generation growing old: Iniesta and Busquets, even Messi, couldn't hold everything together for ever. Signing

Neymar and Suárez may have been a step away from the purity of the Guardiola ideal, but it also, at least temporarily, arrested the decline – perhaps even took them to new heights, a reiteration of the paradigm that a team's greatest moment of self-expression comes just before its decline. Having moved away from the culture of home-grown self-sufficiency towards a more celebrity-based model, though, the club was then placed in an awkward position: should it keep buying, or should it hope another great generation emerged? Barça kept buying, and did so badly, which suggested the blame lay with the board.

They had already found themselves the subject of criticism after the PSG defeat from Dani Alves, who had left for Juventus on a free transfer the previous summer. 'During my final three seasons,' he said, 'I always heard that "Alves was leaving", but the directors never said anything to my face. They were very false and ungrateful. They did not respect me. I was only offered a new deal when the FIFA transfer ban came in. That was when I played them at their own game and signed a deal with a termination clause. Those who run Barcelona today have no idea how to treat their players.'

But just as had happened in January 2015, just when things were at their bleakest, there came an unexpected turnaround. Barça beat Sporting Gijon 6-1, after which Luis Enrique, describing himself as 'exhausted', announced he would leave the club at the end of the season. That same night, Madrid were unexpectedly held to a 3-3 draw at home by Las Palmas: against all expectations, Barcelona suddenly had the league title back in their grasp – providing they beat Madrid in the *Clásico*. They beat Celta Vigo 5-0. Then came the second leg against PSG: surely they couldn't win a third successive game by five goals?

They could. Perhaps it had more to do with PSG's psychological collapse than particularly great play on their own part. Perhaps they did get the rub of some refereeing decisions and they certainly benefited from some curious bounces of the ball, but who cared about that in the immediate aftermath? Not Luis Enrique who, his usual restraint gone, ran onto the field at the final whistle, collapsed, and thrashed like a fish on a deck. Yet while Barça's 6-1 victory over PSG will – rightly – be remembered as one of the greatest of all games, nothing that happened during it suggested those long-term issues had been addressed or solved.

Luis Enrique had switched to a 3-4-3, getting rid of the full-back issues by getting rid of the full-backs. It perhaps made Barça more secure, but it seemed to crowd Messi, who was noticeably quiet against PSG. And it perhaps got them higher up the pitch faster, emphasised their intensity, which was the attribute they most obviously demonstrated that night. They got an early goal as PSG froze under an awkwardly spinning ball and Suárez headed in. They added a second before half-time as Iniesta's backheeled cross bounced in off Layvin Kurzawa. When a Messi penalty, awarded after Meunier slipped and brought down Neymar, made it 3-0 four minutes into the second half, the momentum seemed decisively with Barça. But then Cavani smacked in a half-volley after 62 minutes and Barça went from needing one goal to pull level to needing three not to lose. For 26 minutes, almost nothing happened. The game was flat, finished. Then Neymar belted in a stunning free kick and PSG folded. They completed only four passes in the final seven minutes of the game, three of them from a kick-off. Suárez took advantage of a stupidly raised arm from Marquinhos to dive for a penalty that Neymar converted. And then, in the fifth minute of injury time, Ter Stegen, having gone up for a corner, made a vital challenge in the centre circle to cut off a break and was himself fouled: a sweeper-keeper showing clearly the advantages of having 11 players who can play. The free kick was cleared back to Neymar, who jinked inside and floated a ball over a shambolic PSG backline. Sergi Roberto ran on and controlled his jab-volley past Kevin Trapp.

It was a remarkable night, one that will live for ever in the history of the Champions League and in the collective memory of Barcelona, but it proved oddly meaningless; in fact, it arguably did nothing more than open Barça up to a further beating in the quarter-final. It came, sure enough, against a tough and slick Juventus who capitalised on more lacklustre defending to win 3-0 in Turin before holding Barça to a goalless draw at the Camp Nou.

The advantage Barça had gained in the title race, meanwhile, was squandered long before that as they lost 2-0 at Deportivo La Coruña four days after the recovery against PSG. A subsequent defeat at Malaga effectively ended their La Liga hopes.

The appointment of Ernesto Valverde, a midfielder in Cruyff's Dream Team, was portrayed as some sort of return to the traditional philosophy, but it didn't really play out like that. Barcelona won La Liga with some ease in 2017-18 but never looked comfortable in the Champions League. The 4-4-2 Valverde favoured made them very dependent on Lionel Messi for creativity and strangely flimsy in the centre. Ivan Rakitić was never able to offer Sergio Busquets the protection he needed in midfield and Chelsea had exposed how vulnerable Barça were before Valverde's side squandered a 4-1 first-leg lead to be eliminated by Roma on away goals in the quarter-final. Pressed by a Roma side who would themselves be physically over-powered by Liverpool in the semi, Barça looked slow and sluggish, while the lack of defensive work done by Messi and Luis Suárez was striking. Perhaps that was a result of age, or perhaps it's just what happens once a club starts dabbling with a culture of celebrity. Either way, the days when Guardiola had urged Messi to be not merely the best in the world with the ball but the best without it felt a long time in the past.

\* \* \*

When were the Dutch last truly Dutch? While the other bastions of the Cruyffian style disputed trophies, in its homeland the questions were more existential. There'd been doubts about the style of Marco van Basten's side at Euro 2008, huge doubts about Bert van Marwijk's team at the 2010 World Cup and general bewilderment about Louis van Gaal's use of a back three at the 2014 World Cup. But at least those sides had been in tournaments, at least they'd been competing. Whatever qualms there'd been about Van Gaal's adaptation of the traditional Dutch style soon faded.

Guus Hiddink returned to the job but lasted only a year, by which time the Netherlands, having lost away to the Czech Republic and Iceland, were in serious danger of failing to qualify for the expanded Euro 2016. Danny Blind couldn't stop the rot, suffering home defeats to the Czech Republic and Iceland as well as being hammered 3-0 in Turkey. With two teams from each group to qualify as of right and third-placed teams guaranteed at least a play-off, it had seemed inconceivable that any major side could fail to qualify. The Netherlands finished fourth. It was the first time they'd failed to reach the Euros since 1984.

With France and Sweden in their World Cup qualifying group, the draw had, admittedly not been kind to them. But their form didn't improve and a defeat away to Bulgaria in March 2017 led to the removal of Blind. There was some talk that the Netherlands might turn to Jorge Sampaoli, the Bielsa disciple who had had great success with Chile and went on to become national coach of Argentina, but instead they named the 69-year-old Dick Advocaat. He had a fine record as a manager but it was more of the same: so resolutely were the KNVB sticking to the trusted model that he was the third manager of the previous four they'd appointed who'd played for Sparta Rotterdam in 1981.

By October, with two games of qualifying remaining, Sweden in second led the Dutch by three points. The sides were to meet in Amsterdam in their final game, which meant if the Netherlands won that, goal difference would be the key. The Netherlands had to go to Belarus while Sweden faced Luxembourg. Advocaat expressed confidence. But what, he was asked, if Sweden won easily, effectively putting the Dutch out of contention. 'They won't win 8-0,' he said. 'What a stupid question that is.' They won 8-0.

The crisis in Dutch football has many causes, not least of which is that no country with a population of 17 million can guarantee always to excel; there will always be generations that simply aren't that good at football. Economics play a part, with Dutch clubs constantly looking to sell abroad, meaning the average age of players in the Eredivisie has dropped. 'In my time, if you made your debut at 17 or 18, it was, "Wow! Miracle!"' said Ryan Babel, who made his debut for Koeman's Ajax as a 17-year-old in 2004, 'but now it's normal. The younger players have to be more responsible earlier. That's why some players now are not in their best shape and getting criticised already even though they are still very young.'

As analysis by Pieter Zwart has shown, the Netherlands national team is so dependent on Arjen Robben that between 2014 and 2018 they scored almost a goal a game more when he played than when he didn't. Robben's pace on the counter, indeed, rather than an approach rooted in possession, had underlain the wins over France and Italy at Euro 2008, the second-half performance in the quarter-final win over Brazil at the 2010 World Cup and then the evisceration of Spain in

2014. Worryingly, as Simon Kuper pointed out in an article in *Der Spiegel*, Robben's upbringing wasn't even really Dutch. He grew up in Bedum in the north-east of the Netherlands, near the German border. Had he been born further west, his instinct for dribbling might have been coached out of him, he might have gone through the process Fabio Capello said Zlatan Ibrahimović had undergone at Ajax and lost his individuality. Robben, aged 33, retired after the win over Sweden.

Kuper had no doubt who was to blame. 'The Dutch game,' he wrote, 'has fallen into the hands of an old boys' club of former players who don't even want to keep up with the best foreigners.' Harking back always to the golden age of the seventies and Total Football, it has not evolved as Guardiola, Mourinho, Luis Enrique and even Van Gaal had evolved. For a long time the best Dutch football has been played in Spain. Which is perhaps why, after missing out on a second successive international tournament, the KNVB turned to a coach who had been there when the philosophy that shaped the modern game was forged: Ronald Koeman.

Koeman, though, had lost his faith. He laughed when asked at his introductory press conference whether he would revert to the classic 4-3-3 and, while he praised what Guardiola was doing at Manchester City, set up in both of his first two games, friendlies against England and Portugal, with a back three and little intention of controlling possession. For the national side, the lessons of Rinus Michels are a distant memory.

For the truest believers, the most devout Cruyffians, it is an increasing struggle to find a club that will let them take over the whole process. The Cruyff Football project is now working in China with the Beijing Montessori Institute. 'We have invested all our money in this company,' said Ruben Jongkind, 'and we try to spread the legacy of Cruyff around the world, the legacy of football of course, the kind of football, but also how we can develop players beyond this kind of football. How can we develop total humans? Not only the player but the player who has also the behavioural characteristics of a Cruyffian footballer such as creativity, problem-solving skills, positive growth mindset, self-regulation skills, respect, thinking outside only the small world of football, helping others to become better. How can we connect the educational process to football and take football as a point of departure for education? That's basically our mission. And how we do it is by developing players, and we develop coaches by giving coaching courses and workshops.'

Perhaps it will work. Perhaps by the 2030 World Cup, there will be a genuine threat from a China side playing positionally intelligent, hard-pressing, possession-based, post-Cruyffian football. But for now, the Netherlands is going through a period of doubt and pragmatism.

* * *

When the circumstances are right, though, post-Cruyffian football can still produce football that is not merely highly effective, but extremely good to watch, and can hint towards pre-eminence. After his disappointing first season in English football, Guardiola moved swiftly to deal with the evident weaknesses in his Manchester City squad, buying a goalkeeper, Ederson, who was not merely good with his feet but was physically brave and a fine shot-stopper, and three full-backs for a combined total of £115m. Bernardo Silva and, in January, Aymeric Laporte, later added depth to the squad.

José Mourinho sneered about City buying full-backs for centre-forward prices as Manchester United bought a centre-forward, Romelu Lukaku, for £75m and strengthened the spine with the holding midfielder Nemanja Matić and the central defender Victor Lindelöf.

His point about money, of course, was valid – up to a point. City's success has been fuelled by the sovereign wealth of Abu Dhabi, and it's entirely reasonable to question the nature of the regime whose reputation the football club is effectively laundering, but United have also spent vast sums on players. In the two seasons after Guardiola and Mourinho arrived in Manchester, City spent a net £350m and United £255m. That's only a snapshot, of course, of an ongoing process but it does suggest that, while City spent more than United, it wasn't so much to make their success inevitable. The more important issue, anyway, is the targeted nature of City's spending. City did not do what PSG did and simply go out and spend eye-watering sums on two of the most vaunted forwards in the world. They targeted their spending with a thought always to the collective.

There was a joke doing the rounds in the summer of 2017 that featured Guardiola approaching Sheikh Mansour and telling him he could make City the most successful club in Europe playing football of extraordinary beauty. Enthused by the vision Guardiola described, Mansour asked how he could make it reality. 'All I need,' the gag had Guardiola reply, 'is the best two players in the world in every position.' It was a jibe with enough truth to resonate but it was just a joke. There was something almost tawdry about PSG's expenditure, the sense that there wasn't much substance behind the bling exposed when Real Madrid cuffed them aside in the last 16 of the Champions League, while City used their resources to bring into being a remarkable incarnation of the post-Cruyffian philosophy. Just as undeniable as the money spent was the fact that Guardiola's system and his coaching had made players better.

City began 2017-18 with a back three, seemingly as a way of getting both Sergio Agüero and Gabriel Jesus into the side, and used it three times in the first four league games. It brought a 2-0 win at

Brighton, a 1-1 draw at home to Everton (in a game City dominated) and then a 5-0 victory over Liverpool but it was rarely seen after that. The success against Liverpool was nowhere near as emphatic as the scoreline made it seem. City had been leading 1-0 but were under pressure when Sadio Mané, stretching to bring down a bouncing ball, kicked Ederson in the head and was sent off, after which Liverpool couldn't cope with City's movement. The next week Guardiola selected a 4-3-3 and beat Watford 6-0 at Vicarage Road. For the couple of months that followed, with Kevin De Bruyne and David Silva superb in 'free 8' roles, creating almost like old-fashioned inside-forwards in front of Fernandinho, City were sensational. They won a record 18 league games in a row, scoring 58 goals as they did so.

But Mourinho's United had also begun the season well. They won six of their first seven games in the league, scoring four in four of them, as well as against Burton Albion in the League Cup and CSKA Moscow in the Champions League. They were tough and physically imposing, outlasting opponents and picking them off on the break late in games. Of the 21 goals they scored in those first seven league matches, ten had come after the 80th minute.

Then they went to Anfield. Although they would go on to have an excellent season, Liverpool at the time were struggling. Defeat at City had been the start of a run of seven games in all competitions in which they'd won only one and hadn't kept a clean sheet. They were vulnerable. With City's form making clear that it would take a huge points tally to win the league and that any slip-up could be decisive, it was an opportunity for United to take advantage of the schedule and win at a difficult venue, to gain a slight advantage and apply some pressure. They didn't take it. Rather they sat back, looked to absorb pressure that never really came and managed just one significant chance. Mourinho blamed Jürgen Klopp for not 'breaking' the game but he was the coach in the position of power, he was the one bearing a responsibility to win.

The following week an out-of-sorts United lost at Huddersfield and although they then beat Tottenham 1-0, capitalising on a defensive error to score a late goal after another strikingly reactive display, they followed that up by losing 1-0 at Chelsea after another oddly meek display. The gap to City at the top was suddenly eight points. After the Europa League final, Mourinho has spoken of United's success as a victory for pragmatism, but where was that spirit here?

Pragmatism in football ought to mean nothing more than playing in the way most likely to bring success – as Mourinho had at Inter. As Andrés Iniesta once said of Barcelona's style, 'We play the way we do because it suits us. We don't have the players to pull it off playing a different way. People talk about "pragmatic" football; well, for us, this is pragmatic. It's the way we like to play and it's the way we believe we have the best chance of winning.' Pragmatism is not a synonym for defensiveness. It's hard to understand how playing negatively against Liverpool and Chelsea sides who had come to seem vulnerable gave United the best chance of winning – as they had to keep up with City. Mourinho insists on reactive football again and again, even when it means losing ground. Three games in a month against top-six sides were always likely to represent a decisive phase of the season. In them United totalled six shots on target. Mourinho's approach by then was not pragmatic; it was stubbornly dogmatic.

This was the great irony of the whole debate around post-Cruyf-fianism, that while Guardiola was the one criticised for his inflexibility, his unwillingness to countenance a shift away from the principles that had been instilled in him at Barcelona, the manager who actually suffered for his philosophical obstinacy, for his determination to embody the opposite of what Guardiola stood for, was Mourinho.

The title was effectively settled on 10 December, as City went to Old Trafford and again won 2-1. When Marcus Rashford equalised just before half-time, United had had just 25 per cent possession. They had sat deep, been extraordinarily passive and essentially waited for a City mistake. Yet when they did attack late on, City wobbled, Ederson saving a close-range Lukaku shot with his face. By then, though, City led 2-1, both their goals, as though to mock the one-dimensional nature of Mourinho's approach, having stemmed from set plays that United failed to clear.

Mourinho responded in classic Mourinho fashion, complaining about City's supposedly excessive celebrations, leading to a fracas in which milk and water were thrown by City players and City's assistant coach Mikel Arteta suffered a cut to the head. In his post-match interview, Mourinho blamed the referee Michael Oliver for deciding Ander Herrera had dived rather than awarding a penalty when he tumbled over a clumsy challenge from Nicolas Otamendi. By this stage, though, his games were too transparent, and every chance United created late on served only to emphasise the fact that if City had been attacked earlier they may have succumbed.

Although United ended up comfortably second, that was the story of the season. They beat every top-six side and yet they lost to the three promoted sides. They were inconsistent in a weirdly inconsistent way. They were powerful and efficient, but weirdly defensive when there was little reason to be, most damagingly when they lost to Sevilla in the Champions League. As goals flew in elsewhere in the knockout stages – prompting the thought that a team that could actually defend would have a significant competitive advantage – United were both timid and lumbering in Seville, nicking a 0-0 draw thanks largely to the excellence of David de Gea. That, though, rendered them vulnerable to an away goal and Sevilla got two.

But it was also the story for City. They ended the season having had a record 66.4 per cent possession and having completed an average 743 passes per game, 124 more than the next team in the list, Arsenal. They conceded just 27 goals in their 38 league games but, as Van Gaal had pointed out, get beyond their press and they were vulnerable, just as Bayern had been under Guardiola. That first became really apparent at Anfield in the January as Liverpool beat City 4-3, racing into a 4-1 lead with three goals in nine minutes – that familiar burst of goals that kept on undermining Guardiola sides. Much more significant, though, was when Liverpool did the same in the Champions League quarter-final, a blast of three goals in 19 minutes of the first half of the first leg effectively winning them the tie.

In part, the problem was part of a more general trend. In the eight seasons from 2009-10 to 2016-17, 21 of 104 games in the quarter-finals or later of the Champions League finished with a winning margin of three or more; in the eight seasons before that there were only eight. In 2017-18, there were five. Large margins of victory have come to be expected in the group stages of the competition when there is often a significant disparity between the resources of two sides, but that shouldn't be the case in the last eight and beyond.

There would seem to be numerous, inter-related explanations. Although the competitive nature of the Premier League means that it shouldn't really apply to City, the ease with which elite sides from other top European leagues dominate their domestic competition perhaps means that they forget both how to defend and how to fight, an issue compounded by the growing focus on celebrity individuals. Generally untested, they are then exposed when pitched into a more even game, leading to collapses, big scores and wild swings. Alongside runs the general preference in modern football for players at the back who are comfortable on the ball rather than necessarily adept at the more traditional defensive arts. When a team expects, whether for reasons of superiority over the opposition or philosophy, to control possession, of course it makes sense to favour players who are good at using the ball rather than preventing others using it, but that of course renders that team vulnerable when attacks do come.

With Guardiola sides there is an additional factor. They aren't just prone to conceding goals when they come up against the very best, they concede them in clusters – that quick-fire salvo of goals that undid Bayern in semi-finals against both Real Madrid and Barça, and City twice against Liverpool – and, indeed, against Leicester in the league in 2016-17 and Manchester United in 2017-18. That suggests the issue is in part psychological, that for some reason when a Guardiola side faces a setback, it is prone to panic. Perhaps this is the other side of the privileging of the system: that when players subordinate their individuality so absolutely to the team unit, they lose some of the personality that would otherwise enable them to grab a game and yank it back their way; they take on, in other words, the role of obedient schoolboys of which Zlatan Ibrahimović was so scathing at Barcelona. The condition made Guardiola's dismissal from the bench in the second leg of the Champions League quarter-final against Liverpool all the more decisive: he is so active on the touchline, so engaged in the micromanagement of games, that when he is not there to guide his players, they become rudderless.

But none of that renders Guardiola's interpretation of post-Cruyffianism invalid. His philosophy may have a flaw. It may be particularly susceptible to the ferocity of Klopp's approach: Klopp won eight of their first 14 meetings; no other manager has a head-to-head record against Guardiola anywhere near as good. It is, obviously, a style that is applicable only to a certain type and level of player; the criticism that Guardiola wouldn't play that way if he were in charge of Burnley is as irrelevant as sneering that a Formula One driver wouldn't drive like that popping down to the shops in a 20-year-old Fiat Uno. But it is also an approach that has brought seven league titles (and two Champions Leagues) in nine seasons of management, and has produced football of extraordinary beauty while challenging the drift to celebrity and individuality in the modern game.

Elsewhere, perhaps, the post-Cruyffian influence is waning. Mourinho battles on with his *anti-guardiolisme*, fitfully successful but seemingly not quite the force he was, seemingly scarred by the experience of Madrid and not quite able to generate the necessary underdog scrappiness at clubs that are manifestly too big to take on the role of plucky outsider. He may come again, but there was a strain about his first two years at United, a sense of constant struggle that City's excellence, in 2017-18, only heightened.

The traditional homes of the Cruyffian style, meanwhile, are in difficulty. Barcelona won La Liga in 2017-18 but their football was often slow and the limitations of an ageing squad were exposed in the Champions League. The dose of celebrity culture Luis Enrique introduced may not easily be eradicated. At Ajax, the Velvet Revolution ended in acrimony. Bosz, who had briefly breathed life into the club, left for Borussia Dortmund but never convinced while the turmoil in Amsterdam went on. The Netherlands national side is at its lowest ebb in half a century and although it has turned to a post-Cruyffian in Ronald Koeman to rectify the situation, he has been clear that he doubts the traditional philosophy is applicable in this case.

But 20 years after that great confluence of minds in Barcelona, it is the style of football they practised that remains the dominant style. In various forms those principles of pressing and possessing, adapted according to circumstance, underpin the modern game – more universally, thanks to the globalised nature of modern football, than any style has before. Even those who, like Mourinho, have rejected the Cruyffian principles or, like Diego Simeone, Mauricio Pochettino or Jürgen Klopp, come from a different background, have been in some way moulded by it. That's where the reach and influence of Cruyff's philosophy is really seen. It's not just that those who found themselves working together at the Camp Nou have been enormously successful in their own right, it's that every other club and coach at the elite level of the game has in some way had to find solutions to the questions they have asked.

More than two decades after he last held a managerial position, Johan Cruyff's legacy is secure. For all the multiplicity of approaches at the top of the modern game, his remains the most far-reaching influence.

# ACKNOWLEDGEMENTS

All books are part of a collaborative process. This one could not have been written without the help of a huge number of people across the world, who gave their time and wisdom freely. To the dozens of managers, players and coaches who agreed to be interviewed, I'm hugely grateful, but even greater thanks are due to all the journalists who helped out – particularly when you suspect they probably should have been writing their own books about this.

Sid Lowe, as ever, was a garrulous and generous guide, helping to arrange interviews, offering contact details and placing his enormous wealth of Spanish experience at my disposal. The Dutch and Portuguese sections of the book could not have been written without the assistance of Priya Ramesh and Carlos Santos, while Rik Sharma's work digging through old newspapers in Barcelona was invaluable. In Italy, James Horncastle, Federico Bassahún and Paolo Bandini were of enormous help.

Kat Petersen's stern eyebrow was as stern as ever in an initial edit, while Ian Greensill's copy-edit saved me from numerous embarrassments. Thanks also to my editor Matt Phillips and my agent David Luxton, whose slow left-arm spin is slower than even I'd imagined possible.

This book had its roots in an article written for the Swedish magazine *Offside*, so my thanks to them for commissioning it. It took flight with a subsequent article for the *Guardian* written on a cricket tour while in St Peter's Square waiting for the Pope, so my thanks both to my editors there and to my Authors CC teammate Tom Holland, whose capacity to cite chunks of *Paradise Lost* off the top of his head made clear the resonances between José Mourinho and Milton's Satan.

And then there are all the others who have in some way offered assistance, whether in terms of information, argument or logistics. Thanks to: John Brewin, Miguel Delaney, Ken Early, Simon Kuper, Gabriele Marcotti, Andy Mitten, Jack Pitt-Brooke and Kristof Terreur.

# BIBLIOGRAPHY

Ancelotti, Carlo, *Quiet Leadership* (Penguin, 2016)

Balague, Guillem, *Messi* (Orion, 2013)

——*Pep Guardiola* (Orion, 2013)

Bakema, JB, *Thoughts about Architecture* (St Martin's Press, 1981, ed. Marianne Gray)

Barclay, Patrick, *Mourinho* (Orion, 2005)

Barend, Frits and Henk van Dorp, *Ajax, Barcelona, Cruyff: The ABC of an Obstinate Maestro* (Bloomsbury, 1997)

Beasley, Rob, *Mourinho* (Michael O'Mara 2016)

Borst, Hugo, *O, Louis* (Yellow Jersey, 2014)

Burns, Jimmy, *Barça: A People's Passion* (Bloomsbury, 1999)

Claessen, Sjoerd, *Koeman & Koeman* (DCM, 1998)

Condo, Paolo, *The Duellists* (De Coubertin, 2017)

Cruyff, Johan, *My Turn* (Macmillan, 2016)

Damásio, António, *Descartes' Error* (Grosset Putnam, 1994)

Goldblatt, David, *The Ball is Round: A Global History of Football* (Viking, 2006)

Guardiola, Pep, *La meva gent, el meu futbol* (Edecasa, 2001)

Hesse, Uli, *Bayern* (Yellow Jersey, 2017)

——*Tor!* (WSC, 2003)

Honigstein, Raphael, *Das Reboot* (Yellow Jersey, 2015)

Hunter, Graham, *Barça* (BackPage, 2012)

——*Spain* (BackPage, 2016)

Ibrahmović, Zlatan with David Lagercrantz, *I Am Zlatan Ibrahimović* (Penguin, 2013)

Iniesta, Andrés, *The Artist* (Headline, 2016)

Kormelink, Henny and Tjeu Seeverens, *The Coaching Philosophies of Louis Van Gaal and the Ajax Coaches* (Reedswain, 2003)

Kovacs, Ştefan, *Football Total* (Calman-Levy, 1975)

Kuper, Simon, 'The Dutch Style and the Dutch Nation,', *The Blizzard*, Issue Zero

——'Pep's Four Golden Rules', *The Blizzard*, Issue Nine

Kuper, Simon and David Winner, 'Comparing Apple with *Oranje*', *The Blizzard*, Issue Three

Lourenço, Luis, *José Mourinho* (Dewi Lewis Media, 2004)

Lowe, Sid, *Fear and Loathing in La Liga* (Yellow Jersey, 2013)

——'The Brain in Spain' in *The Blizzard*, Issue One

Meijer, Maarten, *Louis van Gaal* (Ebury, 2014)

Modeo, Sandro, *L'Alieno Mourinho* (ISBN Edizioni, 2013)

Mourinho, José, *Mourinho* (Headline, 2015)

Müller, Salo, *Mijn Ajax: Openhartige Memoires van den Talisman van Ajax in den gouden Jaren '60 en '70* (Houtekiet, 2006)

Neto, Joel, *Mourinho* (First Stone, 2005)

Perarnau, Martí, *Pep Confidential* (Arena, 2014)
  *Pep: The Evolution* (Arena, 2016)

Robson, Bobby, *Farewell but not Goodbye* (Hodder & Stoughton, 2009)

Soriano, Ferran, *The Ball Doesn't Go In By Chance* (Palgrave, 2011)

Torres, Diego, *The Special One* (HarperSport, 2014)

Van Gaal, Louis, *Biografie & Visie* (Publish Unlimited, 2009)

Williams, Tom, 'An Englishman Abroad' in *The Blizzard*, Issue Twenty-Seven

Wilson, Jonathan, *Angels with Dirty Faces* (Orion, 2016)

——*Inverting the Pyramid* (Orion, 2008)

Winner, David, *Brilliant Orange* (Bloomsbury, 2000)

Zanetti, Javier, *Giocare da uomo* (Oscar, 2016)

# INDEX

Abelardo 38
Abidal, Éric 120, 127, 128, 173–4, 189
Abramovich, Roman 64, 83, 84–5, 86–7,
    191, 220, 260, 268, 269, 275
AC Milan 1, 20, 44, 79, 104, 131, 132,
    134, 144
Afellay, Ibrahim 168
Agger, Daniel 86
Agüero, Sergio 268, 284, 292, 299–300,
    312
Ajax FC (*see also individual competitions;*
    *individual managers*):
    Beenhakker joins 44
    Beenhakker leaves 99
    Bosz takes over at 293
    Buckingham as manager of 8
    commissioners resign from 209
    crisis point in 100–1
    Cruyff as technical advisor to 16
    Cruyff becomes manager of 17
    Cruyff criticises 205
    Cruyff leaves, as manager of 20,
        44
    Cruyff player at 9–12 *passim*, 17
    Cruyff's oblique control of 194
    De Boer becomes manager at 207
    goals by under Cruyff 19
    Ibrahimovič leaves 101
    Jol manages 194
    Jol resigns as manager of 207
    Koeman joins, as manager 89
    Koeman joins, as player 90–1
    Koeman leaves 103
    Koeman–Van Gaal tension within
        88–9, 100, 102
    league win by 47
    Michels at 8–11
    notable victories of 19, 92, 211
    Reynolds as manager of 8
    title drought of 210
    UEFA Cup won by 49

and Van Gaal director's appointment
    208–9
Van Gaal joins, as manager 44
Van Gaal joins, as player 42
Van Gaal joins, as technical director
    88
Van Gaal leaves 102
Alaba, David 252, 256, 279
Albiol, Raul 161
Alonso, Pichi 21, 25
Alonso, Xabi 72, 155, 162, 163, 166, 192,
    195, 237, 257
Alves, Dani 118, 121, 123, 127, 128, 144,
    146, 160, 161, 167, 170, 184, 242, 250,
    253, 303, 305
Amor, Guillermo 3, 22, 26, 52
Ancelotti, Carlo 225, 234, 247
Aragonés, Luis 20, 21
Arbeloa, Alvaro 163, 167, 187
Archibald, Steve 20–1
Argentina 16, 111, 112, 156, 164, 184n,
    223, 224n, 308
Arsenal FC 39, 83, 107, 142, 159–60, 214,
    220, 234, 259, 261, 267, 270, 283, 293
Aston Villa FC 79, 86, 221, 273, 280
Athens FC 1–2, 8
Athletic 28, 37, 178–9, 180, 185, 226, 252
Atlético 2, 3, 22, 30, 141, 191, 222, 225,
    226, 227, 244, 252, 255–7
Auxerre 50, 103
AZ 43, 148, 196, 197–9, 214, 216, 262

Baía, Vítor 53–4, 55, 56, 57, 60, 73, 74,
    75–6
Bailly, Eric 286
Bakero, José Mari 22
Balotelli, Mario 133
Barcelona FC (*see also individual*
    *competitions; individual managers*):
    academy of, *see* La Masia
    bad buying by 305